ENHANCED BEINGS

Today, scientists are using CRISPR/Cas9 and other molecular editing tools to alter human gametes and embryos, a practice known as human germline modification. In the near future, these efforts may lead to the birth of children with better health, improved memories, and extended lifespans. However, critics claim that human germline modification exceeds divine and natural boundaries, transforms reproduction into manufacture, and yields apocalyptic outcomes such as the collapse of democracy. *Enhanced Beings: Human Germline Modification and the Law* analyzes and critiques these objections on both biological and political grounds. Professor Kerry Lynn Macintosh discusses the hidden psychology behind the objections and describes the laws that affect this new technology. Provocative and timely, *Enhanced Beings* argues that bans on human germline modification pose a threat to scientists and science, parents, children, foreigners, and society.

Kerry Lynn Macintosh is Professor of Law at Santa Clara University School of Law. She received her BA from Pomona College and her JD from Stanford Law School. Professor Macintosh is the author of *Human Cloning: Four Fallacies and Their Legal Consequences* (2013) and *Illegal Beings: Human Clones and the Law* (2005). She has also published articles about infertility, assisted reproductive technologies, and embryonic stem cell research. Professor Macintosh is a member of the American Law Institute, a law reform organization.

Enhanced Beings

HUMAN GERMLINE MODIFICATION AND THE LAW

KERRY LYNN MACINTOSH

Santa Clara University

CAMBRIDGE
UNIVERSITY PRESS

University Printing House, Cambridge CB2 8BS, United Kingdom

One Liberty Plaza, 20th Floor, New York, NY 10006, USA

477 Williamstown Road, Port Melbourne, VIC 3207, Australia

314–321, 3rd Floor, Plot 3, Splendor Forum, Jasola District Centre, New Delhi – 110025, India

79 Anson Road, #06-04/06, Singapore 079906

Cambridge University Press is part of the University of Cambridge.

It furthers the University's mission by disseminating knowledge in the pursuit of education, learning, and research at the highest international levels of excellence.

www.cambridge.org
Information on this title: www.cambridge.org/9781108471206
DOI: 10.1017/9781108557818

© Kerry Lynn Macintosh 2018

This publication is in copyright. Subject to statutory exception and to the provisions of relevant collective licensing agreements, no reproduction of any part may take place without the written permission of Cambridge University Press.

First published 2018

Printed in <country> by <printer>

A catalogue record for this publication is available from the British Library.

Library of Congress Cataloging-in-Publication Data

ISBN 978-1-108-47120-6 Hardback
ISBN 978-1-108-45729-3 Paperback

Cambridge University Press has no responsibility for the persistence or accuracy of URLs for external or third-party internet websites referred to in this publication and does not guarantee that any content on such websites is, or will remain, accurate or appropriate.

To Mark Donald Eibert

Contents

Acknowledgments		*page* viii
	Introduction	1
	PART I OBJECTIONS TO HUMAN GERMLINE MODIFICATION	9
1	Therapy and Enhancement	11
2	Transgressing Boundaries	30
3	Transforming Reproduction into Manufacture	39
4	Stratifying Society	48
5	Endangering Democracy, Society, and the Species	62
	PART II PSYCHOLOGICAL ORIGINS AND CONSEQUENCES OF OBJECTIONS TO HUMAN GERMLINE MODIFICATION	89
6	Psychological Essentialism	91
7	Envy	107
	PART III HUMAN GERMLINE MODIFICATION AND THE LAW	121
8	Existing Laws and Regulations	123
9	Future Laws and Regulations	146
10	Prohibiting Human Germline Modification Harms Scientists and Science, Parents, Children, Foreigners, and Society	157
	Conclusion	180
Index		183

Acknowledgments

In writing and publishing this book, I have received assistance from many people. Gary Spitko and Stephanie Wildman, my colleagues at Santa Clara University, reviewed my drafts. Several other academics read the book manuscript for Cambridge University Press. Kyle Glass, Alexander Patent, and Monica De Lazzari provided able research assistance. All of these individuals contributed substantive comments that improved the book. Dean Lisa Kloppenberg and Santa Clara University School of Law provided encouragement and support for my research.

My editor, John Berger, helped me secure the publication contract with Cambridge University Press. My content manager, Rebecca Jackaman, shepherded the book through the publication process. Others at Cambridge worked to market and publicize the book. In addition, Karthik Orukaimani and Linda Benson of Integra Software Services ably served as project manager and as copyeditor, respectively.

I thank all of these individuals and organizations for their kindness, generosity, diligence, and professionalism. Without them, this book would not exist. Last but not least, I thank my husband and children for their support and understanding as I worked on this complex and challenging project.

Introduction

Suppose one man has sexual intercourse with one woman. A spermatozoon fertilizes an egg and creates an embryo with 46 chromosomes.[1] These chromosomes are studded with *genes*: discrete passages of deoxyribonucleic acid (DNA) coding for the amino acid chains that form proteins.[2] Proteins build cells; cells create tissues; and, ultimately, tissues become a baby.[3] Other than the choice of mate, no design is involved. Because this process accounts for most births, this book describes it as *standard reproduction*.

An alternative to standard reproduction may soon emerge. In *human germline modification* (HGM), scientists use molecular editing tools to alter the genes in human *gametes* (sperm and eggs) or embryos.[4] Such gametes or embryos can be used to conceive babies with modified traits (*HGM for reproduction*) or to perform lab research (*HGM for research*).

Bioethicists, lawyers, and policymakers have debated the costs and benefits of HGM for reproduction for many years.[5] Until recently, this debate was academic because efficient editing technology did not exist.[6] However, in 2015, Chinese researchers published the results of an experiment in which a molecular editing tool known as CRISPR/Cas9[*] was applied to human embryos.[7] The goal was to cut the beta-globin gene (HBB), which when mutated causes a blood disorder known as beta thalassemia,[8] and repair the break with a new sequence of DNA. Upon testing 54 surviving embryos, the researchers found that the CRISPR/Cas9 tool cut the HBB

---

[*] CRISPR/Cas9 has many uses. For example, in addition to HGM, it can be applied to cells in culture or used to create or cure experimental animals. ELIZABETH PENNISI, The CRISPR Craze, 341 SCIENCE 833, 834–35 (2013); MARGARET KNOX, The Gene Genie, 311 SCI. AM. 42, 45–46 (December 2014). Here is a simplified explanation of how it works: suppose a researcher wishes to disable a specific gene in the nucleus of a cell. She creates a synthetic guide ribonucleic acid (gRNA) molecule complementary to the gene's sequence and attaches the gRNA to the Cas9 enzyme. Using one of various methods, she introduces the complex into the nucleus of the cell. The gRNA leads the Cas9 enzyme to the relevant DNA sequence, which the enzyme then cuts and disables. If the researcher wants to substitute a new DNA sequence, she can add it to the gRNA/enzyme complex in the hope that the cell will use it as a template to repair the cut. ANDREW POLLACK, A Powerful New Way to Edit DNA, NEW YORK TIMES (March 3, 2014), www.nytimes.com/2014/03/04/health/a-powerful-new-way-to-edit-dna.html

gene in 28. However, only 4 took up the new DNA, and those 4 were *mosaic*, incorporating the new DNA in some cells but not others.[9] Seven other embryos repaired the cut on their own using HBD, an endogenous gene with a sequence similar to that of HBB.[10] Also, the CRISPR-Cas9 tool sometimes cut the DNA in the wrong place, leading to off-target mutations.[11] The researchers concluded that further study was needed before the CRISPR/Cas9 tool could be applied to human embryos in a clinical setting.[12]

A stunning reality overshadowed this modest conclusion: the Chinese researchers had dared to modify human embryos.[13] To be sure, they never intended to create babies and used only nonviable embryos in the experiment.[14] Nevertheless, their work was so shocking that when news of it leaked out, scientists and bioethicists immediately began to comment.[15] Some objected that HGM was unsafe[16] and would lead to human enhancement.[17] Others countered that scientists could continue their research as long as they did not conceive babies through HGM.[18]

HGM research did continue around the world. British and Swedish scientists edited genes in healthy human embryos to study embryonic development,[19] while Chinese scientists explored potential therapeutic uses of HGM.[20] Finally, in 2017, two years after the first experiment, an international team of scientists from the United States, Korea, and China reported major advances in editing human embryos.[21]

The international team obtained donor sperm from a man who carried a mutation that causes hypertrophic cardiomyopathy, a dangerous condition in which the heart muscle develops thicker walls.[22] The team hypothesized that mosaicism could be reduced if editing were performed when only a single copy of the mutated gene was present; accordingly, it injected the CRISPR/Cas9 tool together with the sperm directly into eggs.[23] Fifty-eight embryos were analyzed. The team did not detect the mutation in 42 embryos, or 72.4 percent. (In comparison, 47.4 percent of control embryos created with the sperm lacked the mutation.[24]) Only 1 of the 42 embryos was a mosaic.[25] Even better, the team did not detect off-target mutations in the embryonic cells it examined,[26] perhaps because it modified the CRISPR/Cas9 tool so that the cutting enzyme was present in a purified form and dissipated more quickly.[27]

Hard on the heels of this report, Chinese scientists announced that they had applied a new technology called *base editing* to cloned human embryos.[28] Unlike CRISPR/Cas9, which cuts and repairs DNA, base editing uses enzymes to change a mutated nucleotide base into the standard one.[29] The embryos in the experiment contained a mutation that causes beta thalassemia. The scientists found that the mutation was corrected in more than 20 percent of the embryonic cells tested.[30]

While some scientists innovated, others pondered the policy implications. In 2017, the National Academy of Science (NAS) and the National Academy of Medicine issued a report about human genome editing, including HGM (

hereinafter NAS Report).[31] The report opined that research on human gametes and embryos could proceed subject to existing ethical rules and legal regulations.[32] Clinical trials performed to conceive children without a serious disease or condition might be acceptable if reasonable alternatives were not available and research subjects were closely monitored for health and safety.[33] However, the report advised that regulators should not authorize clinical trials for other purposes, such as enhancement, at the present time.[34]

These recommendations are generally consistent with federal law in the United States. HGM for research is permitted,[35] and HGM for reproduction is not yet banned (although federal regulators cannot receive applications for clinical trials at present).[36] However, political forces may lead to changes in the law. Conservatives who wish to protect human embryos may demand that the US Congress ban all HGM, including basic research.[37] Liberals who favor research but wish to prevent the birth of modified babies may insist that Congress ban HGM for reproduction,[38] as other countries have already done.[39]

Too often, both sides of the political divide ignore a simple fact: when human beings are motivated to procreate, they do what it takes to circumvent laws that get in the way. For example, within the United States, residents of states that prohibit gestational surrogacy travel to states with more permissive laws.[40] Likewise, citizens of foreign nations that ban donor gametes and gestational surrogacy travel to places where those technologies are legal.[41]

Therefore, this book proceeds on the basis of two assumptions: first, scientists may eventually acquire enough technical expertise and genetic knowledge to make HGM reasonably safe for mothers and babies; and second, if the United States bans HGM, those who wish to use it may travel to China or other nations for treatment. As a consequence, children with modified genomes will be born and raised here, go to school here, and (upon reaching adulthood) work here. This book describes such individuals as *children of HGM*.

Analysis proceeds in three parts. Part I discusses HGM for reproduction as a matter of public policy. Chapter 1 presents hypotheticals in which parents use HGM to conceive children with therapeutic or enhancing modifications. Next, Chapters 1, 3, 4, and 5 collect complaints about such interventions into four categories. The first, the hubris objection, addresses claims that adults who use HGM transgress divine and natural boundaries, leading to bad outcomes. The second, the manufacture objection, asserts that adults who employ HGM transform human reproduction into manufacture. The third, the stratification objection, charges that children of HGM and their descendants will produce class divides and social inequalities. The fourth, the apocalypse objection, includes allegations that children of HGM will bring about catastrophic outcomes, such as the collapse of democracy or genocide. Chapters 2 through 5 subject these objections and related concerns to critical analysis and link them to negative stereotypes about children of HGM.

Some critics may assert a fifth objection: HGM is hazardous to human embryos.[42] Many will die in the lab or be transferred to women but fail to come to term. But harm to embryos is a general concern: it applies to most embryo research and many assisted reproductive technologies.[43] Therefore, this book does not examine this objection in detail, although it mentions it where relevant.

Part II shifts the focus to the psychological origins and consequences of the four objections and related concerns. Chapter 6 explains that the objections are consistent with, and likely the product of, a heuristic called "psychological essentialism." Thus, stereotypes about children of HGM derive or draw power from essentialism. Chapter 7 claims that predictions of social stratification and apocalyptic outcomes encourage people to envy and mistreat children of HGM.

Part III addresses the laws of HGM in the United States. Chapter 8 presents existing federal and state laws that affect HGM for research and reproduction. Next, Chapter 9 describes future laws that Congress or state legislatures may enact in an effort to stop HGM. Finally, Chapter 10 discusses the harms that bans impose on scientists and science, parents, children, foreigners who travel to the United States, and society. This book concludes that education is a safer and more effective means of preventing abuses of HGM.

Notes

1. KERRY LYNN MACINTOSH, Chimeras, Hybrids, and Cybrids: How Essentialism Distorts the Law and Stymies Scientific Research, 47 ARIZ. ST. L.J. 183, 192 (2015).
2. Genetics Home Reference, U.S. NATIONAL LIBRARY OF MEDICINE, What Is a Gene? (May 2, 2017), https://ghr.nlm.nih.gov/primer/basics/gene.
3. KERRY LYNN MACINTOSH, HUMAN CLONING: FOUR FALLACIES AND THEIR LEGAL CONSEQUENCES 1–2, 28 (2013).
4. This definition excludes mitochondrial replacement techniques (MRT), even though some classify such techniques as a form of human germline modification. See SUSANNAH BARUCH ET AL., HUMAN GERMLINE GENETIC MODIFICATION: ISSUES AND OPTIONS FOR POLICYMAKERS 14 (2005). MRT bypass the defective mitochondria found in some eggs to prevent the birth of children who would otherwise inherit debilitating mitochondrial diseases. MRT are excluded from discussion here because they pose a more limited and technology-specific set of policy and legal issues. The Institute of Medicine recently issued a report opining that clinical trials of MRT could be ethical under specific circumstances. COMMITTEE ON THE ETHICAL AND SOCIAL POLICY CONSIDERATIONS OF NOVEL TECHNIQUES FOR PREVENTION OF MATERNAL TRANSMISSION OF MITOCHONDRIAL DNA DISEASES, BOARD ON HEALTH SCIENCE POLICY, INSTITUTE OF MEDICINE, MITOCHONDRIAL REPLACEMENT TECHNIQUES: ETHICAL, SOCIAL, AND POLICY CONSIDERATIONS (ANNE CLAIBORNE, REBECCA ENGLISH, & JEFFREY KAHN EDS., National Academies Press 2016).

5. Some have embraced HGM as a means of controlling our own evolution. *See, e.g.*, RONALD BAILEY, LIBERATION BIOLOGY: THE SCIENTIFIC AND MORAL CASE FOR THE BIOTECH REVOLUTION (2005); GREGORY STOCK, REDESIGNING HUMANS: OUR INEVITABLE GENETIC FUTURE (2003); LEE M. SILVER, REMAKING EDEN: CLONING AND BEYOND IN A BRAVE NEW WORLD (1997). Others have insisted HGM is an evil to be avoided. BILL MCKIBBEN, ENOUGH: STAYING HUMAN IN AN ENGINEERED AGE (2004); FRANCIS FUKUYAMA, OUR POSTHUMAN FUTURE: CONSEQUENCES OF THE BIOTECHNOLOGY REVOLUTION (2003).
6. *See* NICHOLAS WADE, Scientists Seek Ban on Method of Making Gene-Edited Babies, NEW YORK TIMES (March 29, 2015), www.nytimes.com/2015/03/20/science/biologists-call-for-halt-to-gene-editing-technique-in-humans.html (asserting that until recently, concerns about HGM have been theoretical); *see also* PRESIDENT'S COUNCIL ON BIOETHICS, Beyond Therapy: Biotechnology and the Pursuit of Happiness 37–40 (2003) (dismissing visions of designer babies as improbable given technical challenges and limited knowledge of genetic and environmental factors).
7. PUPING LIANG ET al., CRISPR/Cas9-mediated Gene Editing in Human Tripronuclear Zygotes, 6 PROTEIN & CELL 363 (2015).
8. *Id.* at 364. The mutation disrupts production of the beta hemoglobin protein, a component of the hemoglobin A that red blood cells need to carry oxygen. If a child inherits the mutated gene from both parents, she will suffer from severe anemia. AMERICAN MEDICAL ASSOCIATION, FAMILY MEDICAL GUIDE 616 (4th ed. 2004).
9. LIANG ET AL., *supra* note 7, at 366.
10. *Id.*
11. *Id.* The source of these off-target effects was unclear. Imperfections in CRISPR/Cas9 technology might have been to blame. JOCELYN KAISER & DENNIS NORMILE, Embryo Engineering Study Splits Scientific Community, 348 SCIENCE 486, 487 (2015). Alternatively, the off-target effects might have stemmed from the use of nonviable embryos in the experiment. DAVID CYRANOSKI & SARA REARDON, Chinese Scientists Genetically Modify Human Embryos, NATURE NEWS (April 22, 2015), www.nature.com/news/chinese-scientists-genetically-modify-human-embryos-1.17378.
12. LIANG ET AL., *supra* note 7, at 364.
13. KAISER & NORMILE, *supra* note 11.
14. The researchers obtained tripronuclear zygotes from fertility clinics. Each of the abnormal zygotes contained two sperm nuclei and one oocyte nucleus. These zygotes had the capacity to mature into blastocysts but not babies. LIANG ET AL., *supra* note 7, at 364, 369.
15. GRETCHEN VOGEL, Embryo Engineering Alarm, 347 SCIENCE 1301 (2015).
16. *E.g.*, EDWARD LANPHIER ET AL., Don't Edit the Human Germ Line, 519 NATURE 410, 411 (2015); *see also* ERIC S. LANDER, Brave New Genome, 373 N. ENG. J. MED. 5, 6–7 (2015) (questioning safety of the technology and expressing opposition to clinical applications that change human gene pool).

17. LANPHIER ET AL., *supra* note 16, at 411. The authors of the article cited in this note have a motive to oppose HGM. They perform research aimed at correcting genetic mutations within somatic cells, which they believe can save lives without transmitting modifications to future generations. They fear that public backlash against HGM could derail their work. *Id.*

18. For example, in 2015, an International Summit on Human Gene Editing concluded that HGM research could proceed but advised that babies should not be conceived until safety was established, benefits identified, societal consensus achieved, and regulatory oversight imposed. ORGANIZING COMMITTEE FOR THE INTERNATIONAL SUMMIT ON HUMAN GENE EDITING, On Human Gene Editing: International Summit Statement, NATIONAL ACADEMIES (December 3, 2015), www8.nationalacademies.org/onpinews/newsitem.aspx?RecordID=12032015a.

19. NORAH M. E. FOGARTY ET AL., Genome Editing Reveals a Role for OCT4 in Human Embryogenesis, 550 NATURE 67 (2017) (reporting United Kingdom experiment in which scientists disabled OCT4 to study effect on embryonic development); ANNEESA AMJAD, Swedish Scientist Edits Genomes of Healthy Human Embryos, 870 BIONEWS (September 26, 2016), www.bionews.org.uk/page_704671.asp (describing Swedish experiment in which scientist edited genes to observe effect on embryonic development).

20. In 2016, one Chinese research team reported that it added a gene variant conferring resistance to HIV infection to nonviable human embryos. XIANGJIN KANG ET AL., Introducing Precise Genetic Modifications into Human 3PN Embryos by CRISPR/Cas-mediated Genome Editing, 33 J. ASSISTED REPROD. & GENETICS 581 (2016). In 2017, another Chinese team stated that it corrected genetic mutations in viable human embryos. LICHUN TANG ET AL., CRISPR/Cas9-mediated Gene Editing in Human Zygotes Using Cas9 Protein, 292 MOLECULAR GENETICS AND GENOMICS 525 (2017).

21. HONG MA ET AL., Correction of a Pathogenic Gene Mutation in Human Embryos, 548 NATURE 413 (2017).

22. *Id.* at 414; HEIDI LEDFORD, CRISPR Fixed Disease Gene in Viable Human Embryos, 548 NATURE 13 (2017). Hypertrophic cardiomyopathy has been implicated in the deaths of young athletes. Unfortunately, the mutation that causes the condition is dominant. Even if only one parent carries the mutation, a child can inherit the condition. *Id.*

23. MA ET AL., *supra* note 21, at 415.

24. *Id.* at 416.

25. The mosaic embryo repaired four of its cells using DNA that the team added to the CRISPR/Cas9 tool to serve as a template. It repaired its other three cells with reference to the normal DNA of the egg. *Id.*

26. *Id.* at 417. As another scientist pointed out, however, off-target mutations could be present even if the researchers did not detect them. LEDFORD, *supra* note 22, at 14.

27. MA ET AL., *supra* note 21, at 418; LEDFORD, *supra* note 22, at 13.

28. PUPING LIANG ET AL., Correction of β-thalassemia Mutant by Base Editor in Human Embryos, PROTEIN & CELL, doi: 10.1007/s13238-0170475-6 (2017).
29. JON COHEN, 'Base Editors' Open New Way to Fix Mutations, 358 SCIENCE 432 (2017).
30. LIANG ET AL., *supra* note 28.
31. NATIONAL ACADEMY OF SCIENCES & NATIONAL ACADEMY OF MEDICINE, Human Genome Editing: Science, Ethics, and Governance (2017).
32. *Id.* at 142.
33. *Id.* at 145–46, Recommendation 5-1. This recommendation came subject to other conditions, which can be summarized as follows: the edited genes caused or contributed to a serious disease or condition; the genes were changed to types linked to normal health; data existed to show the risks and health benefits of the procedure; researchers had plans to track research subjects and their descendants over time; the work was transparent without compromising patient privacy; health and social risks and benefits were continually reevaluated with the benefit of public input; and oversight ensured that the technology was not used for purposes other than averting serious diseases or conditions. *Id.*
34. *Id.* at 147–48.
35. Chapter 8, Sections A.1, A.2, A.3.a.
36. For a discussion of the role of the Food and Drug Administration in regulating HGM for reproduction, see Chapter 8, Section A.1.
37. For a discussion of a total ban and who might favor it, see Chapter 9, Section A.1.
38. *E.g.*, Center for Genetics and Society, Genetically Modified Humans? Seven Reasons to Say "No," (May 7, 2015), www.geneticsandsociety.org/biopolitical-times/genetically-modified-humans-seven-reasons-say-no.
39. *See id.* (claiming more than 40 countries ban HGM that affects future generations); BARUCH ET AL., *supra* note 4, at 39 (citing Australia, Austria, Brazil, Canada, Costa Rica, Finland, France, Georgia, Germany, Hungary, Italy, Japan, the Netherlands, Norway, Slovenia, Spain, Sweden, Switzerland, and the United Kingdom as nations that prohibit HGM in most cases).
40. VICTORIA R. GUZMAN, A Comparison of Surrogacy Laws of the U.S. to Other Countries: Should There Be a Uniform Federal Law Permitting Commercial Surrogacy? 38 HOUSTON J. INT'L L. 619, 626–28 (2016).
41. RICHARD F. STORROW, Assisted Reproduction on Treacherous Terrain: The Legal Hazards of Cross-border Reproductive Travel, 23 REPROD. BIOMEDICINE ONLINE 538, 539 (2011).
42. *See* BRENDAN FOHT, Experiments on Human Embryos Offer Little Hope for Curing Genetic Diseases, NAT'L REVIEW (February 4, 2016), www.nationalreview.com/article/430771/genetic-modification-embryos-morally-wrong-still (asserting that HGM for research exploits the unborn); *but see* CHRISTOPHER GYNGELL ET AL., The Ethics of Germline Gene Editing, 34

J. OF APPLIED PHILOSOPHY 498, 504 (2016) (arguing that HGM for research should proceed even if it is not safe for embryos).

43. See MICHAEL J. SANDEL, Embryo Ethics – The Moral Logic of Stem-Cell Research, 351 N. ENG. J. MED. 207, 208 (2004) (discussing embryo losses in stem-cell research and assisted reproduction).

PART I

Objections to Human Germline Modification

Part I introduces the debate over human germline modification (HGM) for reproduction. It contains five chapters. Chapter 1 aims to provide context. It presents scenarios in which prospective parents might be tempted to use HGM to alter their embryos. It also explores the disputed distinction between therapy and enhancement.

The remaining four chapters describe and critique four objections to HGM. Chapter 2 presents concerns that HGM transgresses divine and natural boundaries and leads to bad outcomes. Chapter 3 outlines the assertion that HGM transforms reproduction into manufacture. Chapter 4 discusses the theory that HGM leads to social stratification. Finally, Chapter 5 describes claims that HGM leads to apocalyptic consequences: the collapse of democracy, eugenics, societal ossification, and genocide. Each chapter also includes concerns that are related to the objection under discussion.

In documenting the four objections, this book relies on governmental and academic publications. For example, it cites the report on human genome editing that the National Academy of Sciences and National Academy of Medicine published in 2017 (NAS Report).[1] That report discusses the ethics of HGM in light of current scientific developments, including the CRISPR/Cas9 tool.

This book also draws upon older sources that discussed HGM long before effective molecular editing tools were available. In 1997, Professor Lee Silver became one of the first to speak out on potential uses of cloning and genetic engineering in human beings.[2] His vision provoked a backlash from academics and others who began to outline the four objections.[3] These critics included the President's Council on Bioethics, a body that advised President George W. Bush on controversies arising out of advances in biomedical science and technology.[4] In 2003, the President's Council issued a report on biomedical enhancements that addressed some of the issues considered herein.[5] In 2004, it released a report on assisted reproductive technologies that also addressed HGM.[6] Although technology has advanced since these reports were published, the ethical reasoning in them remains relevant today.

9

This book respects the eminent academics and experts who have endorsed the four objections and related concerns. However, in this part, it argues that most of the objections and concerns are exaggerated, speculative, or based on questionable biological or political premises. Moreover, this book contends that the objections and concerns promote negative stereotypes about children of HGM, which it enumerates herein.

1

Therapy and Enhancement

Human germline modification (HGM) has many potential uses in human reproduction. One day, scientists may use CRISPR/Cas9, base editors, or other molecular editing tools to ensure that children are born healthy. More speculatively, they may be able to facilitate the birth of children with traits deemed desirable or superior.

This chapter begins with an overview of the medical and technical challenges inherent in HGM. Next, it offers several hypotheticals that illustrate possible uses of HGM. For clarity's sake, it organizes these uses into two categories, therapeutic and enhancing. This chapter closes by acknowledging some difficulties with the therapy/enhancement distinction.

A MEDICAL AND TECHNICAL CHALLENGES

Suppose that John and Mary Smith wish to use HGM to conceive a child with modified traits. To assist them, doctors and technicians must have access to the stuff of life: sperm, eggs, and/or embryos created by combining sperm with eggs.

Modified sperm can be created through various means. For example, technicians may remove spermatogonial stem cells (SSCs) from John's testes, edit them, and return them to the testes to mature into modified sperm.[7] John and Mary can then conceive children with desired traits through sexual intercourse. However, this method may prove unpopular: the only way to ensure that John does not sire a child with *unmodified* sperm is to irradiate his testes to destroy the original SSCs still present there.[8]

Alternatively, technicians may edit sperm directly. For this to happen, John must generate a sample through masturbation.[9] A doctor can transfer the modified sperm to Mary via a process known as intrauterine insemination (IUI).[10] If a modified spermatozoon finds and fertilizes Mary's egg, the embryo (and eventual child) will bear the desired modification.

Eggs and embryos can also be modified if couple undergoes a cycle of in vitro fertilization (IVF) to give technicians access to the eggs and embryos outside the body.[11] Mary must take powerful fertility drugs to stimulate her ovaries to produce multiple eggs and endure a surgical procedure to retrieve the eggs.[12] Technicians can modify her eggs and combine them with John's sperm to produce embryos, or combine the eggs and sperm first before modifying the resulting embryos. At the end of the process, a doctor must transfer one or more embryos to Mary's uterus for gestation.[13]

As the foregoing account indicates, IVF is complicated and hard on the woman. It is expensive also: a single cycle costs around $12,400 on average[14] and that figure does not include the fertility drugs, which cost $3000 to $5000 more.[15]

IVF would be less burdensome if human eggs could be generated from induced pluripotent stem cells (iPSCs) derived from skin or other somatic cells.[16] Scientists have already made mouse eggs from iPSCs in the lab and used those eggs to generate offspring.[17] But even if scientists learn how to make artificial human eggs in the lab, federal regulators must approve them for safety and efficacy before they can be put to reproductive use in humans.[18] Artificial eggs may end up being more expensive to use than natural eggs, given the cost of regulation, lab processes, and liability insurance.

Thus far, it may seem that using modified sperm to fertilize eggs inside the woman is the cheapest and easiest way to conduct HGM. However, if Mary carries a dangerous genetic mutation in her eggs, modifying John's sperm will not help solve that problem. Moreover, in cases where parents wish to give their child a desirable or enhanced trait, it may be necessary to edit both sperm and egg so that the child receives two copies of a particular gene.

Although IVF is expensive, it offers two advantages over fertilization that occurs inside the woman. First, technicians can ensure fertilization by using a glass needle to inject each egg with a single spermatozoon, a process known as intracytoplasmic sperm injection (ICSI).[19] ICSI may be helpful if modified sperm are not as capable of fertilizing eggs as standard sperm. Second, IVF creates embryos outside the body, where they can be screened for genetic or chromosomal abnormalities through a process known as preimplantation genetic diagnosis (PGD).[20] PGD is also expensive, adding another $2500 to $6000 to the tab.[21] However, it may protect John and Mary against the possibility that an edited gamete is flawed and has produced a dysfunctional embryo.[22]

B THERAPEUTIC AND MEDICAL USES

Having examined methods of performing HGM, this chapter turns to possible uses. In bioethics, a distinction is often drawn between therapeutic and enhancing uses of technology.[23] This distinction can be problematic; however, this chapter temporarily adopts it as a convenient means of organizing uses of HGM into categories. Therapeutic and medical uses will be discussed first.

Therapy is an intervention that treats a person who suffers from disease, disability, or impairment with the goal of bringing him back to normal health and fitness.[24] For example, if a person is infected with a dangerous virus or bacterium, a course of antiviral or antibiotic drugs will counter the infection and restore the person to good health. American attitudes toward medical interventions are generally positive: people usually find it ethical to treat disease and most respect physicians as healers.[25]

1 HGM to Eliminate Genetic Disease

Some hereditary diseases are caused by the mutation of a single gene, including Huntington disease, sickle cell disease, and cystic fibrosis.[26] A person who harbors such a mutation can transmit it to offspring via sperm or eggs.[27] Once perfected, CRISPR/Cas9 or base editors could be used to correct deleterious genetic mutations in human gametes or embryos.[28]

The correction of a mutation does not treat a disease in an existing person and bring her back to a state of normal health and fitness. Rather, it secures health and fitness from the outset by preventing the transmission of a genetic disease to a child. Because it focuses on achieving normal health and fitness, HGM of this sort can be considered therapeutic. Two scenarios illustrate possible applications.

a) Huntington disease

Suppose Mary Smith inherits a normal huntingtin (HTT) gene from her father and a mutated HTT gene from her mother. Inheritance of Huntington disease follows an *autosomal dominant* pattern: one copy of a mutated HTT gene is enough to cause the disease, even when paired with a normal gene.[29] Thus, when Mary undergoes genetic testing and learns of the mutated gene, she realizes that in middle age, she may develop a dire condition that includes chorea, emotional disturbance, loss of cognition, and death.[30]

John Smith, Mary's husband, carries the normal HTT gene on both his chromosomes. However, as noted previously, even one copy of a mutated HTT gene is enough to cause Huntington disease. On average, the process of meiosis, which generates haploid germ cells, will distribute the mutated HTT gene to half of Mary's eggs; the other half will receive her healthy HTT gene.[31] Thus, any child of Mary and John has a 50 percent chance of inheriting Huntington disease.[32]

To avoid the risk of giving birth to a child who will inherit the disease, Mary and John have two choices. Today, they can use IVF to create a panel of embryos and screen them via PGD to see which ones carry the mutated HTT gene. Embryos without the mutation can be transferred to Mary; those with the mutation can be discarded. In the minds of some, this solution is adequate.[33] However, if Mary and John believe, as many Americans do, that human life is sacred from the moment of conception, they may resist this strategy.[34] Moreover, if Mary had inherited the mutated HTT gene from *both* of her parents, *all* her eggs and embryos would be affected, and PGD could not solve the problem.[35]

In the near future, Mary and John may consider an alternative solution that involves HGM. For example, perhaps a technician will retrieve eggs from Mary and use the CRISPR/Cas9 tool to edit the genetic mutation in them.[36] More speculatively, the technician might cull skin cells from her, induce them to become pluripotent stem cells, correct the HTT gene in the stem cells, and transform the corrected stem cells into eggs.[37] Once the eggs are corrected, they can be fertilized with John's sperm, yielding healthy embryos and allowing Mary to give birth to a healthy child. Here and in future chapters, this child will be called Ariel.

Alternatively, the technician may correct the genetic mutation in the affected embryos themselves.[38] The corrected embryos can then be transferred to Mary, allowing her to give birth to a healthy child. However, direct editing of embryos presents a special risk: mosaicism, in which a genetic mutation is corrected in only some cells of an embryo.[39] PGD provides a genetic profile of an embryo based on a single excised cell. Removing too many cells destroys the embryo; hence, PGD is not an effective means of screening for mosaicism.[40] Until scientists discover how to edit embryos without creating mosaics,[41] editing gametes is a safer strategy.

b) Sickle Cell Disease

DNA is composed of nucleotides, which include one of four chemical bases: guanine, cytosine, adenine, and thymine.[42] A point mutation occurs when one nucleotide base is changed, added, or subtracted.[43] A point mutation in the beta-globin gene (HBB) causes sickle cell disease,[44] a disorder in which sickle-shaped red blood cells break down, leading to anemia, jaundice, organ damage, and pulmonary hypertension.[45]

Sickle cell disease is an *autosomal recessive* disorder. If a person inherits one normal HBB gene and one mutated HBB gene, he can be healthy; however, he is a carrier who can pass the mutated HBB gene to his offspring.[46] If a person inherits *two* copies of the mutated HBB gene (one from each parent), he will have sickle cell disease.[47]

The Centers for Disease Control and Prevention estimate that approximately 100,000 people in the United States have sickle cell disease.[48] Thus, it is possible that two such individuals will meet, fall in love, and decide to procreate together. Suppose John Smith possesses two copies of the mutated HBB gene and all his sperm carry the mutation. His wife Mary also has two copies of the mutated HBB gene, so all her eggs bear the mutation. The joining of two such gametes will produce embryos that inherit two copies of the mutated HBB gene, and the disease. One hundred percent inheritance makes it impossible to use PGD as a means of picking and choosing among these embryos.[49]

HGM offers an alternative. Suppose John and Mary undergo IVF and create a panel of embryos. Technicians use base editing to correct the point mutation in their embryos.[50] Subsequently, the embryos are transferred to Mary. One implants in her womb and grows to become a healthy baby girl. Again, the name Ariel will be used to describe this child.

Alternatively, the technician helps the couple correct the point mutation in their sperm and eggs prior to fertilization. Once the mutation is corrected in the gametes, all embryos conceived with them will carry standard HBB genes.[51] So long as the editing process is safe and effective, John and Mary will welcome a healthy child into their family.

2 HGM to Confer Immunity

Another potential use of HGM deserves consideration. Parents already provide their children with vaccinations that shield them from smallpox and polio and also lesser ailments such as measles, mumps, and chicken pox. Similarly, some theorize that HGM may one day be used to confer viral or bacterial immunity upon children.[52]

Note that vaccinations do not *treat* disease, as therapies do; rather, they *prevent* disease by conferring immunity. Because vaccinations improve upon the normal function of the human body, one could consider them to be enhancements.[53] However, vaccinations aim to secure good health, and some might perceive them as falling within the realm of therapy.[54]

Similarly, if HGM can be used to confer immunity at birth, one could view it as an enhancement. Yet, when its purpose is to secure good health, HGM shares a common goal with therapy. Moreover, as previously discussed, the public generally approves of medical interventions. Thus, it seems reasonable to discuss the use of HGM to confer immunity alongside therapeutic applications of the technology.

To illustrate, suppose John and Mary Smith worry that their child could reach adulthood only to become infected with human immunodeficiency virus (HIV). To reduce that risk, they elect HGM.[55] Ninety-five percent of infections with HIV-1 (the predominant type)[56] result when the virus enters a cell with the help of a receptor called CCR5.[57] Knowing this, when John and Mary undergo IVF, they ask the technician to give each embryo two copies of a protective variant of the CCR5 receptor gene.[58] Nine months later, Mary gives birth to a son named Blake who is immune to most HIV-1 infections.[59]

Although this hypothetical project may sound like science fiction to some readers, Chinese researchers are already working on it. In 2016, the researchers used CRISPR/Cas9 to introduce the protective variant into nonviable human embryos.[60] In their most successful trial, four of twenty-six embryos absorbed one copy of the desired gene; however, they also found standard copies or unanticipated mutations at the same location.[61] Conceding that scientific concerns remained, the researchers claimed it was important to work with human embryos to improve the technology.[62]

To be sure, a standard CCR5 receptor may protect against viruses other than HIV-1.[63] Therefore, a technician may compromise by giving Blake only one copy of the mutated gene in an effort to confer some protection against HIV-1 infection.[64] But even that strategy may backfire if it still renders Blake more susceptible to other viruses.[65] Time will tell whether HGM emerges as a safe way to confer viral or bacterial immunity or is best abandoned in favor of cheaper and more reliable strategies such as vaccination.

C ENHANCING USES

Enhancement is an intervention that changes and perhaps improves upon the normal functions of the human body and mind.[66] Unlike therapy, which has positive associations, enhancement carries negative connotations. The word calls to mind excessive cosmetic surgeries and steroids taken by cheating athletes.[67] Often viewed as frivolous at best and unethical at worst, enhancement occupies a contested niche in the medical and biotechnological realm.[68] Thus, it is not surprising that news of the CRISPR/Cas9 tool being applied to human embryos has provoked opposition from those who fear that parents may use the tool to create so-called designer babies.[69]

However, as explained earlier, IVF is expensive and difficult for the woman. Moreover, before any babies can be designed, the CRISPR/Cas9 tool and other editing systems must be made safe and reliable for use in human reproduction. Federal regulation of those tools or systems presents a serious barrier, as discussed in Chapter 8, Section A. Even if the technology is approved for use in humans, editing gametes or embryos will require specialized training, lab equipment, and liability insurance, all of which will further add to the expense. Lastly, scientists must develop in-depth knowledge regarding the products and effects of the genes that contribute to specific traits, and parents must trust in their expertise.

Parents who carry dangerous genetic mutations may be willing to shoulder medical and financial burdens to protect their children from a lifetime of sickness and suffering. Enhancements are another story. Which traits will parents be tempted to buy despite the time, expense, and risk involved?

Some believe parents will alter superficial traits such as hair or eye color,[70] but the potential gains are simply not worth the expense and risk, particularly when hair dye and colored contact lenses are readily available. Similarly, although a handsome face can bring success in life, an average face performs well enough that risky attempts to engineer craniofacial structure seem unwarranted.[71] Plastic surgery is an alternative remedy for children born with unusual physical traits that lead to teasing and low self-esteem.[72]

Height also has been suggested as a target for modification.[73] Research links height to professional and educational success, particularly for males.[74] Moreover, roughly 80 percent of variation in adult height is attributable to genes.[75] This statistic makes height seem like a good candidate for genetic modification. However, the genetics of height are not simple or straightforward. Recently, researchers identified

697 genetic variants that account for around 20 percent of the heritability of height.[76] These genes have weak effects, indicating that engineering taller offspring would be a complex endeavor.[77] Where there is complexity, there is additional risk, suggesting that a few extra inches are not worth the gamble.

Nevertheless, a minority of parents may be tempted to engineer traits believed to be closely related to success and survival. General intelligence would be very difficult to engineer, for reasons explained next. However, two other traits that parents may wish to modify will be discussed: capacity for memory and learning and maximum lifespan.

1 General Intelligence

Psychologists have long known that when an individual undergoes multiple tests of diverse cognitive abilities, her results will tend to correlate. For example, if she tests well on vocabulary, she is likely to test well on general knowledge questions or arithmetic too.[78] Psychologists attribute this correlation to an underlying core trait that is known as general intelligence or general cognitive ability.[79]

General intelligence is associated with educational, career, and financial success.[80] If genes play a role in the development of general intelligence, prospective parents might be interested in modifying their embryos to enhance the trait. And indeed, studies of twins and other family members indicate that intelligence has a genetic basis.[81]

Identical (monozygotic) twins, conceived when a fertilized egg splits, have the same DNA; fraternal twins (dizygotic), conceived when two sperm fertilize two eggs, share only some of the same DNA (half on average).[82] This genetic distinction is reflected in the intelligence quotients (IQs) of identical twins and fraternal twins. The IQs of identical twins raised together correlate at .86 (where 1.0 indicates the same scores); the IQs of fraternal twins raised together correlate at the lower rate of .60.[83]

To be sure, genes are not the only factor that goes into a complex trait such as general intelligence. The IQs of identical twins raised apart correlate at .72, which is lower than the .86 correlation for the IQs of identical twins raised together.[84] Such results show that environmental factors that are shared (such as socioeconomic status) play a role in determining general intelligence.[85] Even when identical twins are raised together, their IQs are not exactly the same, suggesting that environmental factors that are not shared (such as peer group) also contribute to general intelligence.[86]

Biometric analyses of twin and family data confirm that genes and environment contribute to general intelligence.[87] Genetic factors are responsible for approximately 50 percent of variation in intelligence among individuals.[88] But realizing that genes play a role in determining general intelligence is one thing; identifying and editing the specific genes involved is quite another.

Some genetics helps explain the problem. As explained in Section B.1.b, DNA is composed of nucleotides that include chemical bases. A human gene that codes for a specific protein may include anywhere from a few hundred to 2 million chemical bases.[89] *Single nucleotide polymorphism*, or SNP, is a term used to describe a variation in a single base.[90] Most SNPs have no impact, but those that are located within a gene may alter its function.[91]

Recently, a group of international researchers assessed the genomes of 106,736 highly educated individuals and identified three SNPs strongly associated with cognitive performance.[92] The researchers estimated that each copy of each SNP could be associated with a 0.3-point gain on an IQ test.[93] In the unlikely event that an individual had two copies of all three SNPs, the increase in IQ would be at most 1.8 points.[94]

As if that were not discouraging enough, the researchers believe hundreds or even thousands of SNPs work together to affect cognitive performance.[95] In other words, like height, general intelligence is a *polygenic trait* that is the product of multiple genes.[96] With so many SNPs involved, as well as environmental factors, general intelligence would be extremely difficult to engineer.

Where hundreds or thousands of genes work together, there may be a way to manipulate them together. For example, researchers in the United Kingdom recently discovered two gene networks that influence cognitive function not only in individuals afflicted with neurodevelopmental disorders but also in healthy controls.[97] The researchers speculated that master regulator switches controlled the genes in the networks, opening up the possibility of managing the networks via those switches.[98] Someday, perhaps parents will hire technicians to manipulate regulatory switches within their gametes or embryos in an effort to increase the intelligence of their offspring. For now, however, this prospect remains more theoretical than real.

2 HGM to Improve Memory and Learning

Even if general intelligence cannot be engineered, components of that trait might be. For example, the international research team found that 12 SNPs associated with cognitive ability are located near various genes related to the nervous system.[99] Four of these genes are linked to a neurotransmission pathway that contributes to *synaptic plasticity*,[100] which is a basis of memory and learning.[101]

Suppose John and Mary Smith hire a technician to add these or related SNPs to their gametes or embryos in an effort to enhance memory and learning.[102] Mary becomes pregnant. When a daughter is born, the Smiths name her Cora.

This project faces certain challenges. For one, manipulating a dozen SNPs located near four genes is riskier than correcting a single mutated gene that causes genetic disease. An error in the process could harm rather than benefit the child. For another, a single gene can affect more than one trait, an event known as *pleiotropy*.[103]

Altering SNPs in an attempt to improve memory and learning could result in unplanned and undesired changes to other traits.[104] Much remains to be learned about molecular tools and human genetics before this type of enhancement can be practiced safely.

3 HGM to Extend Lifespan

This section would not be complete without a look at lifespan. *Maximum lifespan* refers to the maximum number of years that a member of a particular species can live.[105] The oldest human being on record is Jeanne Calment of France, who died in 1997 at age 122.[106] Thus, this book assumes that the maximum lifespan for unmodified human beings is 122 years.

Maximum lifespan is distinct from *life expectancy*, which is the average number of years that a person of a specific age has left to live.[107] During the twentieth century, average life expectancy at birth rose from 48 to 78 years.[108] But this increase in life expectancy indicates only that medicine has advanced so that fewer people die young.[109] According to researchers who reviewed data on supercentenarians (those 110 years or older) from Japan, France, the United States, and the United Kingdom, the annual maximum reported age at death from 1968 to 2006 averaged around 114.9, meaning that Calment was an outlier.[110] Noting that maximum reported age at death had not increased since the mid-1990s, the researchers speculated that human lifespan might be biologically limited.[111] If true, further extension may require genetic modification.

Scientists have used single-gene mutations to significantly extend the lifespan of nematode worms, fruit flies, and mice.[112] However, these mutations sometimes have undesirable side effects, including reduced fertility, diminished size, and vulnerability to cold.[113]

Scientists have not yet applied molecular tools to extend human lifespan, but research continues apace. Twin studies indicate that genes account for 20 to 30 percent of variation in how long people live.[114] Some theorize that polymorphisms in key genes, genomic integrity, and homeostatic mechanisms account for the extreme longevity of centenarians.[115] Scientists have created a searchable online database that lists human gene variants and describes their impact on how long people live.[116] Making sense of all this data will not be easy. When it comes to how long people live, hundreds of genes work together to produce variation[117] and environmental factors are also relevant.[118] But challenges only seem to spur dreamers on. A Silicon Valley company called Calico Life Sciences has declared its intention to extend human lifespan by 100 years.[119] With that in mind, this book offers the following hypothetical.

Suppose John and Mary Smith desire to have children who live as long as possible. While undergoing IVF, the couple requests that gametes or embryos be modified with naturally occurring genetic variants that, in combination, hold the power to increase maximum lifespan. A doctor transfers the resulting embryos to Mary and she bears a son named Devin. The baby reaches developmental milestones and attains maturity at the standard human pace.[120] However, his maximum lifespan is 150 years, which is 28 years longer than the current maximum human lifespan of 122 years.

This hypothetical assumes not only that the technology is safe but also that the modification gives the baby the chance to live to 150 *in reasonably good health*. Parents will not want lifespan extension if it comes at the price of decades of frailty and incapacity; no one wants his or her children to suffer.[121] Fortunately, there are reasons to be optimistic. We already know that the longer a person lives past 100, the shorter his period of disease and disability is.[122] In addition, the same mutations that slow aging in animals also delay the onset of age-related diseases.[123] In November 2017, an international team of researchers reported that members of an Amish community who carried a single copy of a rare genetic variant enjoyed lives that were not only longer but healthier.[124]

D PROBLEMS WITH THE THERAPY/ENHANCEMENT DISTINCTION

This chapter has used the therapy/enhancement distinction as a convenient way to sort possible applications of HGM. The distinction assumes that therapy and enhancement are different and that one can be readily separated from the other. However, as the President's Council on Bioethics once acknowledged, the distinction is problematic for several reasons.[125] This section briefly explains and illustrates some key problems with the distinction.

1 *Therapy and Enhancement Blur Together*

Bioethicists use definitions in an effort to give the concepts of "therapy" and "enhancement" firm boundaries, but real-life examples show that the concepts are blurrier.[126] To see why, consider the hypothetical in which John and Mary Smith edit the genome of their baby boy to confer immunity to HIV-1. The modification gives Blake a powerful immunity that is rarely found in nature and thus can be considered an enhancement.[127] Yet, the modification also has a medical purpose: it protects Blake against HIV-1 infection and secures his good health. The modification does not cure an existing infection and thus is not therapy in the definitional sense, yet, because it achieves the same goal (good health), it is akin to therapy and is best placed in that category for public policy purposes.

Recall also the hypothetical in which John and Mary Smith use HGM to extend the maximum lifespan of their son to 150 years. On its face, this intervention sounds like a classic enhancement. However, as mentioned earlier, researchers have discovered that mutations that slow aging also delay the onset of age-related diseases.[128] If the same genetic modifications that extend lifespan also reduce the odds of cancer, cardiovascular disease, dementia, and other age-related conditions,[129] this use of HGM might be considered therapeutic.

2 Normality Is Hard to Define

The distinction between therapy (which returns the sick or disabled to a normal state of health) and enhancement (which bestows traits that exceed normal function) assumes that normality exists and that we can define what it is.[130] One complicating factor is that many traits fall along a spectrum,[131] suggesting that the term "normal" describes a range.

To illustrate, consider lifespan. Suppose John and Mary Smith have the genetic capacity to conceive a child who can live 85 years at most. They use HGM to conceive a son with a maximum lifespan of 100 years, rather than 150 years. This intervention does not seem like therapy. A lifespan of 85 years is not abnormally low; rather, it comfortably exceeds the average life expectancy at birth of 78 years.[132] Nor does the intervention seem like enhancement. A lifespan of 100 years is not abnormally high; one in 5000 Americans is a centenarian.[133] The therapy/enhancement distinction does not help resolve the legitimacy of this particular use of HGM.

3 Normality Is Mutable

The distinction between therapy and enhancement also assumes that normality is clear and immutable. When it comes to basic health traits, that assumption may be valid. A child either has a genetic disease or does not. He is either free of viral and bacterial infections or is not.

However, the distinction falters when applied to traits that fall along a spectrum, because the range of normal function can shift with time and innovation. For example, suppose a near future in which we discover that nutritional supplements or other environmental interventions can be used to elevate IQ scores nationwide. However, not everyone can benefit from the supplements or interventions. A genetic modification that the public once eschewed as an enhancement of memory and learning may be embraced as a therapy needed to bring a child who might otherwise lag behind into the upshifted normal range.

Likewise, suppose a near future in which medical or public health innovations enable most people to live longer, so that maximum lifespan shifts upward. However, some family lines prove to be resistant to these innovations; members live and die as their ancestors did. A genetic modification that the public once opposed as an enhancement of lifespan may become a therapy used to bring the offspring of these families into the upshifted normal range. In short, that which qualifies as enhancement today may be classed as therapy tomorrow.[134]

E SUMMARY

This chapter has examined potential uses of HGM and selected four uses for discussion: elimination of genetic disease, conferral of viral or bacterial immunity, improvement of memory and learning, and extension of maximum lifespan. These uses are scientifically plausible (though not guaranteed). Also, parents may find these uses appealing enough to pursue despite the effort, expense, and risk involved.

The distinction between therapy and enhancement is prevalent in the bioethics literature. HGM will be viewed through the lens of that distinction. This chapter organizes elimination of genetic disease and conferral of viral or bacterial immunity as therapeutic or medical applications. It classes improved memory and learning and lifespan extension as enhancing applications. However, this chapter also acknowledges that the therapy/enhancement distinction is an unreliable basis for making ethical judgments regarding HGM.[135] The distinction's enduring appeal lies in instinct, rather than logic, as Chapter 6 will explain.

Notes

1. NATIONAL ACADEMY OF SCIENCES & NATIONAL ACADEMY OF MEDICINE, Human Genome Editing: Science, Ethics, and Governance (2017) [hereinafter NAS REPORT].
2. LEE M. SILVER, Remaking Eden: Cloning and Beyond in a Brave New World (1997).
3. E.g., GEORGE J. ANNAS ET AL., Protecting the Endangered Human: Toward an International Treaty Prohibiting Cloning and Inheritable Alterations, 28 AMERICAN J.L. & MED. 151 (2002); MAXWELL J. MEHLMAN, The Law of Above Averages: Leveling the New Genetic Enhancement Playing Field, 85 IOWA L. REV. 517 (2000).
4. Exec. Order No. 13,237, 66 Fed. Reg. 59,851 (November 30, 2001).
5. THE PRESIDENT'S COUNCIL ON BIOETHICS, Beyond Therapy: Biotechnology and the Pursuit of Happiness (2003).
6. THE PRESIDENT'S COUNCIL ON BIOETHICS, Reproduction and Responsibility: The Regulation of New Biotechnologies 110 (2004).
7. MATTHEW H. PORTEUS & CHRISTINA T. DANN, Genome Editing of the Germline: Broadening the Discussion, 23 MOLECULAR THERAPY 980, 981 (2015).
8. CALLISTA L. MULDER ET AL., Spermatogonial Stem Cell Autotransplantation and Germline Genomic Editing: A Future Cure for Spermatogenic Failure and Prevention of Transmission of Genomic Diseases, 22 HUMAN REPRODUCTION UPDATE 561, 568 (2016).
9. The technicians will have plenty of sperm to modify. A single ejaculate within the normal range contains 2.5 milliliters of 40 to 300 million sperm per milliliter. *Male Workup, The Semen Analysis*, RESOLVE, www.resolve.org/about-infertility/male-workup/the-semen-analysis.html?referrer=https://www.google.com/ (last visited November 24, 2016).

10. In IUI, a doctor prepares and transfers sperm into the female patient's cervix or uterus to help her get pregnant. AMERICAN SOCIETY FOR REPRODUCTIVE MEDICINE, Intrauterine Insemination, www.asrm.org/topics/detail.aspx?id=1277 (last visited November 24, 2016).
11. Experts disagree as to whether oogonial stem cells exist. TETSUYA ISHII & RENEE A. REIJO PERA, Creating Human Germ Cells for Unmet Reproductive Needs, 34 NATURE BIOTECHNOLOGY 470, 471 (2016). Thus, it may not be possible to harvest and modify such precursors before returning them to the ovary to mature into eggs inside the body.
12. *See* KERRY LYNN MACINTOSH, Brave New Eugenics: Regulating Assisted Reproductive Technologies in the Name of Better Babies, 257 U. ILL. J.L. TECH & POLIC, 264–65 (2010).
13. *Id.* at 265.
14. AMERICAN SOCIETY FOR REPRODUCTIVE MEDICINE, Frequently Asked Questions About Infertility, www.asrm.org/awards/index.aspx?id=3012 (last visited June 15, 2016).
15. JENNIFER GERSON UFFALUSSY, The Cost of IVF: Four Things I Learned While Battling Infertility, *Forbes* (February 6, 2014), www.forbes.com/sites/learnvest/2014/02/06/the-cost-of-ivf-4-things-i-learned-while-battling-infertility/.
16. HENRY T. GREELY, THE END OF SEX AND THE FUTURE OF HUMAN REPRODUCTION 102 (2016).
17. DAVID CYRANOSKI, Mouse Eggs Made from Skin Cells in a Dish, NATURE NEWS (October 17, 2016), www.nature.com/news/mouse-eggs-made-from-skin-cells-in-a-dish-1.20817. For a more complete discussion of artificial gametes generated from various stem cells, including iPSCs, see SASKIA HENDRIKS ET AL., Artificial Gametes: A Systematic Review of Biological Progress Towards Clinical Application, 21 HUMAN REPRODUCTION UPDATE 285 (2015).
18. GREELY, *supra* note 16, at 158–63.
19. For a detailed account of how ICSI is performed, see SHERMAN J. SILBER, HOW TO GET PREGNANT 260–63 (2005, paperback 2007).
20. To accomplish PGD, a technician must first remove a blastomere (cell) from an early human embryo with eight cells. Doing so does not harm the embryo, which still has enough remaining cells to develop into a healthy baby. *Id.* at 327–31. The excised blastomere is subjected to polymerase chain reaction (PCR) to test for genetic mutations or fluorescent in situ hybridization (FISH) to search for chromosomal abnormalities. *Id.* at 333–34.
21. KATHRYN T. DRAZBA ET AL., A Qualitative Inquiry of the Financial Concerns of Couples Opting to Use Preimplantation Genetic Diagnosis to Prevent the Transmission of Known Genetic Disorders, 23 J. GENETIC COUNSELING 202, 203 (2014).
22. TETSUYA ISHII, Reproductive Medicine Involving Genome Editing: Clinical Uncertainties and Embryological Needs, 34 REPRODUCTIVE BIOMEDICINE ONLINE 27, 29 (2017) (opining that PGD following HGM will be necessary but also questioning its efficacy).

23. PRESIDENT'S COUNCIL ON BIOETHICS, Beyond Therapy: Biotechnology and the Pursuit of Happiness 13–15 (2003) [hereinafter BEYOND THERAPY].
24. Id. at 13.
25. Id. at 13–14.
26. ASHLEY WELCH, Designer Baby Controversy: Scientists Edit Genome of Human Embryo, CBS NEWS (April 24, 2015), www.cbsnews.com/news/designer-baby-controversy-scientists-edit-genome-of-human-embryo/.
  To search for more diseases caused by genetic mutations, see GENETICS HOME REFERENCE, Conditions, U.S. NATIONAL LIBRARY OF MEDICINE (September 1, 2015), http://ghr.nlm.nih.gov/BrowseConditions.
27. GENETICS HOME REFERENCE, What Is a Gene Mutation and How Do Gene Mutations Occur, U.S. NATIONAL LIBRARY OF MEDICINE (October 12, 2015), http://ghr.nlm.nih.gov/handbook/mutationsanddisorders/genemutation.
28. E.g., PUPING LIANG ET AL., Correction of β-thalassemia Mutant by Base Editor in Human Embryos, PROTEIN & CELL, doi: 10.1007/s13238-0170475-6 (2017); HENRY I. MILLER, Germline Gene Therapy: We're Ready, 348 SCIENCE 1325 (2015); BOARD OF EDITORS, Why Embryos Should Not Be Off-Limits, 313 SCI. AM. 10 (July 2015). Even those who oppose HGM for therapy do not object to elimination of disease as such; rather, they believe there are safer ways to achieve the same goal, such as screening embryos for genetic mutations prior to implantation, or using the CRISPR/Cas9 tool to modify the somatic cells of patients who are already born. See ERIC S. LANDER, Brave New Genome, 373 NEW ENG. J. MED. 5, 6 (2015) (advocating screening rather than editing of embryos at risk for genetic mutation); EDWARD LANPHIER ET AL., Don't Edit the Human Germ Line, 519 NATURE 410, 411 (2015) (approving the use of the CRISPR/Cas9 tool to edit somatic cells but not embryos).
29. GENETICS HOME REFERENCE, Huntington Disease, U.S. NATIONAL LIBRARY OF MEDICINE (December 13, 2016), http://ghr.nlm.nih.gov/condition/huntington-disease. "Autosome" is a term used to describe any one of the 22 non-sex chromosomes. When a single copy of a gene located on an autosome can cause a trait or disorder, the trait or disorder is said to be autosomal dominant. GENETICS HOME REFERENCE Autosomal Dominant, U.S. NATIONAL LIBRARY OF MEDICINE (December 13, 2016), http://ghr.nlm.nih.gov/glossary=autosomaldominant.
30. Huntington Disease, *supra* note 29.
31. See, e.g., Bruce Alberts ET AL., MOLECULAR BIOLOGY OF THE CELL 1272–81 (5th ed. 2008) (describing the process of meiosis).
32. Huntington Disease, *supra* note 29.
33. E.g., LANDER, *supra* note 28, at 6.
34. BOARD OF EDITORS, *supra* note 28.
35. LANDER, *supra* note 28, at 6.
36. The correction could be applied to mature eggs or to eggs at the germinal vesicle stage, which would then be matured in the lab prior to use. R. VASSENA ET AL., Genome Engineering through CRISPR/

Cas9 Technology in the Human Germline and Pluripotent Stem Cells, 22 HUMAN REPRODUCTION UPDATE 411, 415 (2016).

37. *Id.*
38. *Id.*
39. Recent experiments in which human embryos were edited with the CRISPR/Cas9 tool yielded mosaics. *E.g.*, LICHUN TANG ET AL., CRISPR/Cas9-mediated Gene Editing in Human Zygotes Using Cas9 Protein, 292 MOLECULAR GENETICS AND GENOMICS 525, 530, 532 (2017); PUPING LIANG ET AL., CRISPR/Cas9-mediated Gene Editing in Human Tripronuclear Zygotes, 6 PROTEIN & CELL 363, 366 (2015).
40. NATIONAL ACADEMY OF SCIENCES & NATIONAL ACADEMY OF MEDICINE, Human Genome Editing: Science, Ethics, and Governance 89 (2017) [hereinafter NAS REPORT].
41. In one recent experiment, scientists edited mouse embryos without generating mosaics. By using electroporation, they speeded introduction of the molecular tool and completed editing before an embryo first replicated its genome. In this manner, they were able to create non-mosaic embryos. MASAKAZU HASIMOTO ET AL., Electroporation of Cas9 Protein/sgRNA into Early Pronuclear Zygotes Generates Non-mosaic Mutants in the Mouse, 418 DEVELOPMENTAL BIOLOGY 1 (2016).
42. GENETICS HOME REFERENCE, What Is DNA? U.S. NATIONAL LIBRARY OF MEDICINE (October 5, 2015), http://ghr.nlm.nih.gov/handbook/basics/dna.
43. "Point Mutation," BIOLOGY DICTIONARY, https://biologydictionary.net/point-mutation/ (last visited on October 30, 2017).
44. BETTY S. PACE ET AL., Sickle Cell Disease: Genetics, Cellular and Molecular Mechanisms, and Therapies, 2012 ANEMIA, Article ID 143594.
45. GENETICS HOME REFERENCE, Sickle Cell Disease, U.S. NATIONAL LIBRARY OF MEDICINE (December 13, 2016), http://ghr.nlm.nih.gov/condition/sickle-cell-disease.
46. *Id.*
47. *Id.*
48. CENTERS FOR DISEASE CONTROL AND PREVENTION Sickle Cell Disease, Data and Statistics, (February 29, 2016) www.cdc.gov/ncbddd/sicklecell/data.html.
49. MILLER, *supra* note 28.
50. *See id.* (anticipating such use of HGM); *see also* TANG ET AL., *supra* note 39 (reporting an experiment in which researchers used the CRISPR/Cas9 tool to correct mutated HBB gene responsible for blood disorder beta thalassemia in viable human embryos).
51. *See* PORTEUS & DANN, *supra* note 7 at 981 (suggesting that spermatogonial stem cells can be edited and used to make sperm for use in IVF).
52. RONALD M. GREEN, BABIES BY DESIGN: THE ETHICS OF GENETIC CHOICE 62–63 (2007).
53. *Id.* at 60.
54. NAS REPORT, *supra* note 40, at 111.

55. *See* LANDER, *supra* note 28, at 6 (acknowledging this scenario).
56. There are two types of HIV, HIV-1 and HIV-2. HIV-1 is found worldwide, while HIV-2 is found primarily in West Africa. HIV-2 is less transmissible and also less likely to result in AIDS. S. NYAMWEYA ET AL., Comparing HIV-1 and HIV-2 Infection: Lessons for Viral Immunopathogenesis, 23 REV. MED. VIROL. 221 (2013).
57. M. MARMOR ET AL., Resistance to HIV Infection, 83 J. URBAN HEALTH 5, 6–7 (2006).
58. Specifically, they request CCR5-Delta 32, which has a 32-base pair deletion. *Id.* at 7.
59. The baby is not perfectly immune because he still can be infected with strains of HIV that gain entrance to cells via a different receptor. *Id.*
60. XIANGJIN, KANG ET AL., Introducing Precise Genetic Modifications into Human 3PN Embryos by CRISPR/Cas-mediated Genome Editing, 33 J. ASSISTED REPROD. & GENETICS 581 (2016).
61. *Id.* at 585.
62. *Id.* at 587.
63. GREEN, *supra* note 52, at 90.
64. MARMOR ET AL., *supra* note 57, at 7–8.
65. LANDER, *supra* note 28, at 6.
66. BEYOND THERAPY, *supra* note 23, at 13.
67. *Id.* at 14, 145.
68. *Id.* at 13–14.
69. *E.g.*, LANPHIER ET AL., *supra* note 28, at 411.
70. *E.g.*, LANDER, *supra* note 28, at 7 (suggesting parents could use HGM to alter hair and eye color).
71. GREEN, *supra* note 52, at 67–70.
72. *E.g.*, AVIANNE TAN, 6-Year-Old Boy Gets 'Life-Changing' Plastic Surgery to Stop Bullying Over His 'Elf Ears', ABC NEWS (Oct. 2, 2015), http://abcnews.go.com/Health/year-boy-life-changing-plastic-surgery-stop-bullying/story?id=34212345.
73. *E.g.*, GREEN, *supra* note 52, at 71.
74. *Id.* at 72; GERT STULP ET AL., Tall Claims? Sense and Nonsense About the Importance of Height of US Presidents, 24 THE LEADERSHIP QUARTERLY 159, 160 (2013).
75. ANDREW R. WOOD ET AL., Defining the Role of Common Variation in the Genomic and Biological Architecture of Adult Human Height, 46 NATURE GENETICS 1173, 1173 (2014).
76. *Id.*
77. LANDER, *supra* note 28, at 7.
78. IAN J. DEARY ET AL., Genetics of Intelligence, 14 EUROPEAN J. HUMAN GENETICS 690, 690, 691 tbl. 1 (2006); MATT MCGUE & IRVING I. GOTTESMAN, Classical and Molecular Genetic Research on General Cognitive Ability, 45 HASTINGS CENTER REPORT (SPECIAL REPORT), September-October 2015, at S25, S25.

79. DEARY, *supra* note 78, at 690; MCGUE & GOTTESMAN, *supra* note 78, at S25.
80. G. DAVIES ET AL., Genome-wide Association Studies Establish That Human Intelligence Is Highly Heritable and Polygenic, 16 MOLECULAR PSYCHIATRY 996, 997 (2011).
81. MCGUE & GOTTESMAN, *supra* note 78, at S26.
82. NANCY SEGAL, ENTWINED LIVES: TWINS AND WHAT THEY TELL US ABOUT HUMAN BEHAVIOR 3–4, 8 (1999).
83. MCGUE & GOTTESMAN, *supra* note 78, at S27 fig. 2 (reporting correlations for twins and other blood relations).
84. *Id.* at S28 fig. 3.
85. *Id.* at S27.
86. *Id.* at S26–S27.
87. *Id.* at S27–S28.
88. *Id.* at S28. Environmental factors that are shared account for 31 to 39 percent of variation in general intelligence among individuals, while those that are not shared contribute another 14 percent. *Id.*
89. GENETICS HOME REFERENCE, What Is a Gene? U.S. NATIONAL LIBRARY OF MEDICINE (May 2, 2017), http://ghr.nlm.nih.gov/handbook/basics/gene.
90. GENETICS HOME REFERENCE, What Are Single Nucleotide Polymorphisms? U.S. NATIONAL LIBRARY OF MEDICINE (December 13, 2016), http://ghr.nlm.nih.gov/handbook/genomicresearch/snp.
91. *Id.*
92. CORNELIUS A. RIETVELD ET AL., Common Genetic Variants Associated with Cognitive Performance Identified Using the Proxy-phenotype Method, 111 PNAS 13790 (2014).
93. *Id.* at 13792.
94. SOCIAL SCIENCE GENETIC ASSOCIATION Consortium et al., FAQs about Common Genetic Variants Associated with Cognitive Performance Identified Using Proxy-Phenotype Method 3, http://ssgac.org/documents/FAQCommonGeneticVariantsAssociatedwithCognitivePerformanceIdentifiedUsingProxy-PhenotypeMethod.pdf (last visited October 7, 2015).
95. *Id.* at 6.
96. NATURE EDUCATION, Definition of Polygenic Trait, Scitable, www.nature.com/scitable/definition/polygenic-polygenic-characteristic-polygenic-trait-90 (last visited May 5, 2017).
97. MICHAEL R. JOHNSON ET AL., Systems Genetics Identifies a Convergent Gene Network for Cognition and Neurodevelopmental Disease, 19 NATURE NEUROSCIENCE 223 (2016).
98. KATE WIGHTON, Intelligence 'Networks' Discovered in Brain for the First Time, Imperial College London (December 22, 2015), at www3.imperial.ac.uk/newsandeventspggrp/imperialcollege/newssummary/news_22-12-2015-10-13-44.
99. RIETVELD ET AL., *supra* note 92, at 13793 (mentioning the genes KNCMA1, NRXN1, POU2F3, and SCRT).

100. Synaptic plasticity is the process by which connections in the brain are strengthened or weakened depending on their use. See ALBERTS, *supra* note 31, at 1395–97.
101. RIETVELD ET AL., *supra* note 92, at 13793 (mentioning the genes KNCMA1, NRXN1, POU2F3, and SCRT).
102. *Cf.* GREEN, *supra* note 52, at 77–78 (describing earlier experiment in which genetically engineered mice exhibited superior learning ability and speculating that genetic modifications to enhance learning would appeal to parents).
103. INGRID LOBO, Pleiotropy: One Gene Can Affect Multiple Traits, Scitable, Nature Education (2008), www.nature.com/scitable/topicpage/pleiotropy-one-gene-can-affect-multiple-traits-569.
104. *Cf.* LANDER, *supra* note 28, at 7 (noting that the same tp53 gene that shields mice against cancer also causes them to age prematurely).
105. Dance with Death, 538 NATURE 6 (2016).
106. *Id.*
107. *Id.*
108. BEYOND THERAPY, *supra* note 23, at 165.
109. Dance with Death, *supra* note 105.
110. XIAO DONG ET AL., Evidence for a Limit to Human Lifespan, 538 NATURE 257, 258 (2016).
111. *Id.*
112. BEYOND THERAPY, *supra* note 23, at 175.
113. *Id.; but see* CYNTHIA J. KENYON, The Genetics of Aging, 464 NATURE 504, 509 (2010) (questioning whether a trade-off between lifespan and reproductive capacity is inevitable).
114. JACOB B. HJELMBORG ET AL., Genetic Influence on Human Lifespan and Longevity, 119 HUMAN GENET. 312 (2006).
115. DIDDAHALLY GOVINDARAJU ET AL., Genetics Lifestyle and Longevity: Lessons from Centenarians, 4 APPLIED & TRANSLATIONAL GENOMICS 23, 30 (2015).
116. HUMAN AGING GENOMIC RESOURCES, Longevity Map: Human Longevity Genetic Variants, http://genomics.senescence.info/longevity/ (last visited October 11, 2015).
117. NIR BARZILAI ET AL., The Place of Genetics in Ageing Research, 13 NATURE REVIEWS 589, 589–90 (2012); GOVINDARAJU ET AL., *supra* note 115, at 25.
118. BARZILAI, *supra* note 117, at 589, 591.
119. MICHAEL SHERMER, Methuselah's Moon Shot: Can Science and Silicon Valley Defeat Death? 315 SCI. AM., 84 (October 2016). Calico's webpage can be accessed at www.calicolabs.com/ (last visited October 7, 2016).
120. *But cf.* BEYOND THERAPY, *supra* note 23, at 182 (hypothesizing each life stage could expand equally, leading to extended dependency in childhood and adolescence).

121. Humans have worried about extended lifespan coming at the price of frailty and incapacity for millennia. According to an ancient Greek myth, Eos, a goddess of the dawn, fell in love with Tithonus, a mortal. She asked Zeus to grant Tithonus immortality, but neglected to request eternal youth for him. As her lover aged, she wearied of caring for him, and she locked him away until he shrank into a cicada. 1 ROBERT GRAVES, THE GREEK MYTHS, 149–50 (rev. ed. 1960).
122. PAOLA SEBASTIANI & THOMAS T. PERLS, The Genetics of Extreme Longevity: Lessons from the New England Centenarian Study, 3 FRONTIERS IN GENETICS, Article 277, at 3 (2012).
123. KENYON, *supra* note 113, at 504.
124. SADIYA S. KHAN ET AL., A Null Mutation in SERPINE1 Protects Against Biological Aging in Humans, 3 SCIENCE ADVANCES, 11, eaao1617 (2017), DOI: 10.1126/sciadv.aao1617.
125. BEYOND THERAPY, *supra* note 23, at 13–16.
126. *Id.* at 14–15.
127. Only 1 percent of Caucasians have two copies of the mutated gene CCR5-Delta 32; 20 percent of Caucasians have one copy. This mutation does not occur naturally in Africans or East Asians. M. MARMOR ET AL., *supra* note 57, at 7.
128. KENYON, *supra* note 113, at 504.
129. BARZILAI ET AL., supra note 117, at 591–92.
130. BEYOND THERAPY, *supra* note 23, at 15.
131. *Id.* at 15.
132. The average life expectancy of an American child born in 2013 is 78.9 years. NATIONAL CENTER FOR HEALTH STATISTICS, CENTERS FOR DISEASE CONTROL AND PREVENTION, U.S. DEPARTMENT OF HEALTH AND HUMAN SERVICES, HEALTH, UNITED STATES 2014, WITH SPECIAL FEATURE ON ADULTS AGED 55–64 102, *available at* www.cdc.gov/nchs/data/hus/hus14.pdf#016 (last visited September 20, 2015).
133. *See* SEBASTIANI & PERLS, *supra* note 122, at 3.
134. *Cf.* BEYOND THERAPY, *supra* note 23, at 16 (speculating that if genetic dwarves use growth hormone to increase their height to the average, those who were once average in height but have become short in relative terms can claim a right to treatment with growth hormone).
135. *See id.* (commenting on therapies versus enhancements, and noting the distinction does not succeed as a moral judgment).

2

Transgressing Boundaries

CRISPR/Cas9 and other molecular editing tools may soon make it possible to modify human gametes and embryos. However, use of human germline modification (HGM) for reproductive purposes runs counter to certain religious tenets. Also, some critics see HGM for reproduction as an offense against nature. Lastly, tinkering with human gametes and embryos – the very stuff of life – can be viewed as an arrogant act that leads to bad outcomes.

These three concerns reflect a sense that human beings should not cross divine or natural boundaries, or meddle in life creation. Therefore, this chapter describes them collectively as the *hubris objection*.[1] It explores the concerns and explains how they associate children of HGM with negative traits.

A GOD

In the Jewish, Christian, and Muslim religious traditions, God creates life.[2] Men and women are facilitators who unite egg and sperm via sexual intercourse to yield embryos that may become babies.[3] But HGM allows men and women to do more than facilitate: by altering gametes and embryos, they attempt to determine the traits of their children. Does this human intervention in a divinely ordained process offend religious principles?

Mainstream religious traditions generally approve of medical care that heals human beings and saves lives.[4] Thus, they may tolerate HGM that prevents disease and disability by eliminating deleterious genetic mutations from gametes or embryos.[5] However, such traditions may oppose HGM when it is used to enhance children.[6]

For example, the Congregation for the Doctrine of the Faith, which promotes and safeguards Roman Catholic doctrine,[7] opposes genetic modification of human gametes at present due to the limited state of research and safety concerns.[8] Interestingly, the Congregation has not foreclosed the future use of HGM to relieve human suffering. However, it opposes nontherapeutic uses of HGM. In its view, modifications that privilege certain traits over others violate the principle human equality and make it harder for people to get along.[9] It adds that human beings should not usurp the role of God as creator.[10]

To be sure, even if therapeutic modifications become safe enough for the Roman Catholic Church to accept, scientists must employ methods consistent with Church teachings. The Church considers in vitro fertilization (IVF) illicit because it divorces human procreation from sexual intercourse and often entails the loss or destruction of human embryos.[11] Thus, a method that entails modifying embryos in the lab is unacceptable.[12] However, the Church may accept a treatment that alters spermatogonial stem cells and returns them to the testes to mature into healthy sperm.[13] Likewise, the Church has not yet decided if gamete intrafallopian transfer (GIFT) is permissible and leaves its use to the conscience of the couple involved.[14] Thus, it may tolerate a GIFT-based process in which eggs are removed from the ovaries, edited, and then placed in the fallopian tubes along with sperm.[15]

Ethicist Ronald Green believes that religious authorities accept therapeutic uses of HGM because they repair the diseases and disabilities stemming from Adam and Eve's original sin.[16] By contrast, they reject enhancing uses because the human genome is of divine origin and its alteration defies the will of God.[17] Similarly, biologist Lee Silver states that those who believe God designed the human species in his image find it sacrilegious to improve upon and perhaps exceed that image. Genetic enhancements are troubling because they reach beyond the current generation and alter the course of human evolution.[18]

The hypothetical scenarios presented in Chapter 1 illustrate the foregoing principles. First, suppose Mary Smith has a genetic mutation that causes Huntington disease. Her doctor retrieves her eggs and corrects the mutation before placing the eggs in her fallopian tubes along with John Smith's sperm. Fertilization occurs, and nine months later, Mary bears a healthy daughter named Ariel. If the editing can be done safely, the Roman Catholic Church may condone this process, because it eliminates a deadly mutation.[19]

Second, assume John and Mary Smith undergo IVF. Their technician gives each embryo two copies of a protective variant of the CCR5 receptor gene. Nine months later, Mary gives birth to a son named Blake who is immune to most HIV-1 infections. Because HGM has a medical purpose in this case, some religious authorities may condone its use. However, because the Smiths used IVF, the Roman Catholic Church would condemn their conduct.

Third, suppose John and Mary Smith add single nucleotide polymorphisms (SNPs) associated with memory and learning to their gametes or embryos. Mary later gives birth to a daughter named Cora. Enhancement does not qualify as healing, so the Roman Catholic Church and other religious authorities are likely to condemn the Smiths' conduct, no matter what method they use.

Fourth, assume John and Mary Smith add lifespan-extending genetic variants to their gametes or embryos. Their son Devin is born nine months afterward.

The reaction of religious authorities is harder to predict in this case. Although lifespan extension is an enhancement, some may accept the modification if it also reduces Devin's susceptibility to disease and disability. One philosopher has suggested that the Christian tradition may tolerate lifespan extension as long as the Biblical maximum set by Methuselah (who reportedly lived to be 969 years old)[20] is not exceeded.[21] Again, however, even if religious authorities accept lifespan extension in principle, they may accept certain methods and condemn others.

B NATURE

HGM is sometimes viewed as an offense against nature. This view holds that evolution has designed an ideal human genome that must be preserved untouched.[22] However, as Professor Green notes, evolution is a mindless process that produces accidents and suboptimal results.[23] The human genome was never perfectly adapted to our ancestral environment and is even more out of synch with the world we live in now.[24] For example, tribalism might have aided the survival of hunter-gatherer societies, but now it foments conflict and genocide.[25]

Jeremy Rifkin argues that mutations that cause diseases should not be eradicated because genetic diversity is valuable.[26] His argument holds a kernel of truth: although the vast majority of genetic mutations are valueless code errors,[27] some do yield an advantage. For example, the gene that causes cystic fibrosis provides resistance to cholera when a person inherits it from only one parent. It is only when a person inherits two copies of the gene from both parents that the cystic fibrosis manifests itself.[28] Nevertheless, it is both callous and unnecessary to condemn an unlucky few to suffer for the good of the species. As the National Academy of Sciences and National Academy of Medicine have noted, the number of people who use HGM to correct genetic mutations is likely to be small and the impact on the gene pool correspondingly slight.[29] Moreover, if loss of specific genetic information is a concern, it would be more compassionate to create a comprehensive databank of human DNA samples, as Professor Green suggests.[30]

If neither evolution nor genetic diversity justifies maintaining a static human genome, is there any other reason why some people consider HGM to be unnatural and wrong? Professor Silver argues that Westerners often treat nature as a God substitute. We see nature as *Mother Nature*: a wise and powerful designer whose plan for humankind must not be disrupted by scientists and their hubristic inventions.[31]

If theories like these drive public policy, they will lead to harsh outcomes. It is one thing to say that John and Mary Smith should not modify their gametes or embryos to produce children with improved memory and learning or extended lifespans. It is quite another to say that they have no right to correct genetic mutations in their gametes that cause Huntington disease or sickle cell disease or other maladies that cause tremendous human suffering.

C THE *FRANKENSTEIN* MYTH

Thus far, this chapter has focused on religious or nature-based concerns about HGM for reproduction. Another, more practical objection must be added here. One sometimes hears that human beings should not play God by meddling in matters that exceed their limited physical and intellectual powers.[32] This warning reminds us that if our reach exceeds our grasp, the results are likely to be bad.

Mary Shelley's novel *Frankenstein; or, The Modern Prometheus* presents the classic example.[33] Dr. Victor Frankenstein scavenges body parts from corpses, assembles them in the form of a man, and animates the whole, only to discover that he has created a hideous, murdering monster.[34] Through its plot, the novel teaches that arrogating godlike powers to oneself leads to suffering and death.[35]

HGM is still in its infancy. There is near-universal consensus that molecular editing tools such as CRISPR/Cas9 should not be used on gametes or embryos destined to become babies. Interestingly, the Frankenstein myth may be a subconscious force behind the cautious approach that currently prevails.

As time passes, and technology improves, scientists may learn how to conduct simple gene edits safely. So, for example, scientists may discover how to correct the mutations that cause Huntington disease or sickle cell disease. At that point, the Frankenstein myth should lose some of its power. However, if the myth lingers, it could distort the regulatory process. As Chapter 8 explains, the Food and Drug Administration claims the power to regulate HGM for safety and effectiveness. If the agency expects bad outcomes, it may skew its evaluation of safety data in that direction, thereby delaying clinical trials of therapeutic modifications and causing human suffering.

Finally, scientists are years away from learning how to enhance complex traits such as memory or lifespan. The Frankenstein myth is most salient and powerful when technology is complicated and entails great risk. This book predicts that the myth will foster enduring opposition to enhancing modifications.

D STEREOTYPES ASSOCIATED WITH THE HUBRIS OBJECTION

Technologies of all kinds can be opposed based on their perceived disadvantages. However, reproductive technologies are unique in that they lead to the birth of human beings. Even when crafted with care, an objection may inadvertently imply that children of HGM have bad traits. This section examines such stereotypes.

1 *Good versus Evil*

If a scientist corrects a genetic mutation in human gametes or embryos, he acts consistently with religious traditions of healing. Depending on the methods he employs, believers may perceive his conduct as acceptable, even beneficial.

However, if he adds SNPs associated with improved memory and learning to gametes or embryos, his attempt to enhance may violate religious tenets. Believers may then condemn his conduct as immoral, sacrilegious, and evil.

Thoughtful believers should realize that the resulting child did not choose to be conceived with an enhanced trait and has committed no sin. Yet, if the child is the product of evil, some may intuitively perceive her as evil, however unfair that may be. Moreover, an uncomfortable question remains: if humankind is made in the image of God, and the child is modified to exceed the human norm, has she transcended the image of God? If so, the child may inspire awe, fear, and rejection rather than the love, warmth, and acceptance that she deserves.

2 Natural versus Unnatural

Some believe that the human genome has evolved to the point where it is in harmony with the environment. For those who hold this view, a scientist who performs HGM despoils an ideal genome and disrupts this harmony. In assessing his transgression, his purpose (therapy or enhancement) is less important than the degree to which he deviates from the standard human genome and its environment. Children who result from his experiments are not to blame for their altered genomes. Nevertheless, the objection may induce some to view their bodies as disharmonious and contrary to the existing natural order.

Next, recall the claim that elimination of harmful genetic mutations undermines human diversity. As discussed earlier, this claim fails because the vast majority of mutations are useless and adequate genetic diversity exists regardless. Moreover, even if this claim were true, children without mutations would pose no further threat to diversity once born. Still, the claim implies that these children do not deserve the good health that their parents selfishly obtained for them.

Finally, those who deify Mother Nature believe that HGM is unnatural and objectionable. Perhaps some will take the next step and infer that children of HGM are also unnatural and objectionable. Whether the genetic modification is accomplished for therapy or enhancement makes little difference. However, the greater the deviation from the standard human genome, the more likely it is that the charge of unnaturalness will stick.

3 Human versus Monster

The warning that arrogant adults should not meddle with the stuff of life does not speak directly to the qualities of children of HGM, who are innocent by-products. Yet, since nothing good can come of arrogance, the children may find it hard to escape the implication that there is something wrong with them. The popularity of the novel *Frankenstein* heightens this risk. The novel and movies made from it[36] condition us to expect that reproductive technologies produce babies who are defective or monstrous. This conditioning has already distorted the human cloning debate, where some falsely claim that all animal clones are abnormal,[37] while others disparage human clones as "Franken-babies"[38] even though none has ever been born.[39] Once children are born through HGM, similar prejudices may extend to them.

E SUMMARY

This chapter has discussed three concerns about HGM for reproduction. First, it may violate religious tenets. However, religious authorities generally view medical therapies as good. Thus, once HGM is perfected, such authorities may tolerate therapeutic modifications but reject enhancing modifications.

Second, HGM for reproduction may be an offense against nature. Various claims fall within this category: the evolution of the human genome in harmony with its environment, the importance of genetic diversity, and the sanctity of nature's plan for humankind. This chapter has questioned these claims on biological and evolutionary grounds.

Third, HGM for reproduction may be an arrogant act that exceeds human competence. The Frankenstein myth, which is deeply engrained in the public consciousness, renders this concern more powerful. As this chapter has explained, the myth may distort regulatory decisions by priming regulators to anticipate bad results.

All three concerns imply that children of HGM have negative traits. If HGM is an evil act that transcends the limits God has placed on humankind, some may view the children as evil or transcendent. If HGM offends nature, others may see the children as disharmonious, undeserving, or unnatural. Finally, if HGM is a form of hubris, still others may perceive the children as defective or monstrous. Part II carries this analysis forward by exploring the psychological origins of the hubris objection and related stereotypes.

Notes

1. The term "hubris" describes the arrogance of those who transgress divine limits on human behavior. "Hubris," BRITANNICA ONLINE ENCYCLOPEDIA (November 14, 2017), www.britannica.com/topic/hubris.
2. RONALD M. GREEN, BABIES BY DESIGN: THE ETHICS OF GENETIC CHOICE 171–72 (2007).
3. *See id.* at 172 (explaining that parents are agents of God, and that God provides human beings with souls after conception).
4. MARK S. FRANKEL & AUDREY R. CHAPMAN, Human Inheritable Genetic Modifications: Assessing Scientific, Ethical, Religious, and Policy Issues. AMERICAN ASSOCIATION FOR THE ADVANCEMENT OF SCIENCE, 27 (2000),

www.aaas.org/sites/default/files/migrate/uploads/germline.pdf (relying on Jewish, Protestant, and Catholic theologians); see GREEN, *supra* note 2, at 173 (speaking of Jewish, Christian and Muslim traditions); JOHN H. EVANS & KATHY HUDSON, Religion and Reproductive Genetics: Beyond Views of Embryonic Life? 46 J. SCIENTIFIC STUDY OF RELIGION 565, 569 (2007) (explaining that Christians do not generally oppose medical research or treatments).

5. See RONALD COLE-TURNER, Religion and the Question of Human Germline Modification, in DESIGN AND DESTINY: JEWISH AND CHRISTIAN PERSPECTIVES ON HUMAN GERMLINE MODIFICATION 1, 15 (RONALD COLE-TURNER ED. 2008) (stating that Christian churches do not object to therapeutic HGM in principle); FRANKEL & CHAPMAN, *supra* note 4, at 29 (noting that official positions of most religions do not reject HGM outright); GREEN, *supra* note 2, at 174 (claiming that there is a consensus that curative applications of HGM fall within religious tradition). In 1983, economist Jeremy Rifkin managed to persuade some Catholic bishops and Protestant leaders to sign a resolution against all HGM. COLE-TURNER, *supra*, at 9–10. However, this dated resolution is inconsistent with official statements from religious authorities. *Id.* at 10–16.

6. See FRANKEL & CHAPMAN, *supra* note 4, at 28 (stating that religious traditions are uneasy about work that alters human nature); COLE-TURNER, *supra* note 5, at 15 (indicating Christian traditions generally oppose genetic enhancement).

7. APOSTOLIC CONSTITUTION, PASTOR BONUS, June 28, 1988, Part III, art. 48, at 33 (Latin-English ed., MICHEL THERIAULT ED. 1999).

8. CONGREGATION FOR THE DOCTRINE OF THE FAITH, Instruction Dignitas Personae on Certain Bioethical Questions ¶ 26 (2008), at www.ewtn.com/library/CURIA/CDF-Dignitas-Personae.pdf [hereinafter DIGNITAS PERSONAE].

9. *Id.* at ¶ 27.

10. *Id.*

11. *Id.* ¶¶ 14–16.

12. *Id.* ¶ 26.

13. See MATTHEW H. PORTEUS & CHRISTINA T. DANN, Genome Editing of the Germline: Broadening the Discussion, 23 MOLECULAR THERAPY 980, 981 (2015) (describing such a method). A theological commission headed by Cardinal Joseph Ratzinger (who later became Pope Benedict XVI) issued a 2003 report on reproductive technologies and other issues. The report suggested that stem cells that develop into sperm might be genetically modified to allow a man to conceive a child via sexual intercourse. GREEN, *supra* note 2, at 173–74, citing International Theological Commission, COMMUNION AND STEWARDSHIP: HUMAN PERSONS CREATED IN THE IMAGE OF GOD (2004), § 90, at www.vatican.va/roman_curia/congregations/cfaith/cti_documents/rc_con_cfaith_doc_20040723_communion-stewardship_en.html (last visited June 8, 2016).

14. JOHN M. HAAS, Begotten Not Made: A Catholic View of Reproductive Technology, UNITED STATES CONFERENCE OF CATHOLIC BISHOPS (1998), www.usccb.org/issues-and-action/human-life-and-dignity/reproductive-technology/begotten-not-made-a-catholic-view-of-reproductive-technology.cfm.
15. *See generally* SHERMAN J. 1991;, HOW TO GET PREGNANT 199–200 (1991; Little, Brown & Co. rev. edn. September 2005, paperback ed. August 2007) (describing GIFT).
16. GREEN, *supra* note 2, at 175–76.
17. *Id.* at 174–76.
18. LEE M. SILVER, CHALLENGING NATURE: THE CLASH OF SCIENCE AND SPIRITUALITY AT THE NEW FRONTIERS OF LIFE 327 (2006).
19. *See* THOMAS A. SHANNON, The Roman Catholic Magisterium and Genetic Research: An Overview and Evaluation, in DESIGN AND DESTINY: JEWISH AND CHRISTIAN PERSPECTIVES ON HUMAN GERMLINE MODIFICATION 51, 64 (RONALD COLE-TURNER ED. 2008) (suggesting the Roman Catholic Church might accept modification to eliminate Huntington disease).
20. *Genesis* 5:25–27.
21. H. Tristram Engelhardt Jr., A TRADITIONAL CHRISTIAN REFLECTION ON REENGINEERING HUMAN NATURE, IN DESIGN AND DESTINY 74, 86 (RONALD COLE-TURNER ED).
22. GREEN, *supra* note 2, at 179.
23. *Id.* at 181–83.
24. *Id.* at 183; *see also* NATIONAL ACADEMY OF SCIENCES & NATIONAL ACADEMY OF MEDICINE, Human Genome Editing: Science, Ethics, and Governance 95 (2017) [hereinafter NAS REPORT], at 95 (noting that some selection pressures that helped shape the human genome are no longer relevant today).
25. GREEN, *supra* note 2, at 183.
26. SILVER, *supra* note 18, at 328.
27. *Id.*
28. GREEN, *supra* note 2, at 97.
29. NAS REPORT, *supra* note 24, at 90.
30. GREEN, *supra* note 2, at 100.
31. SILVER, *supra* note 18, at 325–30.
32. C. A. J. COADY, Playing God, in HUMAN ENHANCEMENT 155, 165 (JULIAN SAVULESCU & NICK BOSTROM, EDS. 2013).
33. MARY SHELLEY, FRANKENSTEIN; OR, THE MODERN PROMETHEUS (1818; Washington Square Press 1995).
34. *See* KERRY LYNN MACINTOSH, ILLEGAL BEINGS: HUMAN CLONES AND THE LAW 15–16 (2005) (summarizing the plot of the novel).
35. The subtitle of the novel reinforces the lesson. Prometheus was a mythical Titan who stole fire from Mount Olympus and gave it to humans. Zeus, who was already unhappy with humankind and its rising powers, reacted in rage, ordering Prometheus bound to a rock so a vulture could tear at his

liver for all eternity. ROBERT GRAVES, 1 THE GREEK MYTHS 144–45 (rev. edn. 1960).
36. *E.g.*, MARY SHELLEY'S *FRANKENSTEIN* (TriStar Pictures 1994); FRANKENSTEIN, THE TRUE STORY (NBC 1973); FRANKENSTEIN (Universal Pictures 1931).
37. MACINTOSH, *supra* note 34, at 55–59.
38. *Id.* at 15.
39. KERRY LYNN MACINTOSH, HUMAN CLONING: FOUR FALLACIES AND THEIR LEGAL CONSEQUENCES 44 (2013).

3

Transforming Reproduction into Manufacture

Critics object to human germline modification (HGM) on the ground that it transforms human reproduction into manufacture.[1] This *manufacture objection* calls to mind *Brave New World*,[2] Aldous Huxley's novel about a future society obsessed with production and consumption. There, human beings are fabricated and conditioned to play a specific labor role within their society: managing Alphas; responsible Betas; and laborer Gammas, Deltas, and Epsilons, each of the latter three classes marked by a decrease in intellectual capacity.[3]

Two concerns are logically related to the manufacture objection. First, some worry that parents who use HGM to design children deprive them of an open future.[4] By selecting traits suited to particular achievements or occupations, parents undermine the autonomy of their children and foreclose other life plans that they might have pursued.[5]

Second, others fear that such children will feel pressure to satisfy parental expectations.[6] *Gattaca*,[7] a film in which parents use preimplantation genetic diagnosis (PGD) to identify and select embryos destined to develop into superior children,[8] illustrates this concern. The film portrays the suffering of a man named Jerome Morrow who expected to be a champion swimmer but placed second in the Olympics. Unable to come to terms with being second best, he hangs his silver medal around his neck and incinerates himself.[9]

This chapter examines the manufacture objection and these related concerns. It also investigates ways in which the objection and concerns distort perceptions of children of HGM.

A REPRODUCTION OR MANUFACTURE

Analysis begins with a comparison of standard reproduction and HGM. Although there are similarities between the two, this section seeks to pinpoint aspects of HGM that make some people perceive it as a manufacturing process.

1 Standard Reproduction

In standard reproduction, one man has sexual intercourse with one woman. A spermatozoon fertilizes an egg, leading to an embryo. The odds are that the embryo will fail due to chromosomal abnormalities.[10] However, if the embryo is viable, it may anchor itself in the woman's uterus and begin to grow. Nine months later, a child is born.

The man and woman do not select the egg, spermatozoon, or embryo. They do choose each other for mating, based on physical or other traits, but the process is otherwise random. Thus, their child possesses a fortuitous assortment of traits. He is a surprise – some might say a gift.[11]

2 HGM

Chapter 1 described various methods of performing HGM. This part presents two. The first deviates only slightly from standard reproduction, while the second is more complicated and involves in vitro fertilization (IVF).

First, suppose a doctor retrieves spermatogonial stem cells from a man. A lab technician uses CRISPR/Cas9 to modify the stem cells, and the doctor returns them to the man's testes to mature into modified sperm.[12] Thereafter, the man has sexual intercourse with a female partner. If a viable embryo is conceived, a child is born nine months later. This method may satisfy religious authorities who believe reproduction should be achieved via sexual intercourse.[13] However, it does not allow embryos to be screened for the desired genetic modification.

Second, suppose a woman takes fertility drugs. A doctor retrieves multiple eggs from her ovaries. A lab technician unites the eggs with sperm obtained from the woman's male partner and cultures the products until they become embryos.[14] But this is not a typical IVF cycle: another technician has used CRISPR/Cas9 to modify the gametes prior to conception, or to alter the embryos afterward, and PGD is employed to identify those embryos that have the desired genetic profile. Thereafter, the doctor transfers one or more embryos to the woman. Nine months later, a child is born.

3 Comparative Analysis

Whether accomplished through the first or second method, HGM aims to achieve the birth of a healthy child in nine months, as standard reproduction does. However, it differs from standard reproduction in four ways.

First, instead of a man and woman, HGM requires a man, woman, technicians, and doctors. Second, instead of a room furnished with bed, sheets, and pillows, it requires a lab with sophisticated equipment. In the case of IVF, fertility drugs are also necessary. Third, while standard reproduction is free, HGM is not. Modifying and transferring spermatogonial stem cells to the testes will cost money. HGM performed in the context of IVF will be even more expensive. As Chapter 1, Section A, explained, IVF costs around $12,400 per cycle, and fertility drugs add another $3000 to $5000 to the tab. Editing gametes or embryos will cost extra, and screening embryos prior to transfer will add another $2500 to $6000. Fourth, instead of a child who is a surprise, HGM yields a child who has at least one trait that is chosen and expected.

B TECHNOLOGY AND MONEY

As the foregoing analysis shows, many differences between standard reproduction and HGM come down to technology and money. In evaluating the objection that HGM transforms human reproduction into manufacture, it is helpful to begin with a look at IVF, which also involves technology and money.

Critics have long claimed that IVF treats human reproduction as manufacture[15] and commodifies children.[16] However, the evidence we have does not support these claims. IVF has been practiced since 1978 and more than 5 million babies have been born with its aid.[17] Studies of families formed in this technological manner indicate that parents exhibit warmth toward their children and enjoy good relationships with them.[18] The children are psychologically comparable to sexually conceived peers, and their rates of emotional and behavioral issues are low.[19] Judging by these results, IVF is not a manufacturing process and does not treat children as products.

C DESIGN

However, HGM differs from both standard reproduction and IVF in one important respect. Both sexual intercourse and IVF generate embryos that are a random combination of chromosomes from mother and father. By contrast, in HGM, parents request a trait (or lack of a trait). Technicians then modify gametes (in their precursor or mature form) or embryos accordingly.

Does this element of intentional design nudge human reproduction toward manufacture? Does it raise serious concerns that children may be deprived of an open future or subjected to unreasonable expectations? This section uses the Chapter 1 hypotheticals to explore these questions.

1 HGM to Eliminate Genetic Disease

Parents may use HGM to prevent their children from inheriting a genetic disease. For example, Chapter 1, Section B.1.a, presents a hypothetical involving Mary Smith, who is a carrier for Huntington disease. She and her husband, John, want to protect their offspring from this adult-onset disease and the suffering that goes along with it. Thus, they decide to undergo IVF with HGM. A technician uses

CRISPR/Cas9 to remove the genetic mutation that causes the disease from Mary's eggs. John's sperm fertilizes the modified eggs, and an embryo is transferred to Mary, leading to the birth of a healthy daughter named Ariel nine months later.

Cases of this kind hardly seem worthy of the label "manufacture." Correction of a mutation that causes disease entails only a minor element of design. Moreover, this modification does not deprive Ariel of an open future. Arguably, HGM has increased, rather than decreased, her autonomy because good health opens up opportunities and life plans that otherwise would have been foreclosed to her. Also, if Ariel is born without the mutation, the Smiths' expectations are met. She will not experience ongoing pressure to please her parents.[20]

2 HGM to Confer Immunity

Next, consider the hypothetical described in Chapter 1, Section B.2. John and Mary Smith use HGM to conceive a baby boy named Blake who is resistant to infection with HIV-1. This type of modification does not vary in purpose or effect from vaccines administered to children after they are born. In either case, the intervention is minor and the goal is to protect a child against disease.

Once again, the element of design would appear to be too slight to transform reproduction into manufacture. Likewise, concerns about open future and parental expectations are not compelling in this context. Blake's future may be healthier, but it is not predetermined; he can live his life as he pleases. And if the procedure succeeds, parental expectations are met at birth, and Blake will not feel pressured.

3 HGM for Enhancement

Finally, recall the Chapter 1, Section C, hypotheticals in which John and Mary Smith use HGM to improve their child's memory and learning and/or extend its lifespan. Their deliberate decision to purchase enhancing modifications inches the reproductive process closer to manufacture. Yet, such scenarios are not that scary, perhaps because our society already encourages parents to improve the health and prospects of their offspring in other ways. Pregnant women are urged to eat well, avoid alcoholic beverages, and take prenatal vitamins. Parents are taught how to feed babies properly and told to take them to doctor appointments for examinations and vaccinations. Parents must send children to school, and many enroll their offspring in after-school sports or activities.

Moreover, John and Mary have left most of their offsprings' genomes to chance. Their interventions do not come close to the assembly-line production depicted in *Brave New World*, where the government uses gamete selection, artificial twinning, prenatal modification of embryos (including oxygen deprivation to reduce intelligence), and postnatal behavior modification programs to shape and control the destinies of babies and children.[21] Aldous Huxley seems to have understood that genes alone could not produce the manufactured castes he envisioned.

To be sure, related concerns about open futures and parental expectations remain. These concerns are often debated in general terms, but they should not be. The analysis depends on the character of the specific modification, as the following sections demonstrate.

a) Improved Memory and Learning

Assume the Smiths hire a doctor to add several single nucleotide polymorphisms (SNPs) to their sperm and eggs in an effort to improve memory and learning. Later, a daughter named Cora is born. It seems unlikely that HGM has undermined Cora's autonomy. Her SNPs may enable her to earn better grades or higher scores on standardized tests but do not determine her future. There are simply too many ways in which she can employ her ability to memorize and learn.[22] Logically, this enhancement increases rather than decreases her range of life plans.[23]

The Smiths may expect Cora to earn good grades or high scores on standardized tests. However, a child born to ambitious parents may face such expectations even without genetic manipulation. Today, parents attempt to design their children through environmental interventions, such as expensive private schools, enrichment classes, tutors, and the like.[24] If high expectations are already present, providing Cora with an innate facility for learning or memorization may reduce rather than increase her stress.[25] Furthermore, as John and Mary raise their daughter, they will learn firsthand that child design is not possible. Cora will defy their expectations in myriad ways. By the time she reaches an age where academic success matters, John and Mary may have adjusted their plans for her.

b) Lifespan Extension

Next, suppose the Smiths use HGM to extend lifespan. Subsequently, Mary gives birth to a son named Devin. This modification does not reduce Devin's autonomy or determine his future, even if he has the potential to live longer than the norm. His life could be cut short at any time by an accident or illness. But if he does live longer, the modification will open up opportunities that he otherwise would not have had. Perhaps he will have two careers rather than one, or live to see his great-great grandchildren.

Nor is Devin likely to feel parental pressure to achieve a specific lifespan, for two reasons. First, whether the genetic modification extends his lifespan is beyond his control. Second, a child is most vulnerable to parental pressure while he is a minor living at home. Yet, even the most aggressive parents are not likely to focus on lifespan during the child's early years. By the time Devin is an adult, and old enough for lifespan extension to be relevant, John and Mary Smith may well have died.

John and Mary may steer Devin away from hazardous activities that could lead to early death and create a sense of pressure in that way. However, parents who are protective enough to invest in lifespan extension would probably have subjected their child to such environmental conditioning even if HGM had not been available.

D STEREOTYPES ASSOCIATED WITH THE MANUFACTURE OBJECTION

Like the hubris objection, the manufacture objection addresses the behavior of adults. Yet, HGM is a reproductive technology that may lead to the birth of children. Thus, it is important to consider whether the manufacture objection is associated with any stereotypes about children of HGM.

The argument that HGM transforms reproduction into manufacture strongly implies that children of HGM are manufactured objects rather than human beings.[26] To some readers, this implication may seem unfortunate but harmless. After all, observers will be able to see for themselves that the children look and act like other human beings, which should help dispel the stereotype.

However, as Chapter 6, Section B.1, explains, the intrusion of laboratories, technology, and money into human reproduction may foster the intuition that HGM is manufacture and children born through it are artifacts. Indeed, the manufacture objection may itself be the result of such intuition. Unfortunately, the manufacture objection elevates this intuition to the level of a public policy concern. By dignifying and reinforcing intuition, the manufacture objection encourages the public to stereotype children of HGM as products.

Related concerns discussed in this chapter may inspire additional stereotypes. Specifically, the claim that HGM deprives a child of autonomy and an open future suggests she cannot direct the course of her own life. She is a pitiful puppet of her overbearing parents. The assertion that a child will suffer pressure from parental expectations predicts that she is likely to be anxious and stressed. Those who express such concerns are good people who wish to ensure that children do not suffer. However, if children are destined to be born through HGM, these concerns may paint them in a negative light.

E SUMMARY

This chapter has critiqued the claim that HGM transforms human reproduction into manufacture. IVF, which requires technology and money, has not brought about such a transformation. To be sure, HGM differs in that it adds an element of design. However, when parents correct a deadly genetic mutation, or confer viral immunity on their child, the degree of design is very small. Even when they improve memory and learning or extend lifespan, they leave most of their child's genome to chance. Such interventions fall far short of *Brave New World*, which is the iconic example of reproduction transformed into manufacture.

Related concerns portray HGM as a threat to human happiness. In theory, the technology deprives a child of an open future and subjects him to parental pressure to live up to unreasonable expectations. However, when these concerns are evaluated in the context of specific applications of the technology, they tend to fade away. Genetic modifications that free a child from genetic disorders or viruses or extend lifespan expand available life plans by securing good health and increasing the years available to pursue them. Arguably, genetic modifications that improve memory and learning do the same, by equipping the child to participate in a variety of careers. Furthermore, most of the applications of HGM discussed in this chapter are unlikely to lead to parental pressure. The use of HGM to improve memory and learning may be an exception, but existing environmental methods of shaping a child are probably as or more stressful.

The manufacture objection and related concerns are troubling because they imply that children of HGM have negative characteristics. If people hear and believe that HGM transforms human reproduction into manufacture, they may be encouraged to view children of HGM more as products than human beings. If people hear and believe that HGM deprives children of an open future, or subjects them to parental pressure, they are more likely to assume that such children lack autonomy or are emotionally disturbed. Part II expands upon these themes by investigating the psychological foundations of the manufacture objection and related concerns.

Notes

1. *E.g.*, The President's Council on Bioethics, Reproduction and Responsibility: The Regulation of New Biotechnologies 110 (2004) [hereinafter REPRODUCTION AND RESPONSIBILITY]; *see also* National Academy of Sciences & National Academy of Medicine, Human Genome Editing: Science, Ethics, and Governance 121 (2017) [hereinafter NAS REPORT] (reviewing sources that present this perspective).
2. ALDOUS HUXLEY, BRAVE NEW WORLD (Harper Perennial Modern Classics ed. 2006) (1932).
3. For a description of the various classes, told from the point of view of a Beta, see *id.* at 27–28. The novel captures the roles of the bottom three classes succinctly in a few paragraphs describing factory production of helicopter lights. Gammas operate machinery and assemble parts. Meanwhile, Deltas perform lower-level work, such as packing crates. Epsilons provide labor that is purely physical, such as loading trucks. *Id.* at 169–60.
4. *See* RONALD M. GREEN, *Babies by Design: The Ethics of Genetic Choice* 110–11, 125 (2007) (describing the open future concern).
5. M. MAMELI, Reproductive Cloning, Genetic Engineering and the Autonomy of the Child: The Moral Agent and the Open Future, 33 J. MED. ETHICS 87, 90 (2007).

6. REPRODUCTION AND RESPONSIBILITY, *supra* note 1, at 95–96, 109; *see also* SUSANNAH BARUCH et al., HUMAN GERMLINE GENETIC MODIFICATION: ISSUES AND OPTIONS FOR POLICYMAKERS 36 (2005) (describing concern that parents will view children of HGM as commodities and love them less if they are not perfect).
7. GATTACA (Jersey Films 1979).
8. For an account of how PGD works, see note 14 in Chapter 1.
9. GATTACA, *supra* note 7. *See also* COLIN GAVAGHAN, "No Gene for Fate?": Luck, Harm, and Justice in *Gattaca*, in BIOETHICS AT THE MOVIES 75, 76–77 (SANDRA SHAPSHAY ED. 2009) (discussing Jerome Morrow as a victim of unrealistic parental expectations).
10. TOBY ORD, The Scourge: Moral Implications of Natural Embryo Loss, 8 AM. J. BIOETHICS 12, 16–17 (2008) (explaining that 45 percent to 75 percent of embryos fail, and 30 percent to 60 percent of those failures are due to chromosomal abnormalities).
11. *See* THE PRESIDENT'S COUNCIL ON BIOETHICS, *Human Cloning and Human Dignity: An Ethical Inquiry* 105–06 (2002) (comparing sexual reproduction to human cloning).
12. MATTHEW H. PORTEUS & CHRISTINA T. DANN, Genome Editing of the Germline: Broadening the Discussion, 23 MOLECULAR THERAPY 980, 981 (2015).
13. GREEN, *supra* note 4, at 173–74 (discussing theological commission report that indicated therapeutic modifications to sperm precursor cells may be permissible); *see also* CONGREGATION FOR THE DOCTRINE OF THE FAITH, Instruction Dignitas Personae on Certain Bioethical Questions ¶¶ 12, 26 (2008), available at www.ewtn.com/library/CURIA/CDF-Dignitas-Personae .pdf [hereinafter DIGNITAS PERSONAE] (stressing importance of the conjugal act and disapproving germline cell therapy that occurs during IVF).
14. For these and other details of the IVF process, see SHERMAN J. SILBER, HOW TO GET PREGNANT 169–80, 220–35 (Little, Brown & Co. rev. ed. Sept. 2005, paperback ed. Aug. 2007; originally published 1991).
15. *E.g.*, REPRODUCTION AND RESPONSIBILITY, *supra* note 1, at 44.
16. *See* JUNE CARBONE & JODY LYNEE MADEIRA, Buyers in the Baby Market: Towards a Transparent Consumerism, 91 WASH. L. REV. 71, 74 (2016) (describing but not endorsing this view).
17. Susan Golombok, MODERN FAMILIES: PARENTS AND CHILDREN IN NEW FAMILY FORMS 71–72 (2015).
18. *Id.* at 79–81.
19. *Id.* at 82–85.
20. Suppose HGM fails and a child is born with the mutation that causes Huntington disease. Her parents may feel disappointed but will not pressure the child because she can do nothing to alter the situation. Instead, if the medical professionals who provided the HGM services failed to exercise reasonable care, the parents may bring a lawsuit for wrongful birth. Some states already allow wrongful birth claims against medical professionals who

screen embryos or fetuses and fail to detect genetic or chromosomal abnormalities. *See generally* KATE WEVERS, Prenatal Torts and Pre-Implantation Genetic Diagnosis 24 HARV. J.L. & TECH. 258 (2010) (discussing how prenatal torts involving PGD vary from those arising out of other screening technologies).

21. *See* HUXLEY, *supra* note 2, at 5–29 (detailing the process).
22. GREEN, *supra* note 4, at 129.
23. *See* MAMELI, *supra* note 5, at 91 (making similar point about enhancement of general intelligence).
24. *See* GREEN, *supra* note 4, at 117 (noting parental attempts to enroll children in the best schools and their alma mater).
25. *Id.* at 118.
26. *See* REPRODUCTION AND RESPONSIBILITY, *supra* note 1, at 109–10 (suggesting that a child produced to specification may seem like an artifact).

4

Stratifying Society

Some claim that parents will use human germline modification (HGM) to create children with superior traits. These children will then transmit their genes to descendants, leading to class divides and social inequalities.[1] This chapter critiques this *stratification objection*. It also presents and analyzes two related concerns: first, parents may feel pressure to design their children to meet social standards or keep up with the Joneses;[2] and second, people will not have equal access to HGM, an expensive technology.[3] Last, this chapter discusses stereotypes about children of HGM that are associated with the stratification objection and related concerns.

A DYSTOPIAN VISIONS

Nineteen ninety-seven was a watershed year for biology and bioethics. In February of that year, Ian Wilmut and Keith Campbell reported that they had cloned a lamb from a cell taken from the mammary glands of a long-dead adult sheep.[4] Their experiment demonstrated that mammals were capable of asexual reproduction[5] and ignited speculation about human cloning and other possible developments in human reproduction.

Shortly thereafter, Professor Lee Silver published a book entitled *Remaking Eden* in which he discussed assisted reproduction, cloning, and genetic engineering.[6] He imagined a future in which some parents give their children artificial chromosomes loaded with synthetic genes that provide an advantage in professional and athletic endeavors. Those born without artificial chromosomes are relegated to substandard education and menial labor. With every passing generation, more genes are loaded onto the artificial chromosomes, and the genetic divide widens. By the end of the third millennium, *Homo sapiens* splits into multiple species that can no longer procreate with one another.[7]

That same year, Hollywood provided its own dystopian vision of reproductive technologies. Although not about HGM specifically, the movie *Gattaca*[8] is so frequently cited in bioethical discussions that it deserves mention here. Vincent, the protagonist, longs to become an astronaut but is relegated to janitorial work because he has a heart defect and cannot pass genetic screening. Desirable jobs are reserved for people who are the products of a high-tech eugenics program that uses preimplantation genetic diagnosis (PGD) to provide parents with a detailed genetic analysis of their in vitro fertilization (IVF) embryos prior to selection for transfer.[9] Only by impersonating a member of this superior genetic caste can Vincent achieve his dream. The movie ends on a high note, with Vincent blasting off into space,[10] but it leaves the viewer with the impression that reproductive technologies lead to bad results.

B SPECIFIC APPLICATIONS

After 1997, bioethicists and other experts continued to debate the pros and cons of HGM, including its potential for social stratification.[11] However, shortly after the turn of the millennium, people realized how challenging it would be to edit gametes or embryos, and concerns about HGM subsided.[12] Twenty years later, with the advent of molecular editing tools, HGM has become a front-burner issue once again. But how likely is it that specific applications would lead to social stratification or related concerns? This section builds on the hypothetical scenarios presented in Chapter 1 to answer that question.

1 HGM to Eliminate Genetic Ddisease

Suppose John and Mary Smith undergo IVF. They ask their doctor to edit their gametes or embryos to eliminate genetic mutations that cause maladies such as Huntington disease or sickle cell disease. Nine months later, their daughter Ariel is born healthy. This process will undoubtedly be expensive. Perhaps the Smiths can afford it, but some carriers will be unable to shoulder the financial burden[13] (an unequal access problem examined in more detail Section B.1.b).

Yet, it does not follow that HGM will lead to social stratification. Consider the example of PGD, an embryo screening technology that parents currently use to detect genetic mutations.[14] PGD occurs in conjunction with IVF. As Chapter 1, Section A, explained, a single IVF cycle costs $12,400 on average, plus $3000 to $5000 more for fertility drugs and another $2500 to $6000 for PGD. Total cost ranges from $17,900 to $23,400, with a mean of $20,650.

Unfortunately, most insurers do not cover PGD, and couples who need it may also be denied IVF coverage because they are not infertile.[15] In 2003, the President's Council on Bioethics warned that PGD could lead to a society in which economic and genetic privilege align to separate rich from poor.[16] Yet, PGD has been around for nearly three decades,[17] and its medical use has not divided society.[18]

Indeed, HGM may *decrease* social stratification in two ways. First, parents who use it to eliminate genetic mutations secure for their children the same good health that the vast majority of the population enjoys at birth. By bringing a handful of children up to the norm, HGM combats the unequal distribution of good health found in nature. Second, genetic disorders are a source of economic disadvantage. Sufferers will incur medical expenses. The disorder may also deprive them of gainful employment and disrupt their personal lives. Loved ones may be forced to leave lucrative employment to serve as caregivers. By eliminating such economic disadvantages, HGM contributes to social justice.

a) Competitive Pressure

HGM to eliminate genetic mutations should not raise concerns about competitive pressure. Parents who are *not* carriers of a genetic disease can have healthy children without any medical intervention. They have no reason to edit gametes or embryos to keep up with the Smiths and other carriers.

b) Unequal Access

As mentioned earlier, HGM will be expensive, and some carriers of genetic mutations will be unable to afford it. This unequal access problem has two possible solutions. First, lawmakers can ban HGM and deny access to everyone. However, if HGM can relieve human suffering, a ban is an unreasonable response.[19] Not everyone has equal access to good health at birth, but HGM may be able to change that.[20]

Second, an effort can be made to expand access through health insurance. Insurers should realize that HGM can be cost-effective. For example, suppose HGM is performed in the context of an IVFR cycle and PGD is used to screen embryos. As discussed earlier, the IVF/PGD process costs around $20,000. It is difficult to predict the cost of modifying gametes or embryos at this early stage of the technology. But even if HGM services double the costs from $20,000 to $40,000, the process will still be cheaper than paying for the lifetime medical costs associated with a genetic disease. According to one study, Medicaid spent an average of $1389 per month per patient with sickle cell disease in Florida, roughly half of which was directly related to the disease. The lifetime cost of care was estimated at $460,151,[21] but that estimate may artificially low due to Medicaid's conservative reimbursement rates.[22] In addition to medical care, sickle cell disease imposes other costs, such as wage loss among patients and their caregivers.[23]

To be sure, insurers may not listen. Today, some refuse to pay for a cycle of IVF with PGD even though a couple already has one sick child with an inherited disorder whose treatment has cost hundreds of thousands of dollars.[24] Medical professionals, genetic counselors, and patient advocates may need to bring their facts and figures to state legislatures.[25] Perhaps some will mandate that health insurance cover HGM to prevent genetic disease. And if not, charitable organizations dedicated to the elimination of specific diseases could step forward to help carriers fund the necessary procedures.

2 HGM to Confer Immunity

Now, suppose John and Mary Smith edit their gametes or embryos to ensure that their son Blake is immune to viral or bacterial infection. Not everyone can afford such services. However, HGM of this kind is not likely to lead to social stratification.

Assisted reproduction, which is medicalized and complicated, compares unfavorably with sexual intercourse, which is private and simple. Moreover, many people will have religious objections to HGM[26] or simply balk at the idea of a lab technician meddling with their gametes or embryos. For these reasons, HGM will not become a popular means of acquiring immunity, even if it is free.

When battling a deadly virus or bacterium, public health authorities must find simpler and less intrusive measures. Consider the HIV-1 virus as an example. Sex education, safe sex measures, and antiviral medications are used to reduce its transmission. Attempts to develop a vaccine are ongoing.[27] If a vaccine emerges, it will offer greater protection than HGM, not only because it is cheaper but also because it is easier and quicker and more likely to gain widespread acceptance.

Nevertheless, research in China indicates that some believe there will be a market for genetic modifications that confer immunity to the HIV-1 virus.[28] Some parents may find such modifications worthwhile, especially if they must undergo assisted reproduction for other reasons. Their use of HGM will not create social division between the modified and unmodified because alternatives (sex education, safe sex, and medications) will continue to be available.

Continuing with HIV-1 as an example, some people are free of the virus while others are infected and undergo treatment. That, too, is a type of social divide. Genetic modifications that confer immunity upon even a small percentage of the population will reduce transmission of the virus, thereby decreasing the number of people who endure this divide.

a) Competitive Pressure

HGM is not likely to lead to competitive pressure. Individuals in our society do not compete with one another on the basis of viral or bacterial immunity. Therefore, parents should not have an incentive to confer genetic immunity upon their offspring to enable them to get ahead in the world.

b) Unequal Access

Many parents will not be able to afford an expensive technology such as HGM. Because good health is implicated, health insurers or governments may pay for or subsidize the treatment. However, parents are likely to prefer simpler and less intrusive means of dealing with contagious viruses, such as vaccines. Further, as discussed earlier, even if few parents can afford HGM, conferring immunity upon their offspring will reduce transmission of dangerous viruses or bacteria to others, thereby helping to equalize access to good health, if not HGM.

3 HGM to Improve Memory and Learning

As the focus shifts from medical uses of HGM to enhancement, the analysis also shifts in interesting ways. To illustrate, suppose John and Mary Smith hope to have a child who becomes a wealthy doctor or lawyer. They realize excellent grades and standardized test scores are required to gain admission to top colleges and professional schools. They have heard that certain single nucleotide polymorphisms (SNPs) are linked to genes related to memory and learning.[29] Thus, John and Mary commission a doctor to modify their sperm and eggs to incorporate the relevant SNPs. Thereafter, the couple undergoes IVF using the modified gametes. Nine months later, a baby girl named Cora is born.

At first glance, it is tempting to conclude that John and Mary have bought an unfair genetic advantage for Cora, who seems destined to outcompete and out-earn her unmodified peers. Cora apparently can hand this genetic advantage down to her children, who can in turn hand it down to theirs, and so on. If many other parents do the same, a class of academic superstars will emerge over time.

However, these conclusions are incorrect for three reasons. First, although genes can contribute to academic or career outcomes, they are not the only influences upon our destinies. As Leonard Mlodinow has noted, we humans have a psychological need to control our environment. We believe we are in control even when we are not[30] and underestimate the role chance plays in our lives.[31] In this case, John and Mary are oblivious to the effects that random events may have on Cora. Peers may influence her to neglect her schoolwork in favor of other diversions: sports, fashion, boys, or recreational drugs. But even if she slogs through many years of higher education to earn a medical or legal degree, her path to wealth is not assured. She may not possess the personal skills or ambition required to build and maintain a lucrative practice. She may reject wealth as a measure of success and open a medical clinic in an impoverished neighborhood or pursue a legal career as a public defender.

Some might protest that Cora and others like her still have an unfair genetic advantage, even if they don't use it. But parents will not incur the expense and risk of HGM unless they are confident the advantage will be used. People who understand the role of chance will be less inclined to pay for genes.

Second, even among the wealthy, few parents are likely to purchase this modification because it entails risk. Improved memory and learning may come at the expense of another important trait that declines because the SNPs were added.[32] Human error could even produce a disabled child. Safer measures are available, including early education, private schools, and tutors. Later, when adult children are ready to enter the workforce, wealthy parents can use personal connections to help them obtain appropriate jobs. They also can leave their riches to their children when they die, or establish trusts for the benefit of their grandchildren. Unfortunately, the growing wealth gap between upper-income families and all others bears testimony to the success of such measures.[33]

Third, if the foregoing analysis is correct, and few parents purchase improved memory and learning, a class of academic superstars is unlikely to emerge. Most men and women of reproductive age will be unenhanced. Yet many will be intelligent, physically attractive, or personable enough to attract enhanced partners. Procreation between the enhanced and unenhanced will dilute genes over the generations.

To understand dilution of genes, consider a simplified version of the hypothetical in which John and Mary modify their gametes by substituting a single rare gene associated with superior memory and learning for a standard gene. Cora marries Chester, an unenhanced man. Their gametes arise out of *meiosis*, a process by which the chromosomal complement is halved.[34] If Cora receives two copies of the rare gene, one from each parent, each of her eggs must contain it. Chester's sperm contains the standard gene he inherited from both his parents. The two procreate via sexual intercourse, and nine months later, Dara is born with one copy of the rare gene and one copy of the standard gene.

Assume first that principles of Mendelian inheritance apply, because one gene is dominant and the other is not. If the rare gene is dominant, Dara will have superior memory and learning. If the standard gene is dominant, she will have average memory and learning. If principles of non-Mendelian inheritance apply, and the rare gene is incompletely dominant, her memory and learning will be improved but not superior.[35]

Next, assume that Dara marries Devon, a man who has the standard gene. Dara has one copy of the rare gene and one copy of the standard gene; thus, when meiosis is complete, each of her eggs carries one or the other. Devon's sperm contains the standard gene he inherited from both his parents. If these two procreate, and principles of Mendelian inheritance apply, half of their children will inherit one copy of the rare gene and one copy of the standard gene. Those children will have superior memory and learning only if the rare gene is dominant. If it is not, they will have average memory and learning. Meanwhile, the other half of the children will inherit two copies of the standard gene and will have average memory and learning.[36] Finally, if principles of non-Mendelian inheritance apply, and the rare gene is incompletely dominant, children who receive it will have somewhat improved memory and learning.

Thus, even under the most optimistic scenario in which principles of Mendelian inheritance apply and the rare gene is dominant, only half of Cora's grandchildren will share her rare gene and trait. If those grandchildren also select unenhanced partners, one-quarter of her great-grandchildren will share her rare gene and trait.[37] With every passing generation, the percentage of offspring who possess the rare gene and its associated trait decreases.

Some may protest that Cora will not select unenhanced Chester as her mate. Her rare gene will gain her admission into elite universities where she will meet only men who share her rare gene.[38] But this argument exaggerates the power of genes to determine academic success and overstates the appeal of a technology that is not only expensive but risky. Further, with many people delaying marriage and childbearing into their late twenties,[39] matches between college sweethearts are far from inevitable. Once Cora graduates and enters the working world, she will encounter a more diverse array of potential mates.

To be sure, Professor Silver, who first predicted the emergence of a genetic divide, assumed that enhanced individuals would carry their advantageous genes on artificial chromosomes.[40] In theory, Cora's rare gene could be located on a pair of artificial chromosomes. If she had 48 chromosomes, and Chester had the standard 46, the pair probably would not be able to reproduce.[41] Cora would be limited to partners who also had 48 chromosomes. If she chose to procreate only with those who shared her rare gene, her offspring would receive two copies of it.

However, artificial chromosomes raise additional safety concerns. Their presence could complicate *mitosis*, the process by which cells divide.[42] Moreover, when a person inherits three rather than the standard two copies of a chromosome, disability often results (think of Down syndrome, in which a person has three copies of chromosome 21).[43] Genes loaded onto an artificial chromosome pair could overlap with genes on other chromosomes and produce similar deleterious effects.[44]

In sum, HGM to improve memory and learning is unlikely to lead to social stratification. Other genetic interventions that aim at academic or workplace success will fail to generate class divides for the same reasons.[45]

a) Competitive Pressure

A related question is whether parents will feel pressured to purchase SNPs associated with memory and learning lest their children fall behind peers in school and the workplace. Viewed through the lens of current social trends, this concern may appear valid. College admission has become akin to a high-stakes competitive sport. High school students must navigate a stressful gauntlet of advanced placement courses, high-pressure standardized tests, and extracurricular activities to impress admissions officers.[46] Parents hire expensive tutors and enroll their children in test preparation courses to help them excel. Many resent the pressure and cost but believe they have no choice but to join in the madness.[47]

However, upon closer examination, the analogy is poor. Academic courses, standardized tests, and extracurricular activities require parents and teens to expend money and effort, but such sacrifices occur at a point that is close in time to college admission. Courses, tests, and activities are also time-honored ways of getting ahead; parents used the same methods themselves and are comfortable with them. Finally, courses, tests, and activities are valuable in their own right, adding knowledge, health, and fun to teenage lives. With the exception of certain sports, they involve few physical risks.

HGM requires parents to invest a large sum of money up front and substitute technological reproduction for sex in the hope that their child may reap benefits in the long run. A service that demands significant sacrifices in the present in return for speculative benefits in the future may not gain wide acceptance. Further, parents who achieved success *without* the benefit of technology may conclude HGM is unnecessary. Efforts to persuade them otherwise will come across as a slight to their genetic heritage. Last, HGM promises to confer an ability that the child may never use. Parents must weigh a speculative benefit against the real risk that something could go wrong during the editing, leaving them with a sick or disabled child.

Thus, even if HGM can improve memory and learning, and some parents use it for that purpose, there are good reasons to believe that others will not feel compelled to do likewise. However, this analysis does not exclude the possibility that the parents of unmodified children will feel envious. That topic is taken up in Chapter 7.

b) Unequal access

If HGM turns out to be as expensive as expected, many people will not be able to pay for it out of pocket. Health insurance will not cover procedures designed to enhance memory and learning in otherwise healthy people.[48] Thus, unequal access to this application is likely.

Those who believe that cognitive enhancements are beneficial argue that the solution is to expand access to HGM.[49] Theoretically, the government can subsidize the enhancement for parents who want it. However, the economics are daunting. Professor Maxwell Mehlman calculated in 2000 that it would cost $120 billion per year if all Americans conceived their children through IVF. That staggering sum did not include the additional expense of modifying gametes or embryos.[50]

If the government declines to pay for cognitive enhancement, should this application of HGM be banned? This book contends that the answer is no. As discussed earlier, genes do not equate to academic success and wealth. The government can create opportunity by investing in environmental interventions such as better nutrition, universal education, and vigorous enforcement of laws that safeguard women and minorities against discrimination in schools, workplaces, and other venues.

4 HGM to Extend Lifespan

Finally, suppose John and Mary Smith edit their gametes or embryos to extend maximum lifespan. Their son, Devin, reaches developmental milestones and maturity at the standard human pace. However, he has the theoretical capacity to live until age 150, 28 years longer than the current maximum lifespan of 122 years. If other parents do the same, could the resulting children amass wealth during their long lives and pass it along with their genes to the next generation, creating an economic and biological divide?

The answer is no, for three reasons. First, odds are that Devin and his peers will not live to 150 or anywhere close. Accident, crime, or disease will cut their lives short at an earlier point in time. Consider that only one woman, Jeanne Calment, has reached the current maximum lifespan of 122 years.[51] In 2015, the average life expectancy at birth in the United States was 78.8, or 44 years less.[52] Second, most parents are likely to eschew a modification that does not guarantee long life. If the extended lifespan comes along with good health in old age, market demand may increase. However, first adopters must take a leap of faith since the benefits will not be evident in their own lifetimes. Third, for the reasons discussed in the preceding section, genes that extend lifespan probably will not be conserved within the family line. Devin and others like him will procreate with those who possess standard genes, causing descendants to regress toward the mean.

a) Competitive Pressure

It seems unlikely that parents will feel competitive pressure to design their children for extended lifespan. As explained in Section B.3.a, the process of engineering traits is expensive and risky and delivers only speculative future benefits. Under such conditions, a strong demand for HGM is unlikely to emerge.

Moreover, there are additional reasons to believe that parents will not feel pressure to keep up with the Methuselahs. Early adopters of the technology will have nothing to flaunt in front of their peers. The success or failure of their genetic project will not be determined for 100 years or more after the first modified cohort is born. By then, the parents' unmodified generation will have died out.

However, suppose that a century from now, lifespan extension has been proven to work. Suppose further that some parents are drawn to it even though it offers no guarantee that their children will have long lives. Even then, competitive pressure may not materialize. Lifespan extension will not be as obvious as expensive clothes, fancy cars, and private schools. Parents can impress others simply by lying about how their children are conceived. The truth will not emerge for decades, so liars are unlikely to be exposed.

b) Unequal Access

HGM for lifespan extension raises access concerns. As noted in Section B.3.b, it would be very expensive for government to offer universal access. However, if modified individuals experience a welcome delay in the onset of age-related diseases,[53] Medicare and other health insurance programs may save money on care that otherwise would have been provided. If those who remain healthy longer also work longer, Social Security and other retirement programs may remain solvent longer. The day may come when insurers and governments run a cost-benefit analysis and decide that covering or subsidizing lifespan extension is in their enlightened self-interest.

But even if it turns out that universal access is an impossible dream, it may not matter. Maximum lifespan does not guarantee that a specific individual will enjoy a long life. In addition, there will always be a risk that something can go wrong during the procedure, leading to the birth of a child who suffers or has a shortened life. Such realities will decrease demand for lifespan extension. The general population will continue to have access to simpler and cheaper environmental interventions. Eating right, exercising, maintaining a healthy weight, and avoiding cigarettes and illegal drugs can increase the odds of a long and healthy life.

C STEREOTYPES ASSOCIATED WITH THE STRATIFICATION OBJECTION

This chapter now turns to stereotypes associated with the stratification objection. Its focus contrasts with that of prior chapters. Only scientists and parents can be guilty of transgressing divine and natural boundaries or transforming human reproduction into manufacture; children of HGM are innocents who are stereotyped by association with improper conduct. But the stratification objection implicitly assumes that *the children are the problem*. Class divides and social inequalities exist only if superstars exist.

The stratification objection rests on two stereotypes about children of HGM that originate in biological misunderstandings. First, it assumes the children are superior to others and thus destined to succeed. However, as Section B of this chapter discussed, that is not necessarily true. Genes are not the sole determinants of traits, and traits do not inevitably lead to success. Second, the objection posits that the children are divisive because they can transmit their superior traits to offspring down through the generations. Yet, beneficial genes are likely to be diluted through standard reproduction, unless artificial chromosomes are employed, which is unlikely.

A third stereotype proceeds directly from the stratification objection itself. Once children of HGM have been characterized as superior and divisive, the objection portrays them as a source of class divides and social inequalities. The children are unjust, oppressors whose accomplishments and wealth derive from an unfair advantage. The nature of the injustice depends on the specific use of HGM. For example, children with improved memory and learning create inequalities in schools and the workplace. Children with extended lifespan are unfair because they live longer than everyone else. Even children modified for health reasons are reprehensible, for they are the first step down a slippery slope to enhancements.[54]

This chapter has also reviewed two concerns related to the stratification objection. The concern that parents will feel competitive pressure assumes that children of HGM are superior. That superiority makes them a competitive threat to others and coerces others to modify their own children to keep up.

By contrast, the concern about unequal access focuses on technology, rather than children born from it. Lack of access to therapeutic modifications is troubling, but for the reasons discussed in this chapter, demand for enhancing modifications is likely to be low. In either case, the concern implies that children of HGM are unjust because parental resources give them an advantage over others.

D SUMMARY

Some believe that HGM will lead to social stratification. The foregoing analysis demonstrates that this belief is false. Medical uses, such as eliminating rare genetic diseases or conferring immunity, may *decrease* social stratification by reducing the number of individuals who suffer from disease and its economic consequences. Nor are non-medical uses, such as improvement of memory and learning or lifespan extension, likely to lead to class divides. Although some parents may attempt to enhance their offspring, most will realize that genes cannot promise academic success or long life, and decide HGM isn't worth the expense and risk. Since the enhanced will have access to multitudes of attractive yet unenhanced partners, nightmare visions of Einstein and Methuselah castes separating themselves from the rest of humanity are unrealistic.

This chapter has also reviewed two concerns related to the stratification objection. Competitive pressure, in which parents enhance their children in an effort to outdo one another, is unlikely because HGM is expensive, burdensome, and provides no guarantees. Unequal access is a concern primarily in rare cases where HGM is necessary to prevent the birth of sick children. The concern is best resolved through efforts to extend health insurance, rather than legal bans.

Finally, this chapter has argued that the stratification objection rests upon and propagates inaccurate and damaging stereotypes about children of HGM. Starting from the assumption that such children are superior and divisive, the objection paints them as unjust. Related concerns also breed stereotypes, suggesting that children of HGM are competitive threats, coercive, and recipients of an unfair advantage in life.

Part II investigates the psychological roots of the stratification objection and related concerns. It also explains how the objection and concerns spark envy and other emotions that threaten the health and wellbeing of children of HGM.

Notes

1. SUSANNAH BARUCH ET AL., HUMAN GERMLINE GENETIC MODIFICATION: ISSUES AND OPTIONS FOR POLICYMAKERS 35 (2005); AUDREY R. CHAPMAN, The Implications of Inheritable Genetic Modifications for Justice, in DESIGNING OUR DESCENDANTS: THE PROMISES AND PERILS OF GENETIC MODIFICATIONS 130, 141 (AUDREY R. CHAPMAN & MARK S. FRANKEL EDS., 2003).
2. *See* RONALD M. GREEN, BABIES BY DESIGN: THE ETHICS OF GENETIC CHOICE 162–64 (2007) (describing self-imposed pressure to design children for competitive advantage).
3. BARUCH ET AL., *supra* note 1, at 35.
4. I. WILMUT ET AL., Viable Offspring Derived from Fetal and Adult Mammalian Cells, 385 NATURE 810 (1997).

5. For a fuller description of the experiment and Dolly's life, see KERRY LYNN MACINTOSH, HUMAN CLONING: FOUR FALLACIES AND THEIR LEGAL CONSEQUENCES 1–4 (2013).
6. LEE M. SILVER, REMAKING EDEN: CLONING AND BEYOND IN A BRAVE NEW WORLD (1997).
7. Id. at 4–7, 240–48.
8. GATTACA (Jersey Films 1979).
9. Id.
10. Id.
11. E.g., FRANCIS FUKUYAMA, OUR POSTHUMAN FUTURE: CONSEQUENCES OF THE BIOTECHNOLOGY REVOLUTION (2003); ENGINEERING THE HUMAN GERMLINE: AN EXPLORATION OF THE SCIENCE AND ETHICS OF ALTERING THE GENES WE PASS TO OUR CHILDREN (GREGORY STOCK & JOHN CAMPBELL, EDS. 2000).
12. See e.g., The President's Council on Bioethics, REPRODUCTION AND RESPONSIBILITY: THE REGULATION OF NEW BIOTECHNOLOGIES 110 (2004) [hereinafter REPRODUCTION AND RESPONSIBILITY] (deeming designer babies unlikely in foreseeable future); The President's Council on Bioethics, BEYOND THERAPY: BIOTECHNOLOGY AND THE PURSUIT OF HAPPINESS 37–40 (2003) [hereinafter BEYOND THERAPY] (perceiving the difficulty of inserting genes into embryos or working with artificial chromosomes and concluding that concerns about HGM could be set aside).
13. R. VASSENA ET AL., Genome Engineering through CRISPR/Cas9 Technology in the Human Germline and Pluripotent Stem Cells, 22 HUMAN REPRODUCTION UPDATE 411, 417 (2016).
14. KATHRYN T. DRAZBA ET AL., A Qualitative Inquiry of the Financial Concerns of Couples Opting to Use Preimplantation Genetic Diagnosis to Prevent the Transmission of Known Genetic Disorders, 23 J. GENETIC COUNSELING 202, 203 (2014).
15. Id.
16. BEYOND THERAPY, supra note 12, at 51.
17. PGD was first employed in 1989 to screen embryos for gender thereby sidestepping diseases linked with the X chromosome. REPRODUCTION AND RESPONSIBILITY, supra note 12, at 90.
18. PGD for sex selection is controversial. Some allege sex selection contributes to bias against women. See BEYOND THERAPY, supra note 12, at 65–66.
19. See KEVIN R. SMITH ET AL., Human Germline Genetic Modification: Scientific and Bioethical Perspectives, 43 ARCHIVES OF MEDICAL RESEARCH 491, 508 (2012) (arguing that benefits should not be denied on basis of unequal access).
20. National Academy of Sciences & National Academy of Medicine, Human Genome Editing: Science, Ethics, and Governance 94 (2017) (reporting view that HGM levels the playing field for those at genetic disadvantage).
21. TERESA L. KAUF ET AL., The Cost of Health Care for Children and Adults with Sickle Cell Disease, 84 AM. J. HEMATOLOGY 323 (2009).

22. SAMIR K. BALLAS, The Cost of Health Care for Patients with Sickle Cell Disease, 84 AM. J. HEMATOLOGY 320, 321–22 (2009).
23. *Id.* at 322.
24. Drazba, *supra* note 15 at 207.
25. *Cf. id.* at 209 (arguing that genetic counselors and other professionals should advocate for a national policy that improves access to PGD).
26. *See* Chapter 2, Section A (discussing Roman Catholic beliefs).
27. *See, e.g.*, HIV TRIALS NETWORK, www.hvtn.org/en.html (last visited July 4, 2016) (website of organization dedicated to developing a vaccine against HIV and AIDS).
28. For a discussion of this research, see Chapter 1, Section B.2.
29. CORNELIUS A. RIETVELD ET AL., Common Genetic Variants Associated with Cognitive Performance Identified Using the Proxy-phenotype Method, 111 PNAS 13790, 13793 (2014).
30. LEONARD MLODINOW, THE DRUNKARD'S WALK: HOW RANDOMNESS RULES OUR LIVES 185–88 (2008).
31. *Id.* at 195.
32. *See* Chapter 1, Section C.2 (discussing pleiotropy and the multiple effects genes can have).
33. A 2014 study showed that upper-income families had a median wealth that was 6.6 times higher than that of middle-income families and nearly 70 times higher than lower-income families. These disparities were the largest documented in 30 years. RICHARD FRY & RAKESH KOCHHAR, America's Wealth Gap Between Middle-Income and Upper-Income Families Is Widest on Record, PEW RESEARCH CENTER (December 17, 2014), www.pewresearch.org/fact-tank/2014/12/17/wealth-gap-upper-middle-income/.
34. NEW OXFORD AMERICAN DICTIONARY 1089 (ANGUS STEVENSON & CHRISTINE A. LINDBERG EDS., 3rd ed. 2010). For an account of meiosis and gamete formation, see P.C. WINTER ET AL., GENETICS 137–42 (2nd ed. 2002).
35. *See* P.C. WINTER ET AL., *supra* note 34, at 122–25 (discussing concept of dominance in genetics).
36. *See id.* at 124 (using a Punnett square to predict inheritance under similar facts).
37. To illustrate this point, assume that Dara and Devon produce two children, one with superior (Edward) and another with average memory and learning (Elijah). Assume further that each son produces two babies. Edward will contribute one baby with superior and one with average memory and learning. Elijah will contribute two babies with average memory and learning. Cora now has four great-grandchildren, but only one has superior memory and learning.
38. *Cf.* SILVER, *supra* note 2, at 6 (suggesting that the modified and unmodified occupy different social spheres and do not come into contact with each other).
39. RAE ELLEN BICHELL, Average Age of First-Time Moms Keeps Climbing in the U.S., NPR (January 14, 2016), www.npr.org/sections/health-shots/2016/01/14/462816458/average-age-of-first-time-moms-keeps-climbing-in-the-u-s (reporting that in 2014, the average age of first birth in the United States was

26.3); D'VERA COHN, Marriage Rate Declines and Marriage Age Rises, PEW RESEARCH CENTER (December 14 2011), www.pewsocialtrends.org/2011/12/14/marriage-rate-declines-and-marriage-age-rises/ (stating that in 2011, men and women in the United States married for the first time at the median ages of 28.7 and 26.5, respectively).

40. SILVER, *supra* note 2, at 246.
41. *Cf.* KERRY LYNN MACINTOSH, Chimeras, Hybrids, and Cybrids: How Essentialism Distorts the Law and Stymies Scientific Research, 47 ARIZ. ST. L.J. 183, 191–92 (2015) (explaining that human-animal hybrids are unlikely due to chromosomal mismatch and citing as an example the incompatibility between human beings and chimpanzees, which have 48 chromosomes).
42. BEYOND THERAPY, *supra* note 12, at 39. For a detailed account of how mitosis works, see P.C. WINTER ET AL., *supra* note 34.
43. KERRY LYNN MACINTOSH, Brave New Eugenics: Regulating Assisted Reproductive Technologies in the Name of Better Babies, 257, U. ILL. J.L. TECH & POLICY 261 (2010).
44. BEYOND THERAPY, *supra* note 12, at 39.
45. *See generally* GREEN, *supra* note 2, at 135–65 (discussing Silver's vision and concluding that HGM in general is not likely to lead to social stratification).
46. *See* ALEXANDRA OSSOLA, High-Stress High School, THE ATLANTIC (October 9, 2015), www.theatlantic.com/education/archive/2015/10/high-stress-high-school/409735/ (describing research into the stress that private high school students feel).
47. For an account of the college admissions process, see FRANK BRUNI, WHERE YOU GO IS NOT WHO YOU'LL BE: AN ANTIDOTE TO THE COLLEGE ADMISSIONS MANIA (2015).
48. Health insurers may develop a more accommodating attitude toward interventions that correct genetic learning disorders. *See* GREEN, *supra* note 2, at 154 (suggesting HGM could be used to correct dyslexia or other reading disorders).
49. SMITH ET AL., *supra* note 21, at 510.
50. MAXWELL J. MEHLMAN, The Law of Above Averages: Leveling the New Genetic Enhancement Playing Field, 85 IOWA L. REV. 517, 532 (2000). Professor Mehlman reached this figure by multiplying $30,000 (a rounded average of what it costs to achieve a live birth through IVF) times 4 million (the approximate number of annual births in the United States). *Id.* at 531, 532 n.56.
51. Dance with Death (Editorial) 538 NATURE 6 (2016).
52. JIAQUAN XU ET AL., Mortality in the United States, 267 NCHS DATA BRIEF 1 (December 2016), *available at* www.cdc.gov/nchs/data/databriefs/db267.pdf.
53. *See* CYNTHIA J. KENYON, The Genetics of Aging, 464 NATURE 504 (2010) (claiming that the same mutations that retard aging seem to also delay age-related diseases).
54. *Cf.* EDWARD LANPHIER ET AL., Don't Edit the Human Germ Line, 519 NATURE 410, 411 (2015) (arguing that therapies are a slippery slope to enhancements).

5

Endangering Democracy, Society, and the Species

Some academics and policymakers allege that the use of human germline modification (HGM) to create enhanced beings will bring about catastrophic outcomes. This chapter adopts the term "apocalypse objection" to describe such theories.[1] It singles out four specific claims for analysis and critique: hereditary castes will cause democracy to collapse, HGM will facilitate the reemergence of eugenics, extended lifespans will lead to societal ossification, and violent conflict between the modified and unmodified will lead to genocide. Inability of future generations to consent to HGM is discussed as a related concern. This chapter concludes by explaining how the apocalypse objection and its related concerns are based upon and inspire stereotypes about children of HGM.

A COLLAPSE OF DEMOCRACY

Professor Maxwell Mehlman has argued that HGM for enhancement imperils our democracy. His chain of logic goes something like this: the wealthy can afford to enhance their children but most people cannot. The enhanced achieve more career success and earn more money than the average person. Genetic transmission of this unfair advantage produces hereditary castes that accumulate wealth and power.[2] Demagogues prey on the resentments of the unenhanced majority and promise to correct genetic injustices. Meanwhile, the enhanced minority employs its wealth to manipulate the media.[3] Political chaos escalates into mob rule – or perhaps a sinister genetic autocracy arises. Either way, democracy fails.[4] This risk justifies a ban on HGM for enhancement.[5]

1 Biological Premises

Professor Mehlman's account rests on certain biological premises. Genes must deliver traits that yield career and financial success. HGM must be popular, so that children born through it are numerous enough to affect society. Lastly, the genes involved must be handed down, generation after generation, to produce hereditary castes. This section will use a hypothetical scenario discussed in Chapter 4, Section B.3, to demonstrate that all of these premises are contestable.

Suppose John and Mary Smith want a child who grows up to be a wealthy doctor or lawyer. They go to a fertility clinic and explain they want to design an intelligent child.[6] A doctor explains that general intelligence cannot be engineered due to the large number of genes and environmental factors involved (Chapter 1, Section C.1).⁻ Instead, he offers to add certain single nucleotide polymorphisms (SNPs) linked to memory and learning to their sperm and eggs.[7] John and Mary assent to the procedure and undergo IVF with modified gametes. Nine months later, Mary gives birth to a baby girl named Cora.

Cora may experience only modest gains in memory and learning. However, for the sake of argument, let us assume she is gifted. As Chapter 4, Section B.3, explained, she still may not turn into an academic superstar. Random factors, including peers and cultural influences, will affect how she chooses to spend her time. Even if she buckles down and excels in school, she may not pursue a high-powered professional career or acquire wealth. Her personal values and professional contacts will affect her life outcomes as much or more than her added SNPs. In sum, even if Cora is born with the desired trait, it may not lead her to achieve the kind of professional and financial success that her parents have in mind.

Now, suppose that John and Mary are aware of these limitations, and decide to forgo HGM in favor of environmental measures. From the time Cora is born, they drum into her the goal of becoming a medical or legal professional. Throughout her childhood and adolescence, she attends private schools. The Smiths scrimp and save to send her to the best universities for her undergraduate and graduate studies, and they encourage her to take internships with powerful mentors who can help her get prestigious and lucrative jobs.

To be sure, Cora may rebel against this conditioning. However, the point is that these environmental measures are available and pose less physical risk to Cora than HGM does. Parents who do their research and understand the risks and limitations of HGM are likely to prefer the environmental measures. If HGM is *not* popular, and few children are born with enhancements, the impact on society will be correspondingly small.

If most American parents do *not* enhance their children, the vast majority of men and women in the dating pool will be unmodified. Thus, Cora and others who share her modification will often select unmodified partners. As Chapter 4, Section B.3, explained in detail, with each successive generation, the choice of an unmodified partner further reduces the percentage of descendants who possess the enhancing genes. Hereditary castes will *not* emerge.

Critics may counter that the modified may select partners who share their genes to preserve their genetic heritage. Alternatively, if their partners are unmodified, they can reproduce through HGM as their parents did. True, but every new generation will have a fresh opportunity to deviate from the plan and reproduce with unmodified partners through sex, thereby diluting genes.

As noted in Chapter 4, Professor Lee Silver believes that artificial chromosomes will make it impossible for modified individuals to procreate with unmodified ones.[8] However, this book believes that parents will be slow to buy artificial chromosomes for their children, if they ever do. Artificial chromosomes may harm children by complicating cell division and giving them more copies of a particular gene than is safe.[9] Parents may also have psychological reasons for rejecting artificial chromosomes, a point that will be pursued further in Chapter 6.

2 Political Premise

Professor Mehlman's account also rests on the political premise that equality is necessary for democracy to exist. This section examines that premise in light of two types of equality: outcome and opportunity.

a) Equality of Outcome

Genes make some of us larger, stronger, prettier, smarter, or handier than others. Environmental factors, including culture, ethnicity, family, location, education, and era, further contribute to diversity. Random events also play a role in shaping lives. As a consequence of all these factors, equality of outcome does not exist.[10] Some men and women achieve greater financial and career success than others. Despite this inequality, the United States has survived as a democracy for more than 200 years.

Professor Mehlman argues that extreme disparities breed class resentment and rebellion.[11] However, significant disparities in income and wealth already exist. In 2014, households with incomes in the top 5 percent accounted for 21.9 percent of aggregate national income in the United States.[12] Households with income in the top 20 percent accounted for 51.2 percent of aggregate national income, while those in the bottom 20 percent accounted for only 3.1 percent.[13] Similarly, a 2014 study showed that upper-income families had a median wealth that was 6.6 times higher than that of middle-income families and nearly 70 times higher than lower-income families.[14] Despite these disparities, our democracy endures. Why?

Several answers come to mind. First, citizens can elect legislators to protect their economic interests. For example, California and New York recently enacted legislation to increase the state minimum wage gradually until it reaches $15 per hour.[15] Second, taxes and government programs, such as Social Security and unemployment benefits, reduce income disparities.[16] Third, welfare programs provide a safety net. For example, in the United States, needy individuals and families can receive cash subsidies, housing vouchers, and health coverage through federal programs.[17]

As discussed earlier, if some parents employ HGM in the vain attempt to control the destinies of their children, it is unlikely that a superior genetic caste will emerge.

But even if it does, the majority can use the vote and government programs to reduce income disparities. Income and estate taxes can curb destabilizing accumulations of wealth. Political chaos and mob rule are not inevitable or even probable.

b) Equality of Opportunity

Professor Mehlman also suggests that democracy must have equality of opportunity to thrive. People can tolerate wide disparities in outcome as long as everyone has a fair shot at success.[18] In his view, HGM threatens democracy because it confers an unfair genetic advantage upon the enhanced and their descendants, creating something akin to a caste system.[19]

Setting biological fallacies aside, this argument assumes that democracy cannot exist without equality of opportunity. That assumption is incorrect. Today, a child born into poverty will not receive as good an education as a child born into wealth. When she is old enough to work, she will not have the same connections or job opportunities as her wealthy peer. Yet, our democracy persists, in part due to legislation and welfare programs that protect the disadvantaged.

To summarize this section, HGM will not lead to an authoritarian future. Genes will not ensure success, HGM will not be popular, and hereditary castes will not arise. Moreover, even if HGM does yield inequalities of outcome and opportunity, our democracy can reduce disparities through wage and labor laws, government programs, welfare, and the like.

B EUGENICS

The second apocalyptic claim is that HGM leads to eugenics.[20] Before this chapter explores the meaning of this vague claim, some historical background is helpful. In 1865, Francis Galton opined that the human species could be improved if only individuals with superior characteristics reproduced (*positive eugenics*) while those with inferior characteristics did not (*negative eugenics*).[21] Galton's ideas gained traction along with the nascent science of genetics. In the early twentieth century, American states enacted compulsory sterilization laws targeting convicts, alcoholics, syphilitics, drug addicts, the feebleminded, and others deemed unfit to pass their genes to the next generation.[22] In the 1927 case of *Buck v. Bell*, the US Supreme Court upheld the constitutionality of a mandatory sterilization law.[23]

Unfortunately, Nazi Germany learned from the American eugenics movement.[24] It imposed the Law for the Prevention of Genetically Diseased Progeny and sterilized 300,000 to 400,000 disabled individuals.[25]

Meanwhile, back in the United States, the Supreme Court had a change of heart. In the 1942 case of *Skinner v. Oklahoma*, it invalidated a law that mandated sterilization of some felons but not others.[26] Ruling on the strength of the equal protection guarantee, the Court subjected the classifications in the law to strict scrutiny. It reasoned: "We are dealing here with legislation which involves one of the basic civil rights of man. Marriage and procreation are fundamental to the very existence and survival of the race."[27] In the wake of *Skinner*, the practice of eugenic sterilization faded, though some surgeries occurred as late as the 1960s and 1970s.[28]

Academics have highlighted several aspects of twentieth-century eugenics that made it abhorrent: coercive laws that forced men and women to undergo sterilization; shoddy science that classed behavioral traits (*e.g.*, criminality) as heritable; and persecution of ethnic, racial, and economic groups deemed unfit to procreate.[29] Professor Paul Lombardo, an expert in the legal history of eugenics, has stated that most people find government coercion to be the most objectionable feature of twentieth-century eugenics.[30]

1 Governmental Coercion

With this background in mind, this chapter now explores the meaning of the claim that HGM leads to eugenics. First, the claim may warn against mandatory government programs. If so, it rails against a dystopian future that will never come to pass.

To see why, imagine that a lawmaker introduces a bill *requiring* parents to conceive their children through in vitro fertilization (IVF) with HGM. In support of the law, he cites one or more of the following goals: elimination of genetic diseases, conferral of viral or bacterial immunity, improvement of memory and learning, and/or extension of maximum lifespan. The bill bars conceiving a child via sex.

Voters will strongly object to a proposal that forces would-be parents to undergo an expensive and burdensome medical procedure. As Chapter 4, Section B.1, explained, IVF with fertility drugs and PGD costs around $20,000 per cycle. Modifying gametes or embryos will add more expense. A woman may undergo several IVF cycles before she conceives.[31] Few can afford such services, and the government is unlikely to fund universal access at a price that Professor Mehlman once calculated at $120 billion or more per year.[32] Moreover, the Roman Catholic Church believes that human conception should be the product of sex between man and wife; it disapproves of both IVF and HGM for enhancement.[33] In the United States, approximately one out of five adults is Roman Catholic.[34] Thus, much of the electorate is likely to oppose the government program on moral grounds. A politician who supports the bill in the face of financial and religious opposition will not survive the next election.

Furthermore, if the bill is enacted into law, it will face a constitutional challenge. Since deciding *Skinner*, the Supreme Court has recognized a constitutional right of privacy that includes the right to make reproductive decisions.[35] In cases about birth control and abortion, the Court has acknowledged a right to procreate in *dicta*.[36] A law that places a significant burden on the right to procreate will face heightened scrutiny and may be invalidated.[37]

2 Governmental Pressure

Second, the claim that HGM leads to eugenics may be intended as a protest against government pressure to correct genetic mutations or other abnormalities. To illustrate, consider the hypothetical scenario from Chapter 1, Section B.1.a, in which Mary Smith carries two copies of the mutated gene that causes Huntington disease. Preimplantation genetic diagnosis (PGD) cannot help her because the defective gene is dominant and all her embryos will have it. Now, suppose the government pays, or requires health insurers to pay, for Mary and other carriers of genetic mutations to undergo IVF with HGM. The provision of coverage sends an implicit message that carriers *should* undergo IVF with HGM rather than run the risk of bearing a sick child. Presumably, medical providers will inform carriers of their rights, adding to the pressure Mary and other carriers feel.[38] However, if the government pays, or requires insurers to pay, for these technologies, the problem of unequal access discussed in Chapter 4, Section B.1, is solved. Mary Smith and other carriers are likely to prefer pressure, which they can resist, to lack of access due to financial constraints.

Some might wonder if authoritarian regimes in foreign nations will provide universal access to improved memory and learning in an effort to gain a nefarious edge, thereby influencing the United States to do the same and creating a situation in which Americans feel pressured to enhance their own children. However, that scenario is unlikely. As discussed in Section A of this chapter, genes deliver only potential and not outcomes. Foreigners have other ways to achieve dominance that are cheaper and less intrusive. For example, students from Europe and Asia often outperform Americans on math and science tests.[39] HGM is not currently available, the foreign students must have learned the material better, perhaps due to more effective pedagogy.[40]

3 Stigmatizing the Disabled

Third, the claim that HGM leads to eugenics may express concern that society will become less tolerant of the disabled.[41] Again, imagine that Mary Smith and other carriers correct genetic mutations in their gametes before conceiving their children through IVF. In this scenario, HGM can be construed as medical treatment provided to a future person rather than extinction of an unworthy one. Thus, HGM is less stigmatizing than current prenatal screening methods, including PGD, which lead directly to the discard or abortion of embryos and fetuses with genetic or chromosomal abnormalities.[42]

To be sure, if HGM is used in this manner, fewer people will be born with genetic diseases. As a result of this decline in numbers, those who have the diseases will have less political clout.[43] However, it does not follow that society will fail to support or accommodate these individuals. The Americans with Disabilities Act of 1990 protects those who suffer from disabilities against discrimination.[44]

4 Market Forces

Last but not least, the claim that HGM leads to eugenics may warn against the power of the market to shape a generation. Imagine that HGM becomes just another option within the array of assisted reproductive technologies. Due to expense and risk, most parents do not use it for therapy or enhancement. However, some are attracted to the technology. They decide for themselves which genes to add or delete from their gametes or embryos. The government regulates the technology for safety and efficacy but is otherwise uninvolved.

Decisions made to benefit individuals, rather than the species, are not eugenic in the traditional sense.[45] Moreover, there is no state coercion in this scenario.[46] Without a powerful government deciding which genes are best, there is less potential for the oppression of unpopular ethnic, racial, or economic groups.

Some might retort that the market can impose its own tyranny. If parents design their children according to current trends, diversity may decline. In theory, cohorts may be born with the same eye color, hair color, stature, or other traits.[47] Worse, parents might alter the skin color or features of their children in an effort to make them resemble a dominant racial group.[48] In this manner, market forces could imply that some traits – and people – are more valuable than others.[49]

However, such outcomes are unlikely for three reasons. First, as Chapter 1, Section C, noted, HGM is expensive and risky enough to discourage parents from using it for frivolous reasons. Second, most parents are not interested in designing their children.[50] Fertile men and women could procure sperm or eggs from beautiful, intelligent, tall, and athletic donors of any race and procreate via assisted insemination or IVF, but there is no such trend in our society.[51] Even the infertile prefer gamete donors with traits similar to their own.[52] Lastly, as Professor Ronald Green notes, traits associated with ethnic or racial groups oscillate in popularity and are often treasured as an expression of ethnic or racial pride.[53] HGM will not lead to racial or ethnic homogenization.

C OSSIFICATION OF SOCIETY

For many years, bioethicists and policymakers have debated whether longer lives are good or bad.[54] For example, in 2003, the President's Council on Bioethics issued a report that took a rather gloomy view of the consequences of lifespan extension for individuals and society.[55] More than a decade later, scientists have finally developed editing tools that could theoretically be used to extend maximum lifespan.

This section evaluates the claim that lifespan extension will cause society to ossify. In tracing the contours of this claim, it relies on the President's Council report and other sources that have expressed concerns about longer lives. To provide context, this section begins with information about current demographic trends.

1 Demographic Trends

Average life expectancy at birth in the United States soared from 48 to 78 years during the twentieth century.[56] Improved sanitation and public health measures such as vaccination helped bring about this increase.[57] An upward trend is not inevitable: a baby born in 2015 had a life expectancy of 78.8 years, 0.1 less than the 78.9 years recorded in 2014.[58] Nevertheless, the 30-year gain during the twentieth century remains a major accomplishment.

Meanwhile, fertility rates in the United States have declined. In 1915, 125 babies were born per 1000 women of childbearing age. In 2000, only 67.6 babies were born per 1000 such women.[59] In 2013 and 2015, the fertility rate hit an all-time low of 62.5, half what it was 100 years before.[60] Reasons for the decline are complex. When fewer babies and children die from disease, fertility rates decrease because parents know their children will live.[61] Other reasons include a decline in marriage,[62] reliable contraception, economic recessions, and education and employment opportuniteis for women.[63]

These two trends have contributed to the graying of the United States. By 2015, the elderly (65 years and older) accounted for nearly 15 percent of the population. By 2050, the elderly are projected to constitute about 22 percent of the population.[64] Moreover, this aging trend is a worldwide phenomenon. By 2020, the elderly will outnumber young children (under age 5); by 2050, there will be more than twice as many elderly people in the world as young children.[65]

As if this were not enough, the elderly are themselves growing older. In the United States, the number of people age 90 and over nearly tripled from 1980 to 2010; centenarians increased in number by roughly 65 percent.[66] Noting these latter statistics, the US Census Bureau commented:

> These oldest old people are distinct from the rest of the older population in many sociodemographic characteristics and are more likely to have chronic conditions that require long-term care, thus may consume public resources disproportionately and constitute a heavier burden on informal care often provided by families.[67]

Although many people are living longer, some researchers have reported that annual maximum reported age at death has not changed significantly since the mid-1990s. Rather, it has plateaued at around 114.9 years.[68] Logically, those who worry about the graying of society must find this report reassuring. If death is indeed inevitable, the turning of the generational guard must continue, albeit at a slower pace.

2 Negative Effects of Lifespan Extension

As mentioned earlier, critics have argued that longer lives spell disaster for society. This section considers three possible consequences of lifespan extension: collapse of social welfare programs, creation of a nursing home world, and organizational ossification.[69]

a) Collapse of Social Welfare Programs

The President's Council on Bioethics has suggested that lifespan extension may exacerbate a general trend in which private and public resources flow to the elderly rather than the young.[70] Similarly, but more pointedly, another critic has claimed that longer lives threaten the survival of Social Security and Medicare.[71] Before evaluating the likelihood that HGM will bring about such harms, this section briefly reviews the current status of Social Security and Medicare.

In 2017, the Social Security and Medicare Boards of Trustees reported on the financial status of the Social Security and Medicare programs. They projected that the Social Security trust funds, which generate interest income and can be used to supplement tax revenues, will be depleted in 2034.[72] After that, scheduled tax incomecan pay only around three-quarters of benefits through 2091.[73] Potential means of closing the gap include tax increases and benefits cuts.[74]

Similarly, Medicare faces challenges. Medicare Part A helps the elderly and disabled cover hospital, follow-up home care, skilled nursing facility, and hospice expenses.[75] However, in 2028, the Medicare Hospital Insurance Trust Fund will be exhausted. Program revenue will then cover only 87 percent of program costs.[76]

However, the Council assumes that age-retardation technologies would be widely available and used.[77] This assumption is incorrect, at least insofar as HGM is concerned. Chapter 4, Section B.4, discussed a hypothetical scenario in which John and Mary Smith use HGM to conceive a son named Devin with a maximum lifespan of 150 years. As explained there, genes cannot guarantee Devin will live that long. He will probably die much sooner due to accident or disease. Thus, few parents will pay for lifespan extension. Devin and others like him will be a drop in the bucket compared to the millions of unmodified elderly who require private or public support.

Moreover, as explained in Chapter 1, Section C.3, unless lifespan extension comes packaged with reasonably good health in old age, no one will want it. For the sake of argument, assume that Devin and others with the same modification are indeed healthy and vigorous in their old age. Good health will reduce their need for medical care and enable them to work past the usual retirement age, thereby easing the strain on private and public resources.[78]

As for Social Security and Medicare, it will take years for scientists to discover how to safely modify the genome to extend lifespan, and six or seven decades after that before the first modified cohort is old enough to claim benefits. The financial crisis currently facing those programs will come to a head long before then. If they collapse, HGM will not be the reason.

b) Nursing Home World

Professor Francis Fukuyama, an academic and member of the President's Council on Bioethics,[79] has written about the cumulative effect of biomedical advances that increase life expectancy.[80] Noting the accompanying rise in dementia and dependency on relatives and other caretakers, he predicts that further biomedical advances will lead to a nursing home world in which even centenarians are doomed to spend another 50 years in child-like dependency.[81] This nightmarish vision does not directly address HGM as a method of extending maximum lifespan. However, it is relevant to the overall theme of long lives leading to negative consequences.

Japan offers an example of what Fukuyama has in mind. In 2016, 26.7 percent of its population was age 65 or older.[82] Not surprisingly, dementia is on the rise. By the year 2025, one out of five persons over age 65 is predicted to have dementia.[83] The burden of caring for the demented has fallen largely on spouses and grown children. To reduce this burden, more nursing homes and care workers are needed. However, a national debt more than twice the size of the economy makes it difficult for the Japanese government to infuse more funds into social welfare programs.[84] As the US population ages and its national debt soars,[85] similar social problems may emerge here.

However, HGM differs from biomedical advances that slowly increase life expectancies. It is a reproductive technology that requires parents to make a specific decision to modify their child at the time of conception. As stated earlier, an extended maximum lifespan must come packaged with reasonably good health or no parent will buy it. No sane person will condemn his or her child to spend 50 years as a helpless invalid, or consign his or her grandchildren to serve as unpaid caretakers for decades.

We can all hope that a nursing home world never exists. However, if it does, Fukuyama is correct in sensing that it will arise out of new medical treatments or drugs that keep men and women alive in a frail or demented state for increasingly longer periods of time. The proper response to this horrifying prospect is support for research into treatments or drugs that maintain the physical and intellectual powers of the elderly.

c) Organizational Ossification

The President's Council on Bioethics has speculated that lifespan extension will cause the elderly to postpone retirement, leading them to occupy leadership positions in business, the military, and politics for many decades. Deprived of youth and the innovation and adaptability it represents, key institutions and organizations will stagnate and ossify.[86] Professor Fukuyama has articulated similar views about longer lives and their potential to stymie progress in academic institutions, businesses, and political parties.[87]

Again, current events are relevant. In the United States today, close to half the population quits work by age 63.[88] Eligibility for Social Security begins at age 62,[89] and its guarantee of financial support induces many to retire.[90] These facts suggest that most Americans will step aside for younger generations if financial support is available.

To be sure, certain people are likely to work longer. Blue-collar workers who engage in physical labor generally take Social Security benefits earlier than white-collar workers.[91] College-educated men and women are more likely to stay in the labor force after age 65 than those with less education.[92] Highly educated academics seem to be especially prone to late retirement. In 2013, Fidelity Investments revealed the results of a study it conducted of faculty at institutions of higher education. A whopping 74 percent of those queried planned to retire after age 65, or never retire, for both professional and economic reasons.[93] The graying of academe contributes to higher tuition (as senior professors tend to earn more) and undermines innovation and change.[94]

In the realm of business, Fortune 500 CEOs averaged 57 years of age in 2015,[95] but high-profile leaders can be much older. For example, Warren Buffett still the CEO of Berkshire Hathaway at age 87.[96] Rupert Murdoch became the acting CEO of Fox News Channel and Fox Business Network at age 86 when Roger Ailes resigned.[97]

The elderly are also prominent in political positions, including the three branches of federal government. Donald John Trump and Hillary Rodham Clinton were ages 70 and 69, respectively, on the day of the 2016 presidential election, making them the oldest pair of contenders in American history.[98] Trump became the oldest president-elect in American history.[99] In the 114th Congress (2015–2016), the average age of senators was 61; the average age of representatives was 57.[100] The eldest representative, John Conyers (D-Mich.), was 85 when the 114th Congress commenced; the eldest senator, Dianne Feinstein (D-Cal.), was 81.[101] The US Supreme Court is another place where the elderly tend to linger. During the 35-year period from 1971 to 2006, justices retired at age 78.7 on average.[102]

In short, the elderly already cling to power in academia, high-profile businesses, and politics. The question is whether extending maximum lifespan will materially worsen the ossification. This book contends that the answer is no. As mentioned previously, the vast majority of those modified will not reach maximum lifespan because genes do not equate to long life. And without that guarantee, few parents will be motivated to purchase HGM services.

Moreover, as Ronald Bailey notes, society has ways to encourage renewal and progress. Young people can found new companies; boards of directors, who elect CEOs, have the power to shake up entrenched management; and voters can institute term limits to avoid the endless recycling of politicians.[103] And if tenure encourages too many elderly faculty members to rest on their laurels, universities can curtail it.

To summarize this section, the American population is aging. This aging trend may continue as biomedical advances help people live longer on average. Moreover, the aging trend already has had an impact on social welfare programs and key institutions, making it easy to suppose that HGM will make matters worse. However, it is highly unlikely that HGM will produce a surfeit of centenarians. Even if scientists learn how to manipulate genes in a way that extends the maximum human lifespan, few parents are likely to purchase an expensive and risky modification that does not ensure long lives.

D GENOCIDE

Professors George Annas, Lori Andrews, and Rosario Isasi theorize that human cloning and inheritable genetic alterations lead to genocide and thus must be banned.[104] Toward that end, these authors have drafted an international treaty that requires nations to enact criminal laws to ensure that no one uses human gametes or embryos with inheritable genetic modifications to begin a human pregnancy or gestation.[105] If the treaty became a reality, it would impose a worldwide ban on all uses of HGM, including correction of genetic mutations that cause disease.

In justification, the authors reason that our species has developed a theory of universal human rights, such as human dignity and equality. These rights are rooted in the fundamental sameness of human beings.[106] However, HGM has the power to change humanity's essence by transforming us into a new species.[107] By changing the foundation of human rights, HGM threatens human rights.

Taking note of Professor Silver's theory that HGM will split humanity into more than one species,[108] these authors claim that an enhanced species will view human beings as inferior and enslave or murder them. Alternatively, human beings will launch a preemptive strike and kill as many members of the new species as possible. Either way, HGM leads to genocide.[109] Scientists who modify the human genome are potential bioterrorists, and their experiments are potential weapons of mass destruction.[110]

1 *Speciation*

There is no such thing as an iconic human genome that defines the species. Rather, there are as many human genomes as there are human beings alive.[111] This mix changes constantly under the influence of various factors, such as random genetic mutations, marriages, infidelities, abortions, births, and deaths.[112] As genomes flux, so do species boundaries.[113]

A species can be defined through its procreative isolation. Under this approach, two groups that do not breed together must be different species.[114] This approach does not always work. For example, it incorrectly suggests that two human groups that do not procreate with each other, perhaps for geographic or religious reasons, are independent species.[115] However, because Professor Silver has suggested that artificial chromosomes will lead to reproductive incompatibility, this definition is relevant here.

a) Mainstream Applications

Keeping these two definitions in mind, consider the potential uses of HGM outlined in Chapter 1 of this book. Scientists may delete a genetic mutation that causes disease or excise a gene that serves as a gateway for a dangerous virus. They may add SNPs associated with memory and learning or genetic variants that boost lifespan. If the genes to be deleted or added already exist in humans, the scientists do not alter the human gene pool.[116] Their efforts may yield a novel *combination* of human genes in a single person, but even sexual reproduction can do that.

To change the genetic boundaries of the species in a meaningful way, HGM would have to be employed on a vast scale.[117] For example, if all or most babies in a generation received genetic variants associated with a lifespan of 150 years, the boundaries might be shifted in the direction of longer lives. But the wholesale transformation of even this one trait is unlikely. As Chapter 4, Section B.4, clarified, most parents will skip lifespan extension due to the cost, effort, and risk. Moreover, as Section B.1 of this chapter explained, the government cannot compel parents to purchase lifespan extension for practical, religious, and legal reasons.

In terms of procreative engagement, the risk of species alteration is even slighter. There is no reason to believe that the genetic modifications discussed in this book will compromise a person's ability to procreate with other human beings. But if a particular modification does interfere with procreation, no parent will want it and no regulator will permit it.

b) Bizarre Applications

Some readers may protest that this analysis fails to confront the heart of the problem. The true threat to the species comes from radical modifications that add bizarre genomes and concomitant traits to the mix. For example, what if a scientist modifies human embryos to make babies who have extra limbs? Or what if a scientist culls genes from other animals and introduces them to human embryos to produce chimeras, such as babies who glow in the dark?[118]

Such radical interventions are unlikely. Parents have a natural instinct to benefit and protect their children.[119] Applications that turn offspring into freaks or chimeras run counter to that instinct. The rare parent who is mentally disturbed enough to want a baby who glows in the dark will find that the trait is unavailable. Scientists will not waste money and time developing modifications that the vast majority of parents do not want. And without copious safety and efficacy data, federal regulators will refuse to approve modifications.[120]

But even if radical interventions were realistic, the proposed treaty would be overbroad.[121] It demands criminal laws to prevent initiation of pregnancies via gametes or embryos subjected to inheritable genetic modification. If such laws were enacted, a doctor who removed a genetic mutation from eggs so a woman could give birth to a healthy baby would be considered as much of a bioterrorist as a renegade who altered an embryo to make a baby glow in the dark.

c) Artificial Chromosomes

Professor Silver predicts that HGM will be used in conjunction with artificial chromosomes. Unmodified human beings with 46 chromosomes will not be able to procreate with those who bear 48 chromosomes.[122] If a species is defined by its procreative engagement or isolation, then artificial chromosomes could lead to speciation. Perhaps this is the possibility that haunts the advocates of the treaty.[123]

However, artificial chromosomes raise serious safety concerns. Most parents will hesitate before accepting a pair of artificial chromosomes that can impair cell division or cause gene overlap.[124] Thus, it seems unlikely that artificial chromosomes will ever be popular enough to lead to speciation.

2 Human Rights and Genocide

To complete the discussion, this section addresses the claim that HGM will undercut human rights and lead to genocide. Let us begin with the alleged threat to universal human rights. Every human being alive today has such rights and will continue to have them even if others are born through HGM. Further, children who are born with random genetic mutations or chromosomal variations are human beings with human rights. It follows that children gifted with human gene variants should also qualify as human beings with human rights, even if those variants are attached to artificial chromosomes.

To be sure, human rights do not guarantee peaceful coexistence. Variations in culture, language, philosophy, religion, economic status, and even appearance can incite envy, hatred, violence, and genocide. Examples include ongoing religious cleansing and genocide in Syria and Iraq;[125] ethnic cleansing and genocide committed against Bosnian Muslims in the 1990s;[126] and the persecution and murder of Jews, Roma, homosexuals, and others in the Holocaust.[127]

Predictions of genocide committed by enhanced beings against human beings or vice versa presuppose that it will be easy to discern whether a person belongs to one group or the other. Fortunately, individuals born with genetic modifications will look and act much the same as the rest of the local population. They will not be confined to specific neighborhoods but will be scattered throughout the populace. There will be no skin color or facial features, no ethnic or religious practices, and no ghettos to distinguish them from unmodified persons.

Suppose some parents use HGM to improve memory and learning, and their offspring achieve career and financial success. Will their career success and wealth mark them out from the rest of the population? The answer is no, for one simple reason: most parents will not employ HGM due to the expense and risk. Therefore, the vast majority of successful and wealthy people in the population will be conceived via sex.

Similarly, suppose some parents use HGM to extend the maximum lifespan of their children. The modification will not be obvious to the naked eye. The only way to be certain that a particular individual has it is to wait and see if he or she lives longer than 122 years – and even then, there will be no guarantee, since the unmodified maximum lifespan may be longer than we realize. Whether a 140-year-old person will provoke envy may depend on how healthy he or she is. In a culture obsessed with youth and beauty, pity or revulsion may be more likely reactions. But in any case, violent reactions are unlikely. Some people live to be 100 years old now, and yet there is no movement to battle or murder centenarians.

However, even if genocide is unlikely, another unpleasant possibility exists. Most modified persons may evade detection, but the unlucky few who are outed may suffer discrimination or violence at the hands of those who fear or envy them. In an ironic twist, the four objections and laws based on them render such outcomes likelier by conveying negative messages about HGM and children born through it. These topics are examined in greater detail in Chapters 7 and 10.

E CONSENT OF FUTURE GENERATIONS

Thus far, analysis has focused on four extreme claims of bad outcomes, which this chapter has bundled together under the label of apocalypse objection. This chapter now turns to an oft-voiced concern that is logically related to that objection.

Critics complain that future generations cannot consent to heritable genetic modifications.[128] However, genes mutate on their own all the time without obtaining consent from anyone. Men and women choose sex partners and make other reproductive decisions affecting the gene pool without obtaining consent from future generations.[129] To insist that one generation obtain consent before conceiving the next is to demand the impossible. Perhaps the complaint about lack of consent is nothing more than a cynical attempt to block access to HGM.

If not, the complaint may be more about harm than consent. Harm is a difficult concept to work with where future generations are concerned. HGM cannot harm individuals conceived through it, for they would not exist otherwise.[130] However, HGM could conceivably lead to a future that is worse than an alternative one in which it does not exist.[131] That prospect may be the reason that some express concerns about future generations who cannot consent.

If the concern expresses fear that HGM leads to a worse future, it is too vague to be useful. The apocalypse objection, with its four claims of specific bad outcomes, could give it substance. However, as discussed earlier, theories that HGM derails democracy, inspires a new eugenics, ossifies society, or leads to genocide are based on flawed biological and political premises. Ultimately, there is no reason to believe that HGM leads to a worse future, and thus no reason to obsess about the consent of future generations.

F STEREOTYPES ASSOCIATED WITH THE APOCALYPSE OBJECTION

This section describes stereotypes associated with the apocalypse objection. Stereotypes are organized according to each claim within the objection.

1 Collapse of Democracy and Genocide

On their face, claims that HGM leads to the failure of democracy and/or genocide attack technology. In reality, however, the claims object to the existence of children of HGM. By transmitting superior genes and traits to future generations, the children create genetic divides and/or new species that undermine democracy and incite genocide. In short, the children are superior and divisive, and thus unjust. These are the same core stereotypes associated with the stratification objection. In addition, the claims present the children as violent, anti-democratic, and genocidal.

2 Eugenics

The claim that HGM leads to eugenics incorporates several concerns. The first is that government will force people to reproduce through HGM. As Section B of this chapter explained, such compulsion is unlikely for political, religious, and constitutional reasons. However, from a historical point of view, eugenics is so strongly associated with coercion, discrimination, and Nazism that the label is damning.[132] By using it, critics insinuate that children of HGM are the product of coercion and evil.

A second concern is that governmental subsidies or insurance coverage may pressure carriers of genetic mutations to use HGM. This pressure, which can be resisted, seems preferable to lack of access due to financial constraints. However, by linking HGM to pressure, critics encourage the public to associate children of HGM with coercion.

A third concern alleges that HGM may render society less tolerant of persons born with genetic mutations and diseases. As discussed in Section B.3, HGM repairs gametes or embryos and may be viewed as medical treatment for future children. Thus, HGM is less stigmatizing than PGD or other screening technologies that lead to the discard of affected embryos or fetuses. The real harm flows from the concern itself, which may encourage those who have genetic diseases to experience a sense of devaluation and to blame children of HGM.

Lastly, a fourth concern asserts that parents will design their children according to current trends, creating faddish cohorts that devalue children who do not have popular traits. This concern frames children of HGM as the problem. By associating them with design and fads, it implies they are fungible, artifact-like, and superficial.

3 Society Ossifies

Another apocalyptic claim is that lifespan extension will burden and disrupt society. Allegedly, children with modified lifespans will overburden social welfare programs, languish in nursing homes, and cause key organizations to stagnate. Here again, the children are the problem. The claim stereotypes them as too controlling and selfish to retire. It also portrays them as parasites that destroy social welfare programs and ossify key organizations.

4 Consent of Future Generations

Lastly, the concern about consent of future generations takes aim at hubristic scientists and parents who dare to wield a damaging technology without first obtaining the approval of everyone who may be affected. The children of HGM are not responsible for the decisions that led to their existence. Nevertheless, this concern brands the children as the unwelcome product of anti-democratic decisions. The concern also strongly implies that the children would not have existed in a just world where everyone had a voice.

G SUMMARY

Critics predict HGM will bring about apocalyptic outcomes, such as the collapse of democracy or genocide. The reality is less dramatic. Scientists may eventually learn to improve memory and learning or extend lifespan, but such enhancements cannot guarantee academic achievement, wealth, or long life. Most parents will prefer sexual intercourse, which is pleasant and free, to a pricey technology that offers uncertain benefits. Artificial chromosomes will be especially unpopular due to the physical risks involved. Thus, children of HGM will grow up to find that most of their potential reproductive partners are unmodified. Given these facts, hereditary genetic castes will not emerge to imperil democracy, and there will be no speciation event to spark inter-species war.

Dark visions of eugenics reborn are similarly unpersuasive. The government cannot compel men and women to substitute IVF with HGM for procreative sex. Governmental subsidies and insurance coverage may exert a subtle pressure to use HGM, but the benefits of access outweigh that disadvantage. Correcting genetic mutations in an embryo and bringing it to term is less stigmatizing than existing screening methods. The market will not produce faddish cohorts because most parents will eschew frivolous uses of an expensive and risky technology.

Finally, HGM will not ossify society. Few parents will spend tens of thousands of dollars to purchase genetic variants that cannot guarantee long lives. Children born with extended lifespans will be too few in number to impact social welfare programs and key institutions. If Social Security collapses, nursing homes boom, and centenarians cling to power, the aging of the *unmodified* population will be to blame.

Relatedly, some assert that HGM is wrong because future generations cannot consent. However, no future generation ever consents to actions that the present generation undertakes. Perhaps this concern is a warning against actions that can lead to bad outcomes in the future. However, as this chapter has demonstrated, claims that HGM leads to disastrous outcomes are exaggerated.

Finally, this chapter has explained that the apocalypse objection conveys negative messages about children of HGM. The objection assumes that the children are superior and divisive, and thus unjust. Specific claims promote further stereotypes. For example, warnings about the collapse of democracy and genocide mark children of HGM as violent, anti-democratic, and genocidal. Eugenic fears link the children to coercion, discrimination, and Nazism. Ossification prophecies insinuate that the children are controlling, selfish, and parasitic. The concern about future generations implies that the children are the product of anti-democratic decisions.

Part II digs beneath the surface of the apocalypse objection and its related concern and unmasks the psychological forces behind them. Further, it explores ways in which the objection and concern promote envy and other emotions that place the health and well-being of children of HGM at risk.

Notes

1. The term "apocalypse" can refer either to the final destruction of the world, as foretold in the Book of Revelation of the New Testament or to an incident entailing catastrophic damage or destruction. NEW OXFORD AMERICAN DICTIONARY 73 (ANGUS STEVENSON & CHRISTINE A. LINDBERG EDS., 3rd ed. 2010). This chapter uses the term in the latter sense.
2. MAXWELL J. MEHLMAN, The Law of Above Averages: Leveling the New Genetic Enhancement Playing Field, 85 IOWA L. REV. 517, 526–27, 530–31, 533, 551 (2000).
3. *Id.* at 553.
4. *Id.* at 554.
5. *Id.* at 575.
6. *See* G. DAVIES ET AL., Genome-wide Association Studies Establish that Human Intelligence Is Highly Heritable and Polygenic, 16 MOLECULAR PSYCHIATRY 996, 997 (2011) (stating that educational, career, and financial success are associated with intelligence).
7. *See* CORNELIUS A. RIETVELD ET AL., Common Genetic Variants Associated with Cognitive Performance Identified Using the Proxy-phenotype Method, 111 PNAS 13790, 13793 (2014) (explaining that certain SNPs are associated with cognitive ability, and some are located near genes associated with synaptic plasticity, a basis of memory and learning).
8. LEE M. SILVER, REMAKING EDEN: CLONING AND BEYOND IN A BRAVE NEW WORLD 6, 7, 246 (1997).
9. THE PRESIDENT'S COUNCIL ON BIOETHICS, BEYOND THERAPY: BIOTECHNOLOGY AND THE PURSUIT OF HAPPINESS 39 (2003) [hereinafter BEYOND THERAPY].

10. *See* RONALD BAILEY, LIBERATION BIOLOGY: THE SCIENTIFIC AND MORAL CASE FOR THE BIOTECH REVOLUTION 169 (2005) (noting that human beings are diverse and not the same or equal).
11. MEHLMAN, *supra* note 2, at 550.
12. CARMEN DENAVAS WALT & BERNADETTE D. PROCTOR, UNITED STATES CENSUS BUREAU, INCOME AND POVERTY IN THE UNITED STATES: 2014 9 tbl.2 (September 2015), www.census.gov/content/dam/Census/library/publications/2015/demo/p60-252.pdf.
13. *Id.*
14. RICHARD FRY & RAKESH KOCHHAR, America's Wealth Gap Between Middle-Income and Upper-Income Families Is Widest on Record, PEW RESEARCH CENTER (December 17, 2014), www.pewresearch.org/fact-tank/2014/12/17/wealth-gap-upper-middle-income/.
15. DAVID SIDERS, Jerry Brown Signs $15 Minimum Wage in California, THE SACRAMENTO BEE (April 4, 2016), www.sacbee.com/news/politics-government/capitol-alert/article69842317.html (explaining that California's minimum wage will rise by $1 annually until it reaches $15 in 2022); SEAN KIRBY, New York State Minimum Wage Set to Increase to $15 Per Hour, LABOR & EMPLOYMENT LAW BLOG (April 5, 2016), www.laboremploymentlawblog.com/2016/04/articles/wage-and-hour/new-york-state-minimum-wage-set-to-increase-to-15-per-hour/ (detailing New York plan to increase the minimum wage in New York City and surrounding counties more rapidly than in the rest of the state).
16. DREW DESILVER, The Many Ways to Measure Economic Inequality, PEW RESEARCH CENTER (September 22, 2015), www.pewresearch.org/fact-tank/2015/09/22/the-many-ways-to-measure-economic-inequality/.
17. Under the Temporary Assistance for Needy Families program, the federal government gives block grants to the states, which dispense cash subsidies to qualified individuals. OFFICE OF FAMILY ASSISTANCE, About TANF (October 29, 2015), www.acf.hhs.gov/ofa/programs/tanf/about. The US Department of Housing and Urban Development administers a program through which low-income individuals receive vouchers to cover the cost of renting or even purchasing a home. *Housing Choice Vouchers Fact Sheet*, HUD.GOV, http://portal.hud.gov/hudportal/HUD?src=/topics/housing_choice_voucher_program_section_8 (last visited December 20, 2016). Medicaid provides health coverage to low-income individuals. The program, which is administered by the states, enrolled 72.5 million people in 2014. Overview, MEDICAID.GOV, www.medicaid.gov/medicaid-chip-program-information/medicaid-and-chip-program-information.html (last visited December 20, 2016).
18. MEHLMAN, *supra* note 2, at 550–51.
19. *Id.* at 551–52.
20. *E.g.*, SUSANNAH BARUCH ET AL., HUMAN GERMLINE GENETIC MODIFICATION: ISSUES AND OPTIONS FOR POLICYMAKERS 34 (2005).
21. KERRY LYNN MACINTOSH, Brave New Eugenics: Regulating Assisted Reproductive Technologies in the Name of Better Babies, 257 U. ILL. J.L.

TECH & POLICY 293–94 (2010). Galton derived the word "eugenics" from the Greek term "eugenes," which means good in birth. *Id.* at 294.

22. *Id.* at 294.
23. BUCK V. BELL, 274 US 200 (1927).
24. *See generally* STEFAN KUHL, THE NAZI CONNECTION: EUGENICS, AMERICAN RACISM, AND GERMAN NATIONAL SOCIALISM (1994) (documenting connection between American eugenics movement and Nazi Germany).
25. DIANE B. PAUL, CONTROLLING HUMAN HEREDITY, 1865 TO THE PRESENT 89 (1995).
26. SKINNER V. OKLAHOMA, 316 US 535 (1942).
27. *Id.* at 541.
28. PHILIP R. REILLY, THE SURGICAL SOLUTION 143, 149 (1991).
29. RONALD M. GREEN, BABIES BY DESIGN: THE ETHICS OF GENETIC CHOICE 160–61 (2007); DAN W. BROCK, Is Selection of Children Wrong? in HUMAN ENHANCEMENT 251, 275 (JULIAN SAVULESCU & NICK BOSTROM, EDS. 2013).
30. PAUL A. LOMBARDO, Taking Eugenics Seriously: Three Generations of ??? Are Enough? 30 FLA. ST. U. L. REV. 191, 216 (2003).
31. *See* ANDREW D.A.C. SMITH ET AL., Live-Birth Rate Associated with Repeat In Vitro Fertilization Treatment Cycles, 314 JAMA 2654 (arguing that practitioners should provide more than three to four cycles of IVF because the cumulative live-birth rate continues to climb and reaches 65.3 percent after six cycles).
32. MEHLMAN, *supra* note 2, at 532.
33. *See* CONGREGATION FOR THE DOCTRINE OF THE FAITH, Instruction Dignitas Personae on Certain Bioethical Questions, ¶¶ 6–10, 14–16, 27 (2008), at www.ewtn.com/library/CURIA/CDF-Dignitas-Personae.pdf [hereinafter DIGNITAS PERSONAE].
34. MICHAEL LIPKA, A Closer Look at Catholic America, PEW RESEARCH CENTER (September 14, 2015), www.pewresearch.org/fact-tank/2015/09/14/a-closer-look-at-catholic-america/.
35. JOHN E. NOWAK & RONALD D. ROTUNDA, CONSTITUTIONAL LAW § 14.27, at 797–98 (5th ed. 1995).
36. *See, e.g.*, EISENSTADT V. BAIRD, 405 U.S. 438, 453 (1972) (birth control case stating that the right to privacy protects individuals from government interference with decision to bear or beget a child); CAREY V. POPULATION SERVICES INT'L, 431 U.S. 678, 685 (1977) (birth control case stating that decision whether to bear or beget a child is constitutionally protected); PLANNED PARENTHOOD OF SOUTHEASTERN PENNSYLVANIA V. CASEY, 505 U.S. 833, 851 (1992) (abortion case listing procreation as a personal right protected by Constitution).
37. *Cf.* Carey, 431 U.S. at 688–90 (applying strict scrutiny to invalidate law that restricted distribution of contraceptives to licensed pharmacists); Planned Parenthood of Southeastern Pennsylvania, 505 U.S. at 876–77, 887–98

(applying undue burden standard to invalidate law that required married women to notify spouses that they intended to seek an abortion).

38. *Cf.* NATIONAL ACADEMY OF SCIENCES & NATIONAL ACADEMY OF MEDICINE, Human Genome Editing: Science, Ethics, and Governance 96 (2017) [hereinafter NAS REPORT] (noting concern that parents who eschew HGM could be judged to be negligent).

39. In 2015, 15-year-olds from 71 nations around the world took the Programme for International Student Assessment (PISA). Americans ranked 38th in math and 24th in science, behind students from many European and Asian nations. Drew DeSilver, U.S. Students' Academic Achievement Still Lags That of Their Peers in Many Other Countries, PEW RESEARCH CENTER (February 15, 2017), www.pewresearch.org/fact-tank/2017/02/15/u-s-students-internationally-math-science/.

40. For example, some Asian nations teach math in greater depth. JENNIFER C. KERR, Internationally, U.S. Students Are Falling, U.S. NEWS & WORLD REPORT (December 6, 2016), www.usnews.com/news/politics/articles/2016-12-06/math-a-concern-for-us-teens-science-reading-flat-on-test.

41. NAS REPORT, *supra* note 38, at 96; BARUCH ET AL., *supra* note 20, at 35–36.

42. BARUCH ET AL., *supra* note 20, at 36.

43. NAS REPORT, *supra* note 38, at 96–97.

44. AMERICANS WITH DISABILITIES ACT OF 1990, 42 U.S.C. §§ 12101–12213 (West, Westlaw through P.L. 115–43).

45. BROCK, *supra* note 29, at 274.

46. The competitive pressure that other parents may feel is discussed in Chapter 4, Section B.

47. GREEN, *supra* note 29, at 163.

48. *Id.* at 70–71.

49. Comment, Regulating Human Germline Modification in Light of CRISPR, 51 U. RICHMOND L. REV. 553, 573 (2016).

50. To be sure, subconscious factors can influence mate selection and affect the genes transmitted to offspring. For example, men generally prefer young women as mates due to their reproductive value. DAVID M. BUSS, EVOLUTIONARY PSYCHOLOGY: THE NEW SCIENCE OF THE MIND 135 (1999). Features such as clear skin, sound teeth, and facial symmetry are consistent with youth and health and therefore are considered beautiful. *Id.* at 139–42.

51. NAS REPORT, *supra* note 41, at 98.

52. GREEN, *supra* note 29, at 165.

53. *Id.* at 226–27.

54. For a summary of authors on the left and right who are critical of longer lives, see BAILEY, *supra* note 10, at 49–61.

55. BEYOND THERAPY, *supra* note 9, at 183–97.

56. *Id.* at 165.

57. *Id.*

58. JIAQUAN XU ET AL., Mortality in the United States, 267 NCHS DATA BRIEF 1 (December 2016), www.cdc.gov/nchs/data/databriefs/db267.pdf. This decline

in life expectancy was due to increased mortality, with the highest percentage increases occurring in the categories of Alzheimer's disease, unintentional injuries, stroke, chronic lower respiratory diseases, and suicide. *Id.* at 3, 5.

59. DONNA L. HOYERT ET AL., Annual Summary of Vital Statistics: 2000, 108 PEDIATRICS 1241, 1243 tbl. 1 (2001).
60. JOSH ZUMBRUN, Behind the ONGOING U.S. Baby Bust, in 5 Charts, WALL ST. J. (June 7, 2016), http://blogs.wsj.com/economics/2016/06/07/behind-the-ongoing-u-s-baby-bust-in-5-charts/.
61. WAN HE ET AL., U.S. CENSUS BUREAU, INTERNATIONAL POPULATION REPORTS, P95/16-1, AN AGING WORLD: 2015 7 (2016) [hereinafter CENSUS BUREAU REPORT].
62. *See* SARAH R. HAYFORD, Marriage (Still) Matters: The Contribution of Demographic Change to Trends in Childlessness in the United States, 50 DEMOGRAPHY 1641 (2013) (citing failure to marry as the primary factor accounting for rise of childlessness among women in the late twentieth century).
63. MARK MATHER, Fact Sheet: The Decline in U.S. Fertility, POPULATION REFERENCE BUREAU (July 2012), www.prb.org/publications/datasheets/2012/world-population-data-sheet/fact-sheet-us-population.aspx.
64. CENSUS BUREAU REPORT, *supra* note 61, at 9.
65. *Id.* at 3.
66. *Id.* at 11.
67. *Id.*
68. XIAO DONG ET AL., Evidence for a Limit to Human Lifespan, 538 NATURE 257, 258 (2016).
69. A fourth claim is that long-lived individuals will be less conscious of their own mortality and thus less motivated to renew themselves through children. BEYOND THERAPY, *supra* note 10, at 189. However, logic and evidence do not support this claim. Extending the maximum lifespan may actually increase births if it means that women live longer on average. Women can then procreate in their twenties and early thirties before their fertility declines and go back to work in their forties and fifties when their children are grown, secure in the knowledge that they still have many decades to devote to their chosen professions. *See* KERRY LYNN MACINTOSH, Teaching about the Biological Clock: Age-Related Fertility Decline and Sex Education 22 UCLA WOMEN'S L.J. 1, 4 (2015) (explaining that a woman's fertility begins to decline at age 32).
70. BEYOND THERAPY, *supra* note 10, at 196.
71. *See* BAILEY, *supra* note 11, at 50 (reporting concerns of bioethicist Daniel Callahan).
72. SOCIAL SECURITY AND MEDICARE BOARDS OF TRUSTEES, A Summary of the 2017 Annual Reports, SOCIAL SECURITY ADMINISTRATION, /www.ssa.gov/oact/trsum/ (last visited March 28, 2018). The cited projection considers two funds together: the Social Security Disability Insurance Trust Fund and the Old Age and Survivors Insurance Trust Fund. Alone, the Social Security Disability Insurance Trust Fund will be depleted in 2023. *Id.*
73. *Id.*

74. JEANNE SAHADI, Social Security Trust Fund Projected to Run Dry by 2034, CNNMONEY (June 22, 2016), http://money.cnn.com/2016/06/22/pf/social-security-medicare/.
75. SOCIAL SECURITY AND MEDICARE BOARDS OF TRUSTEES, *supra* note 75.
76. *Id.* Medicare Part B (covering doctor visits, outpatient hospital care, and other services) and Part D (covering prescription drugs) are projected to remain solvent indefinitely because patient premiums and general revenues support them. *Id.*
77. BEYOND THERAPY, *supra* note 9, at 182.
78. BAILEY, *supra* note 11, at 52.
79. *See* BEYOND THERAPY, *supra* note 10, at xi (naming Fukuyama as a member of the Council).
80. FRANCIS FUKUYAMA, OUR POSTHUMAN FUTURE: CONSEQUENCES OF THE BIOTECHNOLOGY REVOLUTION 60–61 (2002).
81. *Id.* at 67–69.
82. REIJI YOSHIDA, Japan Census Report Shows Surge in Elderly Population, Many Living Alone, JAPAN TIMES (June 29, 2016), www.japantimes.co.jp/news/2016/06/29/national/japan-census-report-shows-surge-elderly-population-many-living-alone/#.WTLwH2jyu7o.
83. NATSUKO FUKUE, The Dementia Timebomb: Ageing Japan Faces Healthcare Crisis, AFP (June 1, 2017), www.yahoo.com/news/dementia-timebomb-ageing-japan-faces-healthcare-crisis-030948375.html.
84. *Id.*
85. In 2015, the Congressional Budget Office forecast that the national debt would reach 103 percent of gross domestic product (GDP) by the year 2040. In the history of the United States, national debt has exceeded 100 percent only twice, in 1945 and 1946 after World War II. TERENCE P. JEFFREY, CBO: Debt Headed to 103% of GDP; Level Seen Only in WWII; 'No Way to Predict Whether or When' Fiscal Crisis Might Occur Here, CNSNEWS.COM (July 10, 2015), www.cnsnews.com/news/article/terence-p-jeffrey/cbo-debt-headed-103-gdp-level-seen-only-wwii-no-way-predict-whether.
86. BEYOND THERAPY, *supra* note 9, at 195.
87. FUKUYAMA, *supra* note 80, at 64–67.
88. AMANDA DIXON, The Average Retirement Age in Every State in 2016, SMARTASSET (March 29, 2017), https://smartasset.com/retirement/average-retirement-age-in-every-state-2016.
89. SOCIAL SECURITY ADMINISTRATION, Retirement Planner: Benefits by Year of Birth, www.ssa.gov/planners/retire/agereduction.html (last visited May 9, 2017).
90. *See* DAVID R. FRANCIS, Social Security Causes Earlier Retirement, NATIONAL BUREAU OF ECONOMIC RESEARCH, www.nber.org/digest/jul03/w9407.html (last visited May 9, 2017) (summarizing research from 12 countries indicating that retirements spike within a cohort in the year after social welfare payments become available).
91. MARK MATHER ET AL., Aging in the United States, 70.2 POPULATION BULLETIN 1, 11 fig. 11 (2015), www.prb.org/pdf16/aging-us-population-bulletin.pdf.

92. Id. at fig. 11.
93. Three-Fourths of Higher Education Baby Boomer Faculty Members Plan to Delay Retirement, or Never Retire at All, FIDELITY (June 17, 2013), www.fidelity.com/about-fidelity/employer-services/three-fourths-of-higher-education-baby-boomer-faculty-members. *See also* SHARON L. WEINBERG & MARC A. SCOTT, The Impact of Uncapping of Mandatory Retirement on Postsecondary Institutions, 42 EDUCATIONAL RESEARCHER 338 (2013) (projecting that 60 percent of faculty at a northeastern research university would work past 70, and 15 percent would work past 80).
94. LAURIE FENDRICH, The Forever Professors: Academics Who Don't Retire Are Greedy, Selfish, and Bad for Students, CHRON. OF HIGHER ED., November 14, 2014, www.chronicle.com/article/Retire-Already-/149965.
95. Profile, Warren Buffet, FORBES, www.forbes.com/profile/warren-buffett/ (last visited (March 24, 2018).
96. ERIK SHERMAN, 6 Oldest CEOs in America in 2015, FORTUNE (December 12, 2015), http://fortune.com/2015/12/13/oldest-ceos-fortune-500/.
97. Roger Ailes Resigns as Chairman and CEO of Fox News Channel and Fox Business Network, and Chairman Fox Television Stations, 21ST CENTURY FOX (July 21, 2016), www.21cf.com/news/21st-century-fox/2016/roger-ailes-resigns-chairman-and-ceo-fox-news-channel.
98. JENA MCGREGOR, Clinton and Trump Are the Oldest Candidates Ever. No One Seems to Care, WASH. POST (July 14, 2016), www.washingtonpost.com/news/on-leadership/wp/2016/07/14/clinton-and-trump-are-the-oldest-candidates-ever-no-one-seems-to-care/.
99. BRIANNA CHAMBERS, Donald Trump Is Oldest President-Elect in History, FOX25 (November 10, 2016), www.fox25boston.com/news/donald-trump-is-the-oldest-presidentelect-in-us-history/466031728.
100. JENNIFER E. MANNING, CONG. RESEARCH SERV., R43869, MEMBERSHIP OF THE 114TH CONGRESS: A PROFILE 2 tbl.1 (2016), https://fas.org/sgp/crs/misc/R43869.pdf.
101. Id. at 2.
102. STEVEN G. CALABRESI & JAMES LINDGREN, Term Limits for the Supreme Court: Life Tenure Reconsidered, 29 HARV. J.L. & PUB. POL'Y 769, 782 (2006).
103. BAILEY, *supra* note 10, at 51–52. To be sure, the foregoing analysis does not foreclose the occasional anomaly. In theory, a Supreme Court justice with a maximum lifespan of 150 years, appointed for life at age 50, could hold his or her position for 100 years. However, in practice, such outcomes seem improbable. The oldest Supreme Court justice was Oliver Wendell Holmes, who retired at 90, long before reaching the current maximum lifespan of 122. Frequently Asked Questions (FAQ), Who Was the Oldest Person to Serve on the Supreme Court? SUPREMECOURT.GOV (May 8, 2017), www.supremecourt.gov/faq_justices.aspx.

104. GEORGE J. ANNAS ET AL., Protecting the Endangered Human: Toward an International Treaty Prohibiting Cloning and Inheritable Alterations, 28 AMERICAN J.L. & MED. 151, 173 (2002).
105. *Id.* at 154.
106. *Id.* at 152–53.
107. *Id.* at 153.
108. *Id.* at 160–61.
109. *Id.* at 162.
110. *Id.*
111. KERRY LYNN MACINTOSH, Chimeras, Hybrids, and Cybrids: How Essentialism Distorts the Law and Stymies Scientific Research, 47 ARIZ. ST. L.J. 183, 211 (2015).
112. *See* LEE M. SILVER, Challenging Nature: The Clash of Science and Spirituality at the New Frontiers of Life 328 (2006) (noting that genetic mutations are errors in code and that the gene pool fluctuates along with individual reproductive decisions); Kurt Bayertz, Human Nature: How Normative Might it Be? 28 J. MED. & PHIL. 131, 135 (2003) (citing not only love and marriage but also migration, war, segregation, and prison and death sentences as factors influencing gene pool).
113. ERIC T. JUENGST, What's Taxonomy Got to Do with It? 'Species Integrity', Human Rights, and Science Policy, in HUMAN ENHANCEMENT 43, 50 (JULIAN SAVULESCU & NICK BOSTROM EDS.).
114. JASON SCOTT ROBERT & FRANCOISE BAYLIS, Crossing Species Boundaries, 3(3) AM. J. BIOETHICS 1, 3 (2003).
115. *Id.*
116. R. VASSENA ET AL., Genome Engineering through CRISPR/Cas9 Technology in the Human Germline and Pluripotent Stem Cells, 22 HUMAN REPRODUCTION UPDATE 411, 417 (2016).
117. *Id.*
118. *Cf.* PIMPRAPAR WONGSRIKEAO ET AL., Antiviral Restriction Factor Transgenesis in the Domestic Cat, 8 NATURE METHODS 853 (2011) (reporting experiment in which jellyfish genes were added to cat eggs, yielding cats that glowed in the dark).
119. *See* BUSS, *supra* note 50, at 189 (noting that natural selection induces parents to strive to ensure survival of genetic offspring).
120. For a discussion of Food and Drug Administration authority over HGM for reproduction, see Chapter 8, Section A.1.
121. *See* JUENGST, *supra* note 113, at 51 (noting that the treaty is not limited to transformational modifications).
122. SILVER, REMAKING EDEN, *supra* note 8, at 6, 7.
123. *See* ANNAS ET AL., *supra* note 104, at 160–61 (noting Silver's theory).
124. *See* BEYOND THERAPY, *supra* note 9, at 39.
125. *E.g.,* Amanda Holpuch & John Kerry, Isis Is Committing Genocide in Syria and Iraq, THE GUARDIAN (March 17, 2016), www.theguardian.com/world/2016/mar/17/john-kerry-isis-genocide-syria-iraq; KAPIL KOMIREDDI, Syria's

126. Crumbling Pluralism, N.Y. TIMES (August 3, 2012), www.nytimes.com/2012/08/04/opinion/syrias-crumbling-pluralism.html?_r=1.
126. Bosnian Genocide, HISTORY.COM, www.history.com/topics/bosnian-genocide (last visited May 10, 2017).
127. The Holocaust, HISTORY.COM, www.history.com/topics/world-war-ii/the-holocaust (last visited May 10, 2017).
128. GREEN, *supra* note 29, at 163; R. VASSENA ET AL., *supra* note 116, at 416.
129. KEVIN R. SMITH ET AL., Human Germline Genetic Modification: Scientific and Bioethical Perspectives, 43 ARCHIVES OF MEDICAL RESEARCH 491, 504–05 (2012).
130. Id. at 505.
131. *See id.*
132. BROCK, *supra* note 29, at 274.

PART II

Psychological Origins and Consequences of Objections to Human Germline Modification

CRISPR/Cas9, base editors, and other molecular editing tools have raised the prospect that human gametes and embryos can be modified to suit parental desires, resulting in the birth of modified babies. Theoretically, human germline modification (HGM) can be used for therapy or enhancement. Critics have raised four key objections. They claim HGM transgresses divine and natural boundaries; transforms human reproduction into manufacture; stratifies society; and leads to apocalyptic outcomes such as the collapse of democracy, eugenics, ossification of society, and genocide.

Part I of this book analyzed the therapy/enhancement distinction and the four objections. It concluded that the therapy/enhancement distinction was spurious and that the four objections were either overstated or based on flawed biological and political premises. But key questions remain. For example, why do some people accept a therapy/enhancement distinction that is too fuzzy to be useful? And why do others embrace objections that are erroneous at best and irrational at worst?

This part investigates the psychological origins and consequences of opposition to HGM. It includes two chapters. Chapter 6 describes a heuristic known as "psychological essentialism." After explaining how the heuristic accounts for the therapy/enhancement distinction, it discusses the role of essentialism in inspiring the four objections and related concerns. Because many stereotypes about children of HGM are associated with those objections and concerns, Chapter 6 concludes that essentialism is also responsible for those stereotypes.

Chapter 7 sets forth research on envy. It describes the emotion and details ways in which the human mind seeks to conceal or transmute it. Chapter 7 then applies these lessons to the stratification and apocalypse objections and related concerns and finds that they encourage the unmodified to envy the modified. The envious may vent their resentment by undermining their rivals in subtle ways or through outright physical aggression. Thus, Chapter 7 concludes that these objections and concerns are dangerous.

6

Psychological Essentialism

A *heuristic* is a mechanism that allows the mind to assess problems and situations quickly, but not necessarily accurately.[1] *Psychological essentialism* is one such heuristic. This chapter explains how essentialism has influenced and distorted the HGM debate.

Section A lays a foundation by describing how psychological essentialism is used to evaluate *natural kinds*, such as animals, plants, minerals,[2] and even human beings.[3] It then goes on to examine the therapy/enhancement distinction. Although the distinction is not logical, it is consistent with essentialism. The objection that HGM exceeds human authority and competence is likewise consistent with essentialism.

Section B turns from natural kinds to artifacts. It discusses the role of essentialism in developing intuitive judgments about artifacts. The heuristic illuminates the objection that HGM transforms reproduction into manufacture. It also sheds light on related concerns about children who lack open futures and suffer undue parental pressure.

Section C draws upon the foregoing accounts of natural kinds and artifacts to analyze the psychological roots of two other objections. One claims that HGM leads to class divides and social inequalities and the other predicts apocalyptic outcomes. Section C demonstrates that these objections are generally consistent with essentialist intuitions. It subjects related concerns about competitive pressure, unequal access, and consent of future generations to a similar analysis.

Finally, Section D reexamines negative stereotypes about children of HGM. It argues that stereotypes associated with the four objections and related concerns are the product of psychological essentialism. Section D completes the analysis by identifying additional stereotypes that may arise directly from the heuristic itself.

A NATURAL KINDS

In 1989, Douglas Medin and Andrew Ortony theorized that psychological essentialism could explain how people perceive concepts.[4] According to their theory, people treat a concept as if it contains an essence. This essence is deep rooted and causal, generating superficial traits that we can use to identify things associated with the concept.[5]

To be sure, this essence is not real.[6] It is only a placeholder that the human mind can complete with various theories or beliefs about what causes a thing to have a certain identity.[7] The idea of essence is useful, not because it is scientifically accurate, but because it enables us to identify things by noting surface traits that are linked to core properties.[8] Further, our sensitivity to surface traits that map to core properties may be especially keen when it comes to *natural kinds*.[9]

Other scholars have conducted research with children and adults and verified that people do indeed use psychological essentialism to conceptualize and evaluate natural kinds.[10] In applying the lessons of this research, this chapter will concentrate on a subset of natural kinds known as *living kinds*, such as animals, plants, and human beings.[11]

To see how the heuristic applies to living kinds, consider the following scenario. Suppose you enter a pet store. A green creature flies toward you and lands on your shoulder. The creature has feathers and two scaly clawed feet. Based on these observable traits – flight, feathers, and scaly clawed feet – you conclude that the creature is a bird. This conclusion rests on an unconscious intuition that birds carry a deep-rooted essence that makes them what they are. Moreover, this essence is causal; it generates the traits you observe, such as flight and feathers, and enables you to classify the creature as a bird.

Once you have identified the green creature as a member of the bird kind, you can draw inferences about other, less obvious traits that it must have.[12] For example, suppose you wish to feed the creature. Even though you have no information about what it eats, you may choose seeds, fruit, or insects because members of the bird kind eat those substances.

Psychological essentialism has other interesting features. For example, living kinds have strict boundaries[13] but can include atypical members.[14] For example, suppose the creature you encounter in the pet store has feathers and scaly clawed feet but cannot fly because its wings have been clipped. It is not a typical bird if it cannot fly. However, as long as it carries essence of bird, it still belongs to the bird kind and you still can draw inferences about non-visible traits such as food preference.

Researchers have also found that adults and children are not easily fooled by external appearances. They have a natural tendency to make identifications based on internal qualities.[15] In one experiment, young children decided that a dog is a dog if its fur is removed, and a turtle is a turtle if its shell is removed, but that both lose their identity if insides are removed.[16]

1 The Relationship of Essence to DNA

Having come this far, the reader may assume that deoxyribonucleic acid (DNA) is the true biological equivalent of the deep-rooted essence that causes the traits of a species.[17] However, such an assumption is false for the following reasons.

In psychological essentialism, kind essence does not change.[18] Moreover, this essence is fully present in every individual member of a kind.[19] Thus, the creature in the hypothetical scenario is a bird by virtue of its essence, which all birds share, and it will remain a bird. By contrast, a species classification evolves over time and depends on the traits (and underlying DNA) of an entire population.[20] Thus, the bird in question may possess some of the DNA associated with its particular species, but certainly not all of it. If the classification of its species changed, its membership therein could also change.

However, even though DNA is not a true essence, its characteristics make it an appealing essence placeholder for living kinds. DNA can be perceived as *internal*: it exists not only inside the body but inside each individual cell within the body.[21] DNA is *causal*: organized as genes, it plays an important role in determining traits.[22] DNA *does not change* significantly over time (although the DNA inside an individual cell can acquire a mutation).[23] For example, one does not graduate high school as a human being and discover 20 years later that one has gradually changed into a house cat.

DNA is an appealing placeholder for yet another reason. Anyone who has taken an elementary biology course understands that parents pass chromosomes bearing DNA to their offspring via sperm and egg.[24] This scientific reality aligns with a core principle of essentialism in which parents are believed to transmit kind essence to offspring at birth.[25]

2 The Therapy/Enhancement Distinction

This chapter now turns to the therapy/enhancement distinction discussed in Chapter 1. In bioethics, "therapy" describes an intervention that treats disease, disability, or impairment with the goal of restoring normal health and fitness.[26] By contrast, "enhancement" means an intervention that alters the normal function of the human body and mind.[27]

Thus defined, therapy and enhancement appear to be distinct concepts. Yet, as Chapter 1, Section D, indicated, the two can blur into each other. For example, a genetic modification performed to confer immunity to the HIV-1 virus seeks to secure normal health and fitness yet qualifies as an enhancement. Moreover, normality, which is central to both concepts, is hard to pinpoint, since most traits fall along a spectrum. Also, the normal range can shift with time and innovation, so that enhancing interventions become therapeutic ones.

If the therapy/enhancement distinction persists despite these problems, it may have a psychological basis. *Status quo bias*, that is, the human tendency to resist change, even when change is merited,[28] is one possible explanation. Perhaps therapies that secure normal health are perceived as less transformative – and thus less threatening – than enhancements that improve upon normal function.

However, there is another possible reason for the human tendency to dwell on normality. According to the dictionary, the adjective "normal" describes items that conform to a model or standard of some kind.[29] When used to describe type, accomplishment, appearance, or operation, the adjective is associated with averages or medians rather than extremes.[30] Psychological essentialism posits that the essence of a living kind causes the traits that kind members have. Most kind members will *conform to a standard* or represent an *average or median* within a kind. Creatures that diverge from the standard, or count as outliers, require additional evaluation and may not belong to the kind.

Conditioned to such intuitions, the mind may be drawn to the therapy/enhancement distinction, with its seemingly bright line between restoring and altering normal function. Viewed in an essentialist light, a doctor who applies a therapy to restore a patient's body to normal function may seem to have restored its underlying essence to its proper form. By contrast, a scientist who conducts an experiment that allows a subject's body to exceed normal function may seem to have altered its underlying essence.

Let us apply this theory to HGM for reproduction. Suppose John and Mary Smith ask a doctor to correct a genetic mutation in Mary's eggs that causes Huntington disease. They undergo IVF with the modified eggs and a baby girl named Ariel is born. Ariel conforms to the human standard of health and fitness, with average physical function. The essentialist cannot doubt that Ariel belongs to the human kind, despite the intervention. Therefore, some people will accept this therapeutic use of HGM.

Now, suppose John and Mary ask the doctor to add single nucleotide polymorphisms (SNPs) associated with improved memory and learning to their sperm and eggs. They perform IVF with the modified gametes and a baby girl named Cora is born. If Cora's memory and learning are significantly above average, some may perceive her as abnormal. Essentialism tolerates atypical kind members, so Cora can still belong to the human kind. However, the more she excels, the more likely observers are to question her membership in the human kind. Therefore, many people reject this and other enhancing uses of HGM.

Skeptics may argue that this theory proves too much. Geniuses are rare but society recognizes them as kind members. For example, no one questions that Leonardo da Vinci and Albert Einstein were human. Moreover, human beings undergo non-genetic forms of enhancement every day without being rejected as kind members. Think, for example, of the high school or college student who abuses stimulant drugs to earn higher test scores,[31] or the starlet who undergoes plastic surgery to achieve a more appealing face or figure.

However, a child of HGM may face greater doubts for two reasons. First, as explained earlier, DNA has qualities that make it plausible in the role of essence placeholder. For those who intuitively ascribe the role of essence to DNA, any intervention that alters DNA will rouse suspicion. If the intervention does no more than correct a genetic mutation in human gametes or embryos, it may be tolerated on the ground that it restores essence to its proper form. However, an intervention that goes further and alters standard genes may be viewed as an illicit tampering with that which makes humans human.

Second, in essentialism, reproduction is a means of transmitting kind essence from parent to offspring. The born genius, the college student, and the starlet all obtained human essence from their parents. Drugs ingested or surgery undergone years afterward cannot change their status, even though the purpose may have been enhancement rather than therapy. HGM differs because it takes place in the sensitive context of human reproduction. When this reproductive context is coupled with the plausibility of DNA as an essence placeholder, the heuristic may yield the intuition that the human essence of the resulting child has been altered or even destroyed.

Skeptics may also protest that the vast majority of people simply do not think in such terms. However, conscious thought is not required for the heuristic to function. Most people probably do not realize that they use essentialism to make sense of living kinds, but researchers have proven that they do. Moreover, the vehement opposition to HGM for enhancement supports the conclusion that essentialist instincts are at work. One would expect resistance to a technology that appears to threaten that which we intuitively believe to be the core of our kind.

3 Hubris Objection

Chapter 2 presented several concerns that refer to the authority and competence of human beings to modify the genome. First, as acknowledged in Section A, HGM for reproduction may violate religious tradition. However, because religions generally tolerate therapies, this concern is best understood as an objection to enhancing uses. As the prior section explained, those who accept therapy but not enhancement act consistently with essentialist intuition. Thus, to the extent the hubris objection equates to a warning not to enhance, it may be the product of such intuition.

Second, as discussed in Chapter 2, Section B, some claim that HGM for reproduction offends nature. For example, they argue that the human genome has evolved to be in harmony with the environment. This argument is weak because the human genome is not necessarily in harmony with the needs of modern society. However, the notion of an idealized human genome existing within a complementary environment may be appealing on a psychological level. Like the DNA of which it is composed, the human genome is internal, causal, and relatively constant, traits that make it a plausible candidate for the role of essence placeholder. If the human genome represents human essence, modifications must be opposed because they threaten to disrupt the place of the human kind within an established psychological order in which every creature and natural substance belong to a natural kind.

Lastly, as noted in Chapter 2, Section C, using technology to produce modified babies may seem like the height of human arrogance. This concern makes some sense on a practical level: HGM is in its infancy and safety concerns about its reproductive use are valid. However, when expressed in terms of playing God, the warning against hubris carries an undertone of essentialism. To explain, if fallible scientists and parents insist upon modifying human gametes or embryos, their hubris predicts disastrous results. The more extensive the modifications are, the greater the hubris and greater the potential for disaster. Yet, as explained in the preceding section, it is precisely these more extensive modifications that are most likely to be perceived as an alteration (rather than correction) of essence.

B ARTIFACTS

In its classical form, psychological essentialism is a heuristic used to make sense of natural kinds, including living kinds. Inanimate objects that human beings make, such as cars, computers, and chairs, do not occur in nature and thus do not belong to natural kinds. However, some experts believe that essentialism is also employed to evaluate such artifacts, with the intention of the person who created the artifact functioning as its essence.[32] Others theorize that humans approach artifacts from a design stance. Per this theory, a designer has a plan or intended function for an artifact that determines its surface traits, uses, and type.[33]

A hypothetical will be used to demonstrate. Suppose a company manufactures a six-inch-long plastic stem with soft bristles at one end. This human-made object is an artifact. The company expects its customers to use the artifact to brush their teeth. However, an artist purchases one of these artifacts and uses it to sprinkle paint onto a canvas. If psychological essentialism applies, the company's intention is the essence of the artifact, and this essence drives what it is: a toothbrush. Similarly, according to the design stance theory, the company intended the artifact to function as a toothbrush. That function determines its surface traits (bristles that can scrub), uses (to brush teeth), and type (toothbrush). That the artist uses the artifact for painting does not change its intrinsic character.[34]

Still other experts question whether essentialism applies within the artifact domain.[35] A creator's intention can help an observer categorize an artifact, but artifact kinds lack the rich inductive potential of living kinds.[36] Returning to the earlier example, classification of the object as a toothbrush may illuminate its use but reveals little about deeper, nonobvious properties (perhaps because it does not have many).[37] Moreover, unlike the internal essence of the living kind, the creator's intention is external to the artifact and is not transmitted by reproduction.[38] In other words, one toothbrush will never get together with another and generate offspring that must be toothbrushes.

Even if psychological essentialism is a less powerful heuristic when applied to artifacts, it is worth considering the extent to which it may distort the debate over

HGM. Artifacts are the product of manufacture, and a key objection is that HGM transforms reproduction into manufacture.

1 Manufacture Objection

Therapeutic modifications may involve the correction of a single mutated gene. Enhancing modifications may be more extensive but will still leave most of a child's genome untouched. Moreover, as discussed in Chapter 1, Section C, genes work together with environment to make a person who she is. Thus, the claim that HGM transforms reproduction into manufacture is hyperbole at best.

Nevertheless, the claim is interesting because it appears to be another expression of essentialism. To see why, let us revisit the hypothetical scenario from Chapter 4, Section B.3. John and Mary Smith would like to have a child who grows up to be a wealthy doctor or lawyer. They hire a doctor to add SNPs associated with improved memory and learning to their sperm and eggs. They undergo IVF using the modified gametes. This process is very expensive. However, it works; nine months later, Cora is born.

John and Mary are human beings and Mary gives birth to Cora. Thus, as discussed in Section A.1 of this chapter, the heuristic should give rise to the intuition that John and Mary have reproduced and transmitted human essence to their daughter. However, this process involves design, a laboratory, technology, and money, four elements that are more commonly associated with the production of artifacts such as drugs or devices. Moreover, it confers upon Cora a superior ability that renders her atypical. The more atypical she is, the greater the doubts about her membership in the human kind, and the easier it is for the mind to shift her into the artifact domain. This shift may account for the objection that HGM transforms reproduction into manufacture.

It must be emphasized that labeling reproduction as manufacture does not make it so. Nor is Cora actually an artifact. However, those who instinctively perceive her as one may draw other inappropriate inferences. Researchers have discovered a mode of dehumanization that denies to others traits associated with human nature. In this mode, the dehumanized others are construed as cold rather than warm, inflexible rather than open minded, inert rather than responsive, fungible rather than individual, and superficial rather than deep.[39] It has been suggested that a shift from the social to the technical domain could trigger this mode of dehumanization.[40]

2 Related Concerns

Chapter 3 cited two concerns related to the manufacture objection: lack of an open future and pressure to conform to parental expectations. Continuing with the hypothetical scenario, consider first whether Cora, who has SNPs associated with improved memory and learning, lacks an open future. As Chapter 3, Section C.3, pointed out, this concern is overblown, given the many ways in which such a trait can be used. Cora need not become a wealthy doctor or lawyer. She is free to pursue a life path other than the one her parents chose for her.

However, on an intuitive level, the concern may appear valid. HGM appears to be a form of manufacture, with John and Mary Smith playing the role of creators and Cora as the artifact. The intention of the creators determines not only Cora's traits (improved memory and learning) but also her uses (to achieve educational, professional, and financial success) and type (doctor or lawyer). In this manner, essentialism pigeonholes Cora and credits John and Mary Smith with much more power and control than they actually have.

Now, consider whether Cora may feel pressure to conform to parental expectations. As Chapter 3, Section C.3, noted, parents already use private schools, tutors, and the like to help their children get ahead, so the problem of parental ambition is not new. Critics may fear that the Smiths will treat Cora like an artifact.[41] Yet, because the Smiths must raise Cora and live in close proximity to her, they will be the first ones to realize that she is human and unpredictable. Perhaps those who worry about undue expectations project their own essentialist intuitions about children of HGM onto parents.

C STRATIFICATION AND APOCALYPSE OBJECTIONS

Having established a foundation in the essentialism of natural kinds and artifacts, this chapter now turns to the remaining two objections. Both the stratification objection and apocalypse objection rest on flawed biological premises. This section explores the psychological origins of those premises.

1 Genes, Traits, and Life Outcomes

The stratification objection supposes HGM can create children with superior traits who are destined for success. Biologically, the objection is hard to defend. As discussed in Chapter 1, Section C, genes are not the sole determinants of traits; environmental factors also play a role. Moreover, as Chapter 4, Section B.3, noted, random events affect how a child expresses and employs the traits she has. It is not possible to plug in genes and generate life outcomes such as high grades, professional careers, wealth, or 150 candles on a birthday cake. Parents who understand these facts will not be drawn to HGM.

However, psychology tells a different story. As noted in Section B of this chapter stated, the intention of a creator determines the traits, uses, and type of an artifact. HGM involves design (in the choice of genes), a laboratory, technology, and money. These factors may encourage a perception that scientists and parents who utilize HGM are creators manufacturing an artifact. From there, it is a small step to the intuition that the scientists and parents have determined the child's traits, uses, and type.

For example, as Section B.1 of this chapter recounted, Cora is not an artifact, but tinkering with her genome makes her appear like one. Moreover, as creators, John and Mary Smith seem to have the power to determine her traits (improved memory and learning), uses (to achieve educational, professional, and financial success), and type (doctor or lawyer). If HGM truly could manufacture wealthy doctors and lawyers, predictions of class divides and social inequalities would be more credible. But if its powers are an essentialist mirage, then the stratification objection fails.

Turning next to the apocalypse objection, one finds dire predictions of democratic collapse, eugenics, societal ossification, and genocide. As Chapter 5 explained, these predictions also rest on questionable biological premises. Traits are the product of more than genes, and life outcomes are the product of more than traits.

However, apocalyptic claims seem plausible when children of HGM are viewed through an essentialist lens and consequently perceived as artifacts. For example, if the rich really could design scions with superior minds, bodies, and achievements, a powerful oligarchy could emerge. Speciation would still be unlikely, but violent conflict between the oligarchy and its subjects could occur. If the middle class could handicraft children destined to live for 150 years, a wave of supercentenarians might present new social challenges. And if government really could design supermen and superwomen, it might find it cost effective to subsidize HGM through a voluntary eugenics program.

2 Transmission of Genes

The stratification objection assumes that children of HGM will transmit their genes to descendants, creating class divides and social inequalities. Similarly, the apocalypse objection assumes that gene transmission will produce hereditary castes or even new species, leading to class warfare, democratic collapse, and genocide. However, HGM will be expensive and entail some physical risk to offspring. Parents are unlikely to accept this cost and risk in exchange for modest or uncertain benefits.[42] If few modified children are born, it follows that few modified partners will be available to them at sexual maturity. As Chapter 4, Section B.3, and Chapter 5, Section D.1, argued, procreation with unmodified partners will be more common, resulting in the dilution of genes.

To be sure, artificial chromosomes would change the analysis. A man with 48 chromosomes probably could not procreate with an unmodified woman with 46 chromosomes. He would have to find a partner who also had 48 chromosomes. If enough such pairings occurred, speciation might follow. However, as Chapters 4 and 5 also stated, artificial chromosomes pose additional health risks to children and are likely to be unpopular.[43]

Nevertheless, the stratification and apocalypse objections may persist due to psychological factors that support them. As discussed in Section A.2 of this chapter, the mind may construe genetic modification as an illicit tampering with essence, resulting in the birth of children with an inhuman essence. Moreover, as mentioned in Section A.1 of this chapter parents are believed to transmit kind essence to offspring at birth. Therefore, children born with an inhuman essence would transmit it to their own descendants, perpetuating a new and different kind. Such intuitions are not consistent with genetics, but they do align nicely with the objections, with their dire prophecies of class divides, hereditary castes, and new species.

Professors Annas, Andrews, and Isasi provide an interesting illustration. When they called for an international treaty prohibiting cloning and HGM, they did not discuss biological concepts of species. Instead, they chose to warn against technologies that could change humanity's essence and create a new species.[44] Such reasoning is consistent with essentialist intuitions, although the authors did not reference psychological essentialism specifically.

3 Related Concerns

Concerns related to the stratification objection are subject to a similar analysis. As Chapter 4, Sections B.3 and B.4 pointed out, worries about the competitive pressure that parents feel or unequal access to enhancements presuppose that genes can deliver traits and life outcomes. However, genes are not that powerful. Rather, the concerns are more consistent with essentialist beliefs about artifacts. If parents really could handcraft children with specific traits, uses, and types, pressure to use HGM to keep up with the Joneses would exist and unequal access to HGM would be more troubling.

Similarly, as Chapter 4, Section E, disclosed, the concern that future generations cannot consent is best interpreted as an argument that HGM leads to a worse future. The apocalypse objection includes four specific claims about bad futures and thus can be used to flesh out the argument. But if visions of hereditary castes, eugenics, ossification, and genocide are rooted in essentialism, so must the concern be.

D STEREOTYPES AND ESSENTIALISM

As Part I of this book documented, the four objections and related concerns are associated with derogatory stereotypes about children of HGM. This chapter completes the analysis by exploring the link between these stereotypes and essentialism.

1 Hubris Objection

As discussed in Chapter 2, the hubris objection encompasses three concerns, each of which is associated with stereotypes about children of HGM. Section D.1 of that chapter stated that religious doctrine casts therapeutic uses of HGM as good and enhancing uses as evil. Adults who enhance are the sinners, but an enhanced child risks being tainted with evil by association. Further, if humankind was made in the image of God, an enhanced child appears to be the product of a sacrilegious attempt to transcend that image. Her existence may inspire awe, fear, revulsion, and rejection.

Reverence for nature has inspired a related set of claims. As Chapter 2, Section D.2, reported, HGM allegedly offends nature, despoils the human genome, places humans at odds with their environment, and undermines genetic diversity. Labeling HGM as unnatural raises an unfortunate inference that a child born through it is also unnatural. Moreover, a child whose genome does not conform to an idealized human genome, and whose body is perceived as environmentally disharmonious, may appear to be a threat to the natural order. Even if her parents do no more than delete a harmful genetic mutation, arguments that such mutations contribute to genetic diversity frame her as the product of a selfish process that impaired diversity.

Lastly, as Chapter 2, Section D.3, noted, HGM may seem like a dangerous expression of human arrogance. If HGM is hubris, and hubris leads to bad outcomes, it follows that HGM leads to bad outcomes, namely, a child who is flawed. Further, the Frankenstein myth, which warns against meddling with the stuff of human life, implies that the child is defective or monstrous.

As Section A.3 of this chapter demonstrated, the hubris objection is consistent with, and likely the product of, the essentialism of natural kinds. Therefore, stereotypes associated with the hubris objection are also consistent with, and likely the product of, such essentialism.

2 Manufacture Objection

The second objection is that HGM transforms reproduction into manufacture. As explained in Chapter 3, Section D, the unfortunate – and perhaps unintended – implication is that a child of HGM is a manufactured object. Relatedly, when critics worry that a child of HGM lacks an open future, they suggest that she is a pitiful puppet who has been programmed to act in a certain manner. When critics claim that a child of HGM will suffer from unreasonable parental expectations, the implication is that the child is anxious and stressed. However, as Section B.1 of this chapter explained, the manufacture objection is consistent with, and likely the product of, essentialist perceptions of artifacts. Therefore, stereotypes that flow from the objection are also consistent with, and probably derive from, such essentialism.

3 Stratification Objection

The next objection is that HGM leads to class divides and social inequalities. As explained in Chapter 4, Section C, this stratification objection assumes that a child of HGM is superior to others. Her ability to transmit relative advantage to future generations also makes her divisive. However, as Sections C.1 and C.2 of this chapter indicated, these stereotypes rest on biological premises with roots in the essentialism of both natural kinds and artifacts, as noted in Section C. Once the objection arises, it encourages people to view a child of HGM as unjust, a further stereotype that can be blamed on essentialism.

Two concerns are related to the stratification objection, and both have stereotypes associated with them. As Chapter 4, Section C, revealed, the claim that parents will feel compelled to modify their offspring to keep up with the Joneses assumes that a child of HGM is superior and further depicts her as a competitive threat and coercive. A concern about unequal access implies that such a child is unjust. Section C.3 of this chapter demonstrated that these concerns, and their related stereotypes, are consistent with an essentialist view of the enhanced child as an artifact with superior traits, uses, and types.[45]

4 Apocalypse Objection

Lastly, as Chapter 5 stated, the apocalypse objection incorporates four claims of extreme outcomes: collapse of democracy, eugenics, ossification of society, and genocide. Section F.1 of that chapter pointed out that two of these claims – collapse of democracy and genocide – rest on stereotypes. Not only is a child of HGM assumed to be superior to others, he is also believed to be capable of founding hereditary castes or new species. In short, he is divisive. If these stereotypes are rooted in essentialism, as the prior section argues, it follows that the claims are too. Moreover, these essentialist claims further mark the child as unjust, anti-democratic, and genocidal.

A third claim is that HGM leads to eugenics. As noted in Chapter 5, Section F.2, this claim associates the child of HGM with coercion and marks him as fungible, artifact-like, and superficial. Section C.1 of this chapter argued that the essentialist intuitions about creators and artifacts make it seem plausible that governments can manufacture citizens with specific traits, uses, and types. If the claim derives from such intuitions, so do stereotypes associated with it.

A fourth claim is that HGM leads to ossification of society. As Chapter 5, Section F.3, revealed, this charge assumes that a child of HGM will be controlling, selfish, and parasitic in extreme old age. Long life (as opposed to maximum lifespan) cannot be purchased, so the claim is not credible. However, the essentialist intuition that the child is akin to an artifact may make it seem as if long life can be purchased. If essentialism inspires the claim, it accounts for the stereotypes associated with it.

Chapter 5, Section F.4, discussed one concern related to the apocalypse objection, namely, that future generations cannot consent to HGM. The concern marks children of HGM as the unwelcome product of anti-democratic decisions and implies they would not exist in a just world. But as Section C.3 of this chapter stated, the concern is best understood as an argument that HGM leads to a worse future. Thus, when essentialism inspires apocalyptic claims about the future, it also promotes this concern and the stereotypes that flow from it.

5 Additional Stereotypes

Even if critics had never raised the four objections, psychological essentialism might promote stereotypes about children of HGM on its own, particularly when genetic modifications are enhancing or extensive. Consider first the essentialism of natural kinds. For those who intuitively assign the role of human essence to DNA or the genome, HGM may seem to move children from the human kind into an inhuman category. If such instincts prevail, market demand for HGM will sag. Parents will not utilize a reproductive technology if they sense that it calls the humanity of their offspring into doubt. Artificial chromosomes are particularly likely to provoke revulsion. If a child cannot procreate with ordinary human beings because she has too many chromosomes, her ability to transmit human essence to the next generation is impaired.

Consider next the essentialism of artifacts. In HGM for reproduction, an expensive technological process conducted in a laboratory results in a child with modified traits. Under these circumstances, observers may intuitively perceive parents as creators and the child as an artifact. Unfortunately, as Section B.1 of this chapter explained, human beings who are construed as artifacts are dehumanized as cold, inflexible, inert, fungible, and superficial. Intuitions of this sort may cause parents to shy away from HGM, further suppressing market demand.

E SUMMARY

Psychological essentialism is a heuristic that facilitates intuitive judgments about things in the world. The concept of essence is the engine that drives its operation. Internal and unchanging, essence links members of a kind and causes the visible and invisible traits that they have. Though strongly associated with natural kinds, the heuristic is believed to play a role in conceptualization of artifacts also.

Psychological essentialism operates at a subconscious, intuitive level. The analysis in this chapter indicates the therapy/enhancement distinction is consistent with essentialism, as are the four objections and related concerns. This consistency suggests that the objections and concerns, and stereotypes associated with them, are the product of essentialism. Further, the heuristic itself may encourage beliefs that the children lack human essence or are akin to artifacts.

Stereotypes can harm children of HGM. However, the worst damage will occur only if lawmakers choose to ban HGM on the strength of the four objections. That prospect is considered in more detail in Chapter 10.

Notes

1. ROBERT J. MORRIS, Not Thinking Like a Nonlawyer: Implications of "Recogonization" for Legal Education, 53 J. LEGAL EDUCATION 267, 273 (2003).
2. KERRY LYNN MACINTOSH, HUMAN CLONING: FOUR FALLACIES AND THEIR LEGAL CONSEQUENCES 70 (2013).
3. MYRON ROTHBART & MARJORIE TAYLOR, Category Labels and Social Reality: Do We View Social Categories as Natural Kinds? in LANGUAGE, INTERACTION AND SOCIAL COGNITION 10, 21 (GUN R. SEMIN & KLAUS FIEDLER EDS., 1992).
4. DOUGLAS MEDIN & ANDREW ORTONY, Psychological Essentialism, in SIMILARITY AND ANALOGICAL REASONING 179 (STELLA VOSNIADOU & ANDREW ORTONY EDS., 1989).
5. Id. at 184–86.
6. This recognition that essence is not real distinguishes psychological essentialism from *philosophical* essentialism. Philosophical essentialism is an outdated and abandoned philosophical theory about the true nature of things. It fails because a thing does not in fact possess an essence that makes it what it is. Rather, descriptions of a thing drive what the essence appears to be. *Id.* at 183.
7. Id. at 184.
8. Id. at 185.
9. Id. at 186.
10. *See generally* SUSAN A. GELMAN, THE ESSENTIALIST CHILD: ORIGINS OF ESSENTIALISM IN EVERYDAY THOUGHT (2003) (digesting and relaying data from multiple researchers and articles).
11. This definition excludes inert substances such as water and gold. MACINTOSH, *supra* note 2, at 70.
12. See GELMAN, *supra* note 10, at 27–33 (discussing experiments in which adults and children draw inferences about natural kinds).
13. Id. at 73.
14. Id. at 69.
15. See id. at 75–83 (describing various studies and experiments).
16. Id. at 79–80.
17. Id. at 299.
18. ROTHBART & TAYLOR, *supra* note 3, at 17, 20–21; *but see* GELMAN, *supra* note 10, at 300 (citing view that essentialism does not require categories to be inalterable).
19. GELMAN, *supra* note 10, at 300.

20. *Id.*
21. GENETICS HOME REFERENCE, What Is DNA? U.S. NATIONAL LIBRARY OF MEDICINE (January 10, 2017), https://ghr.nlm.nih.gov/primer/basics/dna.
22. GENETICS HOME REFERENCE, What Is a Gene? U.S. NATIONAL LIBRARY OF MEDICINE (January, 10, 2017), https://ghr.nlm.nih.gov/primer/basics/gene.
23. GENETICS HOME REFERENCE, What Is a Gene Mutation and How Do Gene Mutations Occur, U.S. NATIONAL LIBRARY OF MEDICINE (January 10, 2017), http://ghr.nlm.nih.gov/handbook/mutationsanddisorders/genemutation.
24. A. Jamie Cuticchia, GENETICS: A HANDBOOK FOR LAWYERS 3–4 (2009).
25. GELMAN, *supra* note 10, at 89–95.
26. PRESIDENT'S COUNCIL ON BIOETHICS, BEYOND THERAPY: BIOTECHNOLOGY AND THE PURSUIT OF HAPPINESS 13 (2003) [hereinafter BEYOND THERAPY].
27. *Id.*
28. RONALD M. GREEN, BABIES BY DESIGN: THE ETHICS OF GENETIC CHOICE 8–9, 176 (2007).
29. WEBSTER'S NEW WORLD DICTIONARY OF THE AMERICAN LANGUAGE 1001 (College ed. 1968).
30. *Id.*
31. *See* BEYOND THERAPY, *supra* note 26, at 85 (addressing illicit use of Ritalin and other drugs).
32. *E.g.*, PAUL BLOOM, DESCARTES' BABY: HOW THE SCIENCE OF CHILD DEVELOPMENT EXPLAINS WHAT MAKES US HUMAN 55 (paperback ed. 2005).
33. *Id.*
34. *Cf.* ADEE MATAN & SUSAN CAREY, Developmental Changes within the Core of Artifacts Concepts, 78 COGNITION 1 (2001) (discussing experiments in which adult and child research subjects generally favored intended use over current use in assessing the identity of artifacts).
35. *E.g.*, ROTHBART & TAYLOR, *supra* note 3, at 12–14, 16–18.
36. GELMAN, *supra* note 10, at 49–53, 138–39.
37. *Cf. id.* at 139 (explaining that intention to create pencil does not enable drawing of inferences about pencils in general).
38. *Id.* at 139, 315.
39. Nick Haslam, Dehumanization: An Integrative Review, 10 PERSONALITY AND SOCIAL PSYCHOLOGY REVIEW 252, 256–58 (2006).
40. *Id.* at 261.
41. SUSANNAH BARUCH ET AL., HUMAN GERMLINE GENETIC MODIFICATION: ISSUES AND OPTIONS FOR POLICYMAKERS 36 (2005) (reporting claim that parents will view children of HGM as commodities and love them less if they are imperfect).
42. Critics might counter that essentialist parents will *believe* that they can decide the traits, uses, and types of their children, leading to a stronger market

demand than this book predicts. Even if that is true, once modified children are born, parents will learn through experience that biology is not destiny, suppressing market demand again.
43. *Id.*
44. GEORGE J. ANNAS ET AL., Protecting the Endangered Human: Toward an International Treaty Prohibiting Cloning and Inheritable Alterations, 28 AMERICAN J.L. & MED. 151, 153 (2002).
45. Once CRISPR/Cas9 or other molecular editing tools are perfected, and correction of genetic mutations leads to the birth of healthy children, that outcome will be a scientific fact, and not an essentialist mirage. Thus, concerns about equal access to life and health-sparing applications of HGM are legitimate, and efforts to extend access should be made, as discussed in Chapter 4, Section B.1.b.

7

Envy

The stratification and apocalypse objections posit that human germline modification (HGM) will lead to class divides and social inequalities and/or catastrophic outcomes, such as the collapse of democracy, eugenics, ossification of society, and genocide. As documented in Chapters 4 and 5, these objections and related concerns rest on dubious biological and political premises. Yet they persist, suggesting a psychological source. Chapter 6 explained that they are consistent with essentialist intuitions about natural kinds and artifacts.

This chapter takes the analysis to the next level by investigating the consequences of these two objections and related concerns. It argues that the objections and concerns promote the emotion of envy, thereby encouraging prejudice and aggression against children of HGM. Section A presents the basic elements of envy and discusses the emotion's relation to stereotypes of warmth and competence. Sections B and C describe how the stratification and apocalypse objections and related concerns promote envy of children of HGM. Finally, Section D explains how the objections and related concerns may incite aggression against children of HGM.

A ENVY

In 2007, psychologists Richard H. Smith and Sung Hee Kim surveyed the empirical literature on envy and reached the following conclusions. Envy is an emotion that contains inferiority, hostility, and resentment at its dark core.[1] It originates when a person compares himself with someone else who has something he wants. Envy is more likely to arise when a person cares about the domain of comparison and the rival is otherwise similar to him.[2] Belief that the desired goal cannot be attained may also be a factor. When similarity induces an expectation of success, yet success is out of reach, a painful sense of frustrated possibility results.[3]

Faced with an unflattering comparison, a person who feels inferior may express depressive affect. But if arbitrary and unalterable factors are to blame for his disadvantage, he may experience a subjective sense of injustice that makes him resentful and hostile toward the advantaged one, even though an objective observer would conclude no injustice exists.[4]

Envious resentment, which is rooted in this subjective sense of injustice, is distinct from another emotion that Smith and Kim describe as *resentment proper*. A person experiences resentment proper when she is treated unfairly, judged by accepted and objective standards.[5] So, for example, if a person is barred from education or employment due to her race, she does not experience envy, but rather resentment proper and indignation at the injustice of the situation.

To illustrate how envy works, suppose Alan and Brad live in the same neighborhood as children and grow up together as friends. When the two enter high school at age 14, both are short. Brad experiences a growth spurt and measures six feet two inches by senior year. His height attracts girls and earns him a spot on the varsity basketball team.

Alan stops growing at five feet six inches. He does not care that Brad is a basketball star because sports never appealed to him. However, he does care that Brad gets more female attention. Privately, Alan feels that Brad's height advantage is arbitrary and unjust. He cannot force his own body to grow, so he feels powerless to change the situation. He grows angry and begins to express hostility toward Brad.

Charles, who is five feet ten inches tall, attends high school with Alan and Brad and is good friends with both. Charles does not understand why Alan has suddenly become hostile to Brad. From his objective point of view, Brad has done nothing to merit antagonism.

1 Envy Distinguished from Jealousy

Suppose that Charles ponders the situation and concludes that Alan is jealous of Brad. His description may reflect a semantic problem, as the word "jealousy" can be used to describe envy.[6] However, he may also have confused envy and jealousy, which are distinct emotions.[7]

Jealousy usually occurs when two people compete for the affections of a third person. It is typically more intense than envy and incorporates elements such as fear of loss, suspicion, and rage at the prospect of betrayal.[8] To illustrate, suppose Alan begins to date a pretty girl named Diana. Brad flirts with Diana. Alan experiences an intense mix of suspicion, anger, and fear that Brad will take Diana away from him.[9] In this case, Charles, the outside observer, would be correct to conclude that Alan is jealous of Brad.

2 Envy and Secrecy

Psychological research indicates that people do not like to admit envy to themselves or others.[10] There are several possible reasons to keep quiet. For example, in many cultures, envy is a sin.[11] Moreover, there is a general expectation in our society that people embrace rather than resent the successes of others.[12] Lastly, keeping quiet may provide a competitive advantage.

The last point requires elaboration. Human beings constantly compare themselves with others in relevant domains. Inferior performance relative to others points to low skill and failure.[13] Thus, some psychologists believe envy is adaptive: its sting alerts one to the risk of low skill and failure and motivates efforts to correct or manage the situation.[14]

Varying strategies are available. For example, a person may seek to improve his own performance (to the extent that is possible)[15] or find ways to bolster his public image.[16] Alternatively, he may denigrate the character or accomplishments of the advantaged one and/or find ways to undermine or defeat him.[17] However, to succeed, such strategies require secrecy. As evolutionary psychologists have noted, competitiveness in a particular realm of endeavor is not self-evident and must be discerned from social or physical cues.[18] In a competitive world, admitting envy is a strategic error because it signals inferiority and unmasks attempts to disparage a competitor. Also, attempts to defeat a rival are more likely to succeed if he is unaware of the envy and the desire it represents.[19]

To understand, let us return to the original hypothetical. Alan cannot make himself grow taller, but he can improve his sex appeal through other means: wearing nice clothes, developing a good sense of humor, or obtaining a desirable job. Less positively, Alan may seek to undermine Brad through gossip, claiming Brad is arrogant.[20] Or Alan may secretly compete for the women Brad admires. However, if Alan's envy becomes apparent, these strategies are less likely to succeed. Young women will sense his insecurity, his gossip will be revealed as unreliable, and Brad will be alerted to the competition he represents.

3 Transmutation of Envy into Resentment Proper

Envy is mutable, in part due to the personal sting and social shame associated with it. It can be painful to admit inferiority, even to oneself. Moreover, those who are incautious enough to admit envy to others may meet with social disapproval.[21] Thus, although some people may acknowledge their envy (at least to themselves) and work to improve their status,[22] others will suppress their envy, perhaps before it even seeps into their consciousness.[23]

Suppressed emotions do not necessarily vanish, however. Psychologists Smith and Kim propose that the envious can create a story line that transforms the emotion. For example, by projecting moral flaws onto rivals, the envious can legitimize their own hostility and justify using gossip and other covert methods against rivals. Moreover, the envious may look for ways to characterize the rivals' advantage as the product of an unfair process. Once armed with an account that seems to present an objective injustice, the envious may be able to convince themselves that what they feel is not envy, but rather resentment proper. They may recruit others to their cause and feel emboldened to commit overt acts of aggression.[24]

For example, recall that Alan envies Brad for his height. Privately, he nurses a subjective sense of injustice. Publicly, he compensates by attempting to persuade Charles and other classmates that Brad is arrogant and insensitive. Alan receives ambiguous or evasive responses from his peers, but in his enraged state, he misreads them as assent. Fortified by the false belief that Brad's conduct violates social norms, Alan begins to experience resentment proper and righteous indignation. He considers challenging Brad to a to take him down a notch but ultimately decides that ending the friendship is punishment enough.

4 Stereotypes and Envy

Thus far, this section has explored the basics of envy using a simple hypothetical in which one individual (Alan) envies another (Brad). However, envy is not limited in this fashion. People who belong to groups that are stereotyped in certain ways are more likely to be envied.

Some psychological literature elucidates the point. Psychologists Susan Fiske, Amy Cuddy, and Peter Glick have proposed a stereotype content model that evaluates groups according to their perceived warmth (intentions) and competence (ability to act on intentions). Warmth traits include friendliness, trustworthiness, morality, sincerity, and helpfulness; competence traits include intelligence, efficacy, creativity, and skill.[25] In the United States, certain groups are perceived as high in competence but low in warmth: rich people, Jewish people, Asian people, and professionals who are female or minorities. These competent-but-cold groups are more likely than other groups to provoke envy and jealousy.[26] Within this set, the rich rate lowest in perceived warmth.[27]

Competition affects these stereotypes. A group that constitutes a competitive threat is construed as unfriendly and cold. A helpful, cooperative group is perceived as trustworthy and thus warm. Status also plays a role, with higher-status individuals (*e.g.*, those in prestigious jobs) viewed as more competent, whether or not they are.[28]

B THE STRATIFICATION OBJECTION

As discussed in Chapter 4, the stratification objection claims that parents can use HGM to give their children superior traits. These children then transmit their genes to descendants, leading to class divides and social inequalities. In 2017, the National Academy of Sciences and National Academy of Medicine issued a report (NAS Report) that took this objection seriously. The report noted that some had expressed concerns about heritable enhancements that could cause or exacerbate social inequalities that would persist for generations.[29] It suggested these concerns be considered in deciding whether to authorize clinical trials[30] but in the next breath recommended that regulatory agencies *not* authorize trials for nonmedical (*i.e.*, enhancing) purposes.[31]

As Chapter 4 further explained at length, the stratification objection exaggerates the power of genes. Complex traits such as memory or lifespan are difficult to engineer, depend on more than genes, and do not determine life outcomes. Thus, most parents are likely to conclude that HGM is not worth the expense and risk. The few modified children who are born will procreate with unmodified partners, diluting their genes and reducing the risk that class divides and social inequalities will emerge.

But even if the stratification objection is founded on biological misunderstandings, it may have psychological consequences. The objection teaches that HGM can create a superior class of modified children and descendants, rendering everyone else inferior by comparison. Genetic status is arbitrary and unalterable; therefore, this prophecy of permanent genetic inferiority is likely to prompt resentment and hostility toward modified children. By sowing false beliefs, and causing people to experience inferiority, resentment, and hostility, the objection encourages people to envy those children.

Some might protest that the stratification objection predicts an objectively unjust situation, thereby promoting resentment proper rather than envy. However, for that argument to be correct, uneven distribution of genes, traits, and wealth must violate established social norms. Just the opposite is true: established social norms tolerate uneven distribution of genes, traits,[32] and wealth.[33] Therefore, it is more accurate to say that the objection promotes a subjective sense of injustice that is characteristic of envy.

The stereotype content model discussed in Section A.4 of this chapter points to the same conclusion. The stratification objection presents children of HGM as superior and highly competent. It also predicts class divides and social inequalities, implying that these superior children and their descendants are cold-hearted hoarders of prestige and wealth. This competent-but-cold profile is tailor made to stimulate envy. Thus, when the NAS Report embraced the stratification objection, it unwittingly encouraged the public to envy children of HGM.

1 *Competitive Pressure*

Two concerns are related to the stratification objection. The first is that parents will feel pressure to design their children to keep up with others. However, as Chapter 4 explained in Sections B.3 and B.4, this concern is overstated. HGM entails expense and risk. Few parents will purchase enhancing modifications, and those who do will soon realize that genes cannot deliver life outcomes. If the market for HGM is weak, most parents will not feel pressured to design their children.

Yet, the concern itself deserves scrutiny. According to psychologists, people who strive to keep up with the Joneses are manifesting benign envy.[34] Benign envy lacks hostility as a component and can be viewed as a form of admiration.[35] Thus, by suggesting that parents will feel pressure to design their children, the concern predicts benign envy of children born with enhancing modifications.

Unfortunately, if enough respected academic experts or politicians advance the idea that parents will feel pressured to use HGM to keep up with the Joneses, the public may come to believe it. As a result, when the first modified children are born, some parents will wonder if they present a competitive threat to their own children, and experience benign envy, when they otherwise would not have. One can only hope that the limitations of HGM will be widely reported, so that the concern about competitive pressure does not become a self-fulfilling prophecy.

2 Unequal Access

Chapter 4, Sections B.1 and B.2, noted that governments and insurance companies may find it economical to pay for therapeutic modifications rather than fund cures after diseases develop. However, if they do not, carriers of genetic mutations and others who need but cannot afford such modifications will lack access. The United States does not provide universal health care to its citizens, but it helps the elderly, disabled, and poor through programs such as Medicare and Medicaid.[36] In other words, health care for the needy is a social norm. That being the case, parents who need but cannot afford therapeutic modifications may feel the objective sense of injustice characteristic of resentment proper.

Enhancing modifications such as improved memory and learning or extended lifespan require a different analysis. Governments or insurance companies probably will not pay for them, so access will be limited to parents who are wealthy or willing to make a major financial sacrifice. People may resent and feel hostile toward parents who can afford enhancing modifications and their children. But such feelings are nothing new; they are simply another manifestation of envy directed at the rich. Critics who assert concerns about unequal access stoke this envious fire by implying that it really is possible to buy specific traits and life outcomes for children. Instead, they should be explaining that specific traits and life outcomes cannot be purchased for the reasons articulated in Chapter 4, Sections B.3 and B.4.

C THE APOCALYPSE OBJECTION

The apocalypse objection predicts that HGM and children born through it will cause catastrophic outcomes. Chapter 5 critiqued it at length. Here, the analysis focuses on ways in which the objection promotes envy of children of HGM. This section addresses four claims of bad outcomes: collapse of democracy (claim one), eugenics (claim two), ossification of society (claim three), and genocide (claim four). It also discusses a related concern about consent of future generations.

1 Collapse of Democracy and Genocide

Claim one and claim four have certain commonalities that justify analyzing them together. Claim one predicts that HGM produces hereditary castes that accumulate wealth and power, thereby undermining democracy and inducing autocracy or mob rule. Claim four asserts that HGM leads to speciation. Members of a new species enslave and murder human beings, who then exterminate the new species in self-defense. As demonstrated in Chapter 5, Sections A.1 and D.1, these two claims exaggerate the power of genes to determine traits, and traits to drive life outcomes. Further, they falsely assume that genes and related traits can be transmitted for generations without dilution, until hereditary castes and new species arise.

However, even though claims one and four are incorrect, they may incite envy of those born through HGM. They forecast a terrifying future in which superior castes or species oppress, enslave, and murder ordinary human beings who suffer a relative genetic disadvantage that is arbitrary and unalterable. Unmodified persons who hear these claims and conclude that they have been consigned to an inferior position may experience resentment and anger toward children of HGM. Inferiority, resentment, and hostility add up to envy.

The stereotype content model reinforces this conclusion. Claims one and four depict children whose superior abilities surpass ordinary human competence. Their privilege, anti-democratic tendencies, and willingness to enslave or murder others place them at most frigid end of the warmth spectrum. Some are not even human, a fact that may nudge them off the spectrum altogether. As previously noted, a competent-but-cold profile tends to provoke envy.

Moreover, these particular claims may induce more than envy. In our culture, democracy is a core norm. Slavery and murder are strictly prohibited. Yet, the claims paint children of HGM and their descendants as destroyers of democracy, enslavers, and murderers. Those who believe that children of HGM and their descendants are poised to violate these accepted norms may experience the objective sense of injustice associated with resentment proper.

2 Eugenics

Analysis now shifts to claim two, which asserts that HGM leads to eugenics. This vague claim can be interpreted in various ways, some of which do not promote envy. For example, as discussed in Chapter 5, Sections B.1 and B.2, some may fear that government will compel or pressure parents to reproduce through HGM. And as Section B.3 noted, some do worry that society will become less tolerant or supportive of the disabled. Concerns about coercion and discrimination may be ill founded, but at least they do not encourage envy.

However, as shown in Chapter 5, Section B.4, others argue that parents will purchase popular traits for their children, creating faddish cohorts that devalue those born without the traits. Of course, such outcomes are highly unlikely for the reasons discussed there. Here, the more salient question is whether this concern promotes envy.

The concern predicts that market forces will relegate people with unpopular traits to an inferior position. Inferiority that results from arbitrary and unalterable factors, such as market forces and genes, creates the right conditions for resentment and hostility to arise. Thus, those who heed this concern may feel envious, particularly if they sense that their own traits are currently unpopular. However, the realization that tastes change over time may temper such emotional reactions.

3 Ossification of Society

Claim three is specific to lifespan extension. As Chapter 5, Section C, stated, this claim alleges that if people live longer, they will refuse to retire, and institutions will stagnate. Nursing homes will be packed with supercentenarians. Social welfare programs will collapse from the strain of a burgeoning elderly population.

These prognostications consign the young to an inferior position. They will be shut out of jobs and other powerful positions, such as political office. Social welfare programs will fail before they can benefit. Moreover, their relative disadvantage will be due to arbitrary factors outside their control, such as the genes others received. Thus, claim three encourages the young to feel resentment and anger toward those born with lifespan-extending modifications. And if they do feel inferior, resentful, and hostile, they are envious.

To be sure, the stereotype content model points in a different direction. Generally, the elderly are viewed as incompetent but harmless, a stereotype that evokes pity rather than envy.[37] However, psychologists Susan Fiske and Michael North have found that young people have strong ideas about how old people are supposed to act and resent those who fail to conform. For example, the young already envy and resent elders who refuse to retire and surrender coveted resources such as jobs, seniority, and wealth.[38] Any claim that HGM will make a bad situation worse can only further fan the flames of envy.

4 Consent of Future Generations

Finally, some argue that HGM is wrong because future generations cannot consent to it. As Chapter 5 noted in Section E, future generations do not consent to other reproductive decisions that affect them. Nor can those born through HGM complain of harm, since they would not exist otherwise. Thus, the concern is best interpreted as a claim that HGM leads to a worse future.

Each of the four claims of the apocalypse objection describes a specific way in which HGM leads to a worse future. This chapter has explained that the four claims may provoke envy or even resentment proper. Therefore, to the extent the concern about future generations incorporates these claims, it also holds the same potential to spark such emotions.

D RISKS TO CHILDREN OF HGM

Thus far, the analysis has established that the stratification and apocalypse objections and related concerns incite envy of children born through HGM. The next step is to explore the likely consequences for such children. To render the analysis more vivid and clear, this section utilizes the hypothetical scenario in which John and Mary Smith amend their gametes to include single nucleotide polymorphisms (SNPs) associated with improved memory and learning and produce a daughter named Cora.

Suppose that by the time Cora reaches high school, she has developed superior memory and learning. Her talents encourage her classmates to envy her, and when she is ready for employment her colleagues experience the same uncomfortable emotion. As Section A.2 of this chapter noted, envy may be adaptive. It alerts underperformers to the risk of low skill and failure and motivates efforts to correct or manage the situation. Because genes are not the only determinant of success, the unmodified may search for other methods of leveling the playing field. So, for example, Cora's classmates can study harder or longer, and coworkers can invest more time and effort learning job-related information. They can even undergo mnemonic training to improve their own ability to memorize, at least in the short term.[39]

Unfortunately, by overemphasizing the role of genes in determining life outcomes, the stratification and apocalypse objections and related concerns may discourage such positive responses and leave the envious to react in more negative ways. For example, if Cora's academic or professional rivals are aware of her genetic status and believe they are unable to compete with her, they may seek to undermine or defeat her. Envy research suggests that the rivals will prefer covert methods that Cora is unable to identify and combat. So, for example, they may denigrate her character, belittle her accomplishments, spread false rumors, or secretly work to derail her projects. However, Cora's rivals may also employ overt methods, including physical violence. To explain this last point, this section presents two models that analyze the relationship between envy and aggression.

1 The BIAS Map

Psychologists Fiske, Cuddy, and Glick have related stereotypes and emotions to behavior in a model they call the BIAS (behaviors from intergroup affect and stereotypes) map.[40] To gather data for the map, they conducted a national telephone survey to assess perceptions of various groups. The questions explored the traits and social status of the groups and also investigated emotional and behavioral responses to them. Subjects were not asked about their personal views, but rather to predict how others would respond to each group.[41]

Because competence can attract allies, the psychologists theorized that their subjects would perceive envied groups as beneficiaries of passive facilitation, such as cooperation or association. They also expected that subjects would perceive envied groups as targets for active harm, such as fights or attacks.[42] Survey data showed a significant correlation between envied groups and predictions of passive facilitation. However, the correlation between envied groups and predictions of active harm was not statistically significant.[43] To clarify the point, the psychologists ran another survey that added questions about anger. The results showed that anger *mediated* the relationship between envy and active harm.[44] In other words, envy linked to anger, and anger linked to active harm.

This chapter has explained how the stratification and apocalypse objections and related concerns promote envy of children of HGM. By encouraging the public to envy children of HGM, these objections and concerns may spark anger against them, and anger can lead to physical aggression. The apocalypse objection is particularly dangerous because it portrays children of HGM as destroyers of democracy, enslavers, and murderers. These predictions of extreme norm violations may be baseless; however, as discussed in Section A.3 of this chapter, they can facilitate the elevation of a subjective sense of injustice to an objective one, thereby heightening the risk of violence.

2 Ideological Model of Scapegoating

Psychologist Peter Glick has created his own ideological model of scapegoating. He theorizes that a society faced with economic or social problems will select scapegoats who are perceived as capable and wicked enough to cause the problems.[45] In his view, envious prejudice, which is targeted at groups viewed as cold and competent, predicts scapegoat selection.[46] For example, Hitler and his propaganda built on a long tradition of Christian anti-Semitism to create a superficially plausible account in which devious and powerful Jews caused Germany's financial and social problems.[47] Glick speculates that envious prejudice may also have inspired other genocides, including the slaughter of Armenians in Turkey and Tutsis in Rwanda.[48]

According to Glick, certain conditions fan the flames of envious prejudice and make it more dangerous. Resentment is most likely to boil over when the majority believes that its status has been downgraded relative to that of the envied minority.[49] He also notes the paradox of Nazi propaganda, which simultaneously presented Jews as powerful yet parasitic and inferior. Claims that Jews were flawed allowed Germans to feel superior and regain cultural pride after losing World War I.[50]

This model suggests that the stratification and apocalypse objections and related concerns may have dire consequences for children of HGM. By painting such children as cold but competent, and encouraging others to envy them, the objections and concerns create emotional tinder that can go up in flames at the right spark. That spark can come in the form of a major recession or depression, or as a shutdown of social welfare programs that the government can no longer afford. To be sure, the children will not be to blame for these economic problems. However, the birth of these allegedly superior and privileged beings may make the unmodified feel like their own genetic status has been downgraded, causing them to respond violently to this new and resented minority group.

E SUMMARY

Envy is an emotion characterized by inferiority, hostility, and resentment. Some researchers believe envy is an adaptive response to unfavorable social comparisons. It can spur a person to improve her own position or motivate her to drag a hated rival down. If a person can frame her rival as a transgressor of social norms, she may transmute her envy into resentment proper and persuade others of the righteousness of her cause. Groups as well as individuals can be the targets of envy. Under the right economic and social conditions, envy can lead to aggression and violence.

Chapters 4 and 5 explained that the stratification and apocalypse objections and related concerns are meritless. However, the objections and concerns are not harmless, for they encourage those who believe them to envy children of HGM. The envious often work to undermine the social status and objectives of their rivals, and sometimes attack or fight them. By fomenting envy, the objections and concerns create a risk that children of HGM will be resented, subverted, bullied, and even subjected to physical violence. In evaluating the harms that legal bans on HGM may impose on such children, Chapter 10 will return to this topic.

Notes

1. RICHARD H. SMITH & SUNG HEE KIM, Comprehending Envy, 133 PSYCHOLOGICAL BULLETIN 46, 49 (2007).
2. Id. at 49–50.
3. Id. at 50–51.
4. Id. at 49, 52.
5. Id. at 48.
6. Id. at 47; see NEW OXFORD AMERICAN DICTIONARY 932 (ANGUS STEVENSON & CHRISTINE A. LINDBERG EDS., 3rd ed. 2010) (including a definition of jealousy as feeling envy of another).
7. SMITH & KIM, supra note 1, at 47.
8. Id. at 47–48.
9. Id. at 47–48. To be sure, envy and jealousy can be present at the same time. For example, Alan can simultaneously envy Brad for his sex appeal and be jealous of his attentions to Diana.

10. *Id.* at 54.
11. *Id.* at 48–49. The Ten Commandments of the Old Testament instruct believers not to covet the house, wife, or other possessions of their neighbors. EXODUS 20:17 (King James).
12. SMITH & KIM, *supra* note 1, at 48.
13. *Id.* at 50.
14. *Id.* at 53; SARAH E. HILL & DAVID M. BUSS, The Evolutionary Psychology of Envy, in ENVY: THEORY AND RESEARCH 60, 62–63 (RICHARD H. SMITH ED. 2008).
15. NIELS VAN DE VEN & MARCEL ZEELENBERG, On the Counterfactual Nature of Envy: "It Could Have Been Me," 29 COGNITION & EMOTION 954, 955 (2015).
16. HILL & BUSS, *supra* note 14, at 63–64.
17. *See id.* (describing such methods); *see also* RICHARD H. SMITH, Envy and Its Transmutations, in THE SOCIAL LIFE OF EMOTIONS 43, 48 (LARISSA Z. TIEDENS & COLIN WAYNE LEACH, EDS. 2004) (explaining that an envious person may attack the character of his rival in an attempt to compensate for his own inferior ability).
18. HILL & BUSS, *supra* note 14, at 64.
19. *Id.* at 63–64.
20. *See* SMITH & KIM, *supra* note 1, at 52 (suggesting that an envious person may interpret his emotion as righteous indignation at the alleged arrogance of the advantaged one).
21. SMITH, *supra* note 17, at 53.
22. SMITH & KIM, *supra* note 1, at 56.
23. SMITH, *supra* note 17, at 54.
24. SMITH & KIM, *supra* note 1, at 56–57.
25. SUSAN T. FISKE ET AL., Universal Dimensions of Social Cognition: Warmth and Competence, 11 TRENDS IN COGNITIVE SCIENCES 77 (2007).
26. *Id.* at 80.
27. *Id.* at 80 fig. 1.
28. *Id.* at 81–82.
29. NATIONAL ACADEMY OF SCIENCES & NATIONAL ACADEMY OF MEDICINE, Human Genome Editing: Science, Ethics, and Governance 122 (2017) [hereinafter NAS REPORT].
30. *Id.* at 123.
31. *Id.* Recommendation 6–1.
32. SMITH & KIM, *supra* note 1, at 49.
33. RICHARD H. SMITH ET AL., Subjective Injustice and Inferiority as Predictors of Hostile and Depressive Feelings in Envy, 20 PERSONALITY AND SOCIAL PSYCHOLOGY BULLETIN 705, 710 (1994).
34. SMITH & KIM, *supra* note 1, at 54.
35. *Id.* at 47.
36. Medicare is a complex health insurance program run by the federal government. It covers persons age 65 and older, some disabled persons, and those

with permanent kidney failure. What's Medicare, MEDICARE.GOV, www.medicare.gov/sign-up-change-plans/decide-how-to-get-medicare/whats-medicare/what-is-medicare.html (last visited February 12, 2017). Medicaid is a federal and state program that covers medical costs and provides certain health care benefits for persons of limited means. Medicaid, MEDICARE.GOV, www.medicare.gov/your-medicare-costs/help-paying-costs/medicaid/medicaid.html (last visited February 12, 2017).
37. FISKE ET AL., *supra* note 25, at 80.
38. MICHAEL S. NORTH AND SUSAN T. FISKE, An Inconvenienced Youth? Ageism and Its Potential Intergenerational Roots, 138 PSYCHOLOGICAL BULLETIN 982, 987–88 (2017).
39. In one experiment, subjects who mastered a mnemonic technique altered their brain network functionality and improved their performance on memory tasks. The last measurement of their ability was conducted four months after the memory training ended. MARTIN DRESLER ET AL., Mnemonic Training Reshapes Brain Networks to Support Superior Memory, 93 NEURON 1227 (2017).
40. AMY J.C. CUDDY ET AL., The BIAS Map: Behaviors from Intergroup Affect and Stereotypes, 92 J. PERSONALITY & SOCIAL PSYCH. 631, 632 (2007).
41. See id. at 648 (providing the interview script and items for the phone interviews).
42. *Id.* at 634–35.
43. *Id.* at 637.
44. *Id.* at 643.
45. Peter Glick, Sacrificial Lambs Dressed in Wolves' Clothing: Envious Prejudice, Ideology, and the Scapegoating of the Jews, in UNDERSTANDING GENOCIDE: SOCIAL PSYCHOLOGY OF THE HOLOCAUST 113, 129 (LEONARD S. NEWMAN & RALPH ERBER, EDS. 2002).
46. *Id.* at 130.
47. *Id.* at 129–30.
48. *Id.* at 139.
49. *Id.* at 130.
50. *Id.* at 133–34.

PART III

Human Germline Modification and the Law

Human germline modification (HGM) is a technology in which CRISPR/Cas9, base editors, and other molecular editing tools are utilized to make changes to human gametes and embryos. Part I of this book described four objections to the use of this technology in human reproduction, along with some related concerns. It also explained that the objections and concerns rest upon, or inspire, negative stereotypes about children of HGM.

Part II investigated the psychological roots of the four objections, as well as concerns and stereotypes related to them. It found that the objections, concerns, and stereotypes are likely the product of psychological essentialism. In addition, the stratification and apocalypse objections promote envy of children of HGM and could lead to violence.

Part III turns from technology and psychology to law. Chapter 8 examines existing laws and regulations that restrict HGM on the federal and state levels. Although HGM for research is discussed, the primary focus is on laws and regulations that impact HGM for reproduction. Chapter 9 discusses future laws and regulations that politicians may impose to gain better control over HGM. Its primary focus is on legal bans, and the politics involved in enacting them. Chapter 10 explores the potential impacts of laws that prohibit HGM. It explores the harms that such laws will impose on scientists and science, parents, children, foreigners, and society. Finally, the Conclusion discusses education as an alternative strategy that can reduce inappropriate uses of HGM while imposing fewer harms on society.

8

Existing Laws and Regulations

This chapter reviews existing laws and regulations that restrict human germline modification (HGM) in the United States.[1] Its primary focus is on laws and regulations that make it difficult or illegal to procreate with modified human gametes and embryos. However, because research is a key step along the path to HGM for reproduction, this chapter also discusses laws and regulations that impede the modification of human gametes and human embryos in the laboratory. Laws and regulations regarding related technologies, such as in vitro fertilization (IVF) or preimplantation genetic diagnosis (PGD), are outside its scope.[2]

A FEDERAL LAW

The US Congress has not banned HGM outright.[3] However, as this section explains, federal laws and regulations have the following impacts. First, Congress has barred the Food and Drug Administration (FDA) from receiving applications to conduct clinical trials; thus, HGM for reproduction is temporarily blocked. Second, restrictive federal funding policies discourage scientists from pursuing HGM for research. Third, human subjects regulations affect HGM for research and reproduction, but privately funded entities can evade them.

1 The FDA Claims Authority over HGM for Reproduction

The FDA has the statutory authority to regulate drugs, medical devices, and biological products.[4] In general, the agency must approve new drugs, medical devices, and biological products[5] as safe and effective before they can be distributed in interstate commerce.[6] Clinical trials to demonstrate safety and effectiveness are a key step along the path to FDA approval.[7] Paradoxically, however, one cannot distribute a new drug to investigators for use in a clinical trial before the FDA has approved it. To obtain an exemption, one must submit an investigational new drug (IND) application to the FDA and meet conditions intended to ensure the safety of human subjects in the clinical trial.[8] The FDA treats biological products as drugs and applies this process to them.[9]

In 2015, after Chinese scientists edited the genomes of human embryos,[10] the National Institutes of Health (NIH) summarized the applicable regulatory regime in these words:

> The Public Health Service Act and the Federal Food, Drug, and Cosmetic Act give the FDA the authority to regulate cell and gene therapy products as biological products and/or drugs, *which would include oversight of human germline modification*. During development, biological products may be used in humans only if an investigational new drug application is in effect.[11]

Through this statement, the NIH suggested that an edited human gamete or embryo is a biological product and/or drug within FDA jurisdiction. This assessment is consistent with actions that the FDA has taken through its Center for Biologics Evaluation and Research (CBER), which regulates biological products for human use.[12] In 2001, the CBER sent researchers a letter asserting jurisdiction over "human cells used in therapy involving the transfer of genetic material by means other than the union of gamete nuclei."[13] As an example, it cited gametes or other cells into which genetic material was transferred via a genetic vector.[14] The CBER directed researchers to submit an IND application before using genetically manipulated cells or their derivatives in humans.[15]

Armed with this background, let us consider the implications for HGM. Suppose a scientist uses a molecular tool to remove a genetic mutation from a human gamete or embryo. If the gamete or embryo remains in the lab, the experiment is not being conducted in humans, and no IND is required.[16] However, if the scientist wishes to transfer an edited gamete or embryo to a woman to initiate a pregnancy, he must first submit his IND application to the FDA.

a) Congress Halts FDA Review

Government agencies like the FDA cannot operate unless Congress provides them with funds.[17] These funds may come with strings attached. After the Chinese scientists reported their HGM research in 2015, Congress enacted the Consolidated Appropriations Act, 2016 (2016 Act), which includes this section:

> None of the funds made available by this Act may be used to notify a sponsor or otherwise acknowledge receipt of a submission for an exemption for investigational use of a drug or biological product under § 505(i) of the Federal Food, Drug, and Cosmetic Act (21 U.S.C. 355(i)) or § 351(a)(3) of the Public Health Service Act (42 U.S.C. 262(a)(3)) in research in which a human embryo is intentionally created or modified to include a heritable genetic modification. Any such submission shall be deemed to have not been received by the Secretary, and the exemption may not go into effect.[18]

Note the phrase "created or modified to include a heritable genetic modification." This phrase encompasses two types of research. In the first, a researcher modifies human gametes and uses them to *create* embryos. For example, she could inseminate a woman with modified sperm, thereby creating embryos in her reproductive tract, or she could inseminate eggs with modified sperm in the lab and transfer the resulting embryos to a woman. In the second example, a researcher uses unmodified gametes to create human embryos in vitro. She then *modifies* these embryos and transfers them to a woman.[19]

If a researcher submits an IND application to conduct either type of research, the FDA is deemed never to have received the application. If the agency has not received an application, no exemption is available. A clinical trial cannot proceed without an exemption, so the research is blocked. In this oblique manner, Congress has temporarily halted HGM for reproduction.

Legislative history is sparse. A committee report accompanying an earlier version of the 2016 Act claimed HGM involved unspecified safety and ethical issues and implied that the restriction was a temporary measure while Congress awaited a formal report on HGM from the National Academy of Sciences and National Academy of Medicine.[20] Nevertheless, even after the Academies released their report (hereinafter NAS Report),[21] Congress included the exact same restriction in the Consolidated Appropriations Act, 2017.[22] Conceivably, it could enact the restriction year after year to block HGM for reproduction while sidestepping a messy public debate.

It is bad public policy to grant the FDA jurisdiction over HGM while denying scientists the chance to submit an IND application. Such applications, and agency responses to them, could provide valuable information on the safety and effectiveness of the technology. Moreover, scientists who are faced with a regulatory brick wall may flee with their patients to nations with less stringent regulations.[23] Cross-border reproductive care poses hazards of its own, as discussed in Chapter 10. Therefore, Congress should eliminate the restriction and permit the FDA to receive applications to conduct trials of HGM for reproduction.

b) Limits on FDA Power

Once the FDA begins to receive applications, its responses may depend on the complexity of the proposed modification. For example, as science progresses, it may become possible to correct a point mutation that causes a serious genetic disorder. If foreign clinical trials result in healthy babies, scientists in the United States can file applications supported by the foreign data. If their clinical trials will be safe for babies and mothers, the FDA should allow them to proceed.[24] Eventually, US scientists may amass enough data through their own clinical trials to prove that the process for correcting a point mutation is safe and effective enough to merit FDA approval.

Complex traits, such as memory or lifespan, involve multiple genes, so learning how to engineer enhancements will take more time. Even so, researchers in foreign nations may eventually generate data that scientists in the United States can use to justify their own clinical trials. If those trials establish that an enhancement is safe and effective, the FDA must approve it. It does not have the statutory authority to regulate on the basis of moral or ethical concerns.[25] For its purposes, the four objections discussed in Part I are irrelevant.

To be sure, the FDA has been known to let moral considerations creep in through the back door. For example, it was slow to grant teenage girls access to emergency contraception over the counter, in part due to concerns that the girls would make bad decisions about sex.[26] Access might never have been granted had citizens not sued the agency in federal court.[27]

By analogy, the FDA may ignore, dispute, or manipulate safety data to delay or reject an application to conduct clinical trials involving HGM. Such intransigent behavior may provoke a lawsuit challenging its authority to regulate the technology.[28] However, it could take years for a court to rule against the FDA. Meanwhile, scientists who work at reputable institutions will not run clinical trials without FDA approval.

2 NIH Funding Policy Discourages HGM for Research

FDA regulation does not bar scientists from conducting experiments on gametes and embryos in their labs. However, science costs money. Without federal funding, HGM for research could wither on the vine.

In 2015, the NIH stated that it would not fund research in which gene-editing technologies are applied to human embryos.[29] In justification, it noted safety issues, ethical issues involved in affecting future generations without consent, and lack of convincing medical applications.[30] It also cited the Dickey-Wicker Amendment, a rider to the annual appropriations bill for the Department of Health and Human Services. This rider forbids the use of federal funds to support work in which human embryos are created for research, destroyed, discarded, or subjected to risk of serious injury or death.[31]

The sweep of the NIH funding policy is broad. Suppose a scientist at a research institution wishes to edit a human embryo. Even if he is engaged in pure research, his work cannot be federally funded. Thus, he must segregate his costs so that federal funds provided to other projects at the institution do not indirectly subsidize his work.[32]

Human embryos aside, are federal funds available for research in which human *gametes* are modified? The 2015 NIH statement did not address that question. To find an answer, one must consult a different source: NIH Guidelines for Research Involving Recombinant DNA Molecules (hereinafter NIH Guidelines).[33]

Under the NIH Guidelines, the Recombinant DNA Advisory Council (RAC) must review any proposal to transfer recombinant or synthetic nucleic acid molecules,[34] or DNA or RNA derived from such molecules, into human research participants.[35] However, the NIH Guidelines state that the RAC will not review proposals for germline alteration, which is defined as "a specific attempt to introduce genetic changes into the germ (reproductive) cells of an individual, with the aim of changing the set of genes passed on to the individual's offspring."[36] Thus, if research involves editing human gametes for use *in reproduction*, RAC review is unavailable and NIH funds are out of reach.[37] Indeed, if an institution accepts NIH funds for any recombinant or synthetic nucleic acid molecule research, no scientist working there can edit human gametes for use in reproduction, even if his specific research project is privately funded.[38]

If a scientist plans to edit human gametes purely for research purposes, RAC review is not required[39] and NIH funds theoretically could be available for early-stage projects. Eventually, however, a scientist who edits gametes will want to test their efficacy by creating embryos with them. And as previously mentioned, the Dickey-Wicker Amendment prohibits the use of federal funds to support experiments in which embryos are created for research. Thus, a scientist who wishes to edit human gametes is probably better off finding an alternative source of funding for his project.

To summarize, federal funds are not available for projects in which human embryos are edited. Funds may be available for research in which human gametes are edited, as long as those gametes are not used in reproduction or to create embryos, but the NIH has not directly addressed the point.

To be sure, states and private institutions may fund HGM for research.[40] But without NIH oversight, there will be less transparency and regulatory control.[41] Moreover, the NIH's decision not to fund HGM for research casts a pall on this emerging technology. Scientists who care about their academic careers and employment prospects will veer away from fields that are disqualified from federal funds.

3 The Common Rule Regulates but Does Not Bar HGM for Research and Reproduction

The Department of Health and Human Services has recently revised a body of regulations known as the Common Rule.[42] Fifteen other federal departments and agencies include the Common Rule in their own regulations.[43] This section provides a brief exploration of the revised Common Rule in relation to HGM.

Federally funded research involving human subjects falls within the scope of the Common Rule.[44] As noted in the previous section, the NIH will not fund research in which human embryos are edited. Nor will it fund research in which edited human gametes are used in reproduction. Theoretically, it could fund pure lab research in which human gametes are edited. However, because the NIH does not fund research in which embryos are created, researchers who want to test the viability of edited gametes by creating embryos must find alternative funds. Thus, at first glance, it seems as if the Common Rule is irrelevant to the vast majority of HGM research.

However, this first impression is misleading. If an institution accepts any federal funds for human subjects research, it must provide a written assurance that it will comply with the Common Rule.[45] Moreover, if an institution wishes, it can incorporate the Common Rule into its internal policies, thereby extending the rule's reach to all research projects conducted there.[46] If a scientist who edits human embryos works at such an institution, she will have to comply with the Common Rule even if private funds support her research.

In general, under the Common Rule, an institutional review board (IRB) reviews and preapproves research.[47] Before it gives researchers the green light, the IRB must find that multiple requirements have been met.[48] For example, risks to human subjects must be minimized.[49] Further, risks must be "reasonable in relation to anticipated benefits, if any, to subjects, and the importance of the knowledge that may reasonably be expected to result."[50] Also, researchers must seek and obtain informed consent from subjects.[51] The regulatory requirements for informed consent are complex and will not be listed in detail here. However, one key requirement is that researchers warn subjects about reasonably foreseeable risks or pain they may experience.[52] Researchers must also describe reasonably expected benefits to the subjects or others.[53]

a) HGM for Research

Hypotheticals will be used to illustrate the workings of the Common Rule. Suppose a scientist named Zach works at an institution that accepts federal funds and incorporates the Common Rule into its internal policies. Zach wishes to modify human gametes or embryos in pure research. The question is whether his research involves human subjects.

The Common Rule defines "human subject" this way:

> Human subject means a living individual about whom an investigator (whether professional or student) conducting research:
>
> (i) Obtains information or biospecimens through intervention or interaction with the individual, and uses, studies, or analyzes the information or biospecimens; or
> (ii) Obtains, uses, studies, analyzes, or generates identifiable private information or identifiable biospecimens.[54]

Human gametes and embryos located outside the body are not "living individuals,"[55] but gamete or embryo donors are. If Zach gathers gametes through a physical procedure, he obtains a biospecimen through an intervention; if he interviews a donor to elicit medical history, he obtains information through an interaction.[56] If Zach gains access to medical records associated with donor names, he obtains identifiable private information;[57] if he works with gametes or embryos linked to donor names, he uses or studies identifiable biospecimens.[58] In all these cases, human subjects are involved. However, if Zach works with gametes or embryos from anonymous donors with whom he does not intervene or interact, no human subjects are involved.

Even if human subjects are involved, the IRB at Zach's institution is doubtless familiar with the Common Rule and can guide him. If Zach works with sperm or embryos, obtaining IRB approval should not be too hard. Donors of sperm and existing embryos face no physical risks. Psychological risks, such as disappointment if the research proves unsuccessful, can be ameliorated via informed consent.[59] If the sperm or embryos are linked to names or medical records, Zach can take measures to protect the donors' privacy.[60] Any risks that remain will likely be reasonable in relation to the knowledge expected to result from the experiment.[61]

If Zach wants to experiment on eggs, he may be able to obtain spare eggs that IVF patients donate to research. Such patients have assumed the risks of the IVF process and the donation does not increase their risk. However, suppose he wants to recruit an egg donor who carries a mutation. Fertility drugs must be used to stimulate maturation of multiple eggs, and a doctor must aspirate the eggs with a needle while the donor is sedated.[62] Women who undergo this process face physical risks, such as ovarian hyperstimulation syndrome (OHSS).[63] Zach may find it easier to persuade his IRB that the risks are acceptable if he substitutes a sperm donor with the mutation, as did the international team that reported high levels of success in correcting genetic mutations in embryos in 2017.[64]

b) HGM for Reproduction

Next, suppose Zach wants to conduct a clinical trial involving HGM for reproduction. Specifically, he plans to remove disease-causing genetic mutations from human gametes or embryos before initiating pregnancies. Further, assume molecular tools and knowledge of human genetics advance to the point where each couple enrolled in the trial has reasonably good odds of a favorable outcome, that is, the safe birth of a healthy child. This assumption is realistic for two reasons: parents are unlikely to participate in a clinical trial without good odds of a favorable outcome, and the FDA will not allow a clinical trial to proceed until and unless HGM is safe for the mothers and babies involved.

<u>Gametes and embryos</u>: The gametes and embryos involved in the clinical trial are human; however, as noted in Section A.3.a of this chapter, they are not human subjects in a legal sense. Therefore, the risk that the editing process may damage gametes or embryos is not directly relevant.

<u>Adults</u>: Adults who provide gametes are human subjects for the reasons stated in the prior section on HGM for research. Transferring embryos with genetic modifications to a woman also qualifies as an intervention,[65] so women who attempt to become pregnant through the trial are also human subjects.

To illustrate, suppose that John and Mary Smith join the clinical trial because all of Mary's eggs carry the mutation that causes Huntington disease, as discussed in

Chapter 1, Section B.1, John, who provides sperm, incurs no physical risk. Mary must take fertility drugs, undergo egg retrieval, and submit to embryo transfer. If the procedure is successful, she must endure pregnancy and give birth. All these activities entail physical risks. In addition, the Smiths may incur psychological harm if Mary gives birth to a sick or disabled child.

However, Zach can minimize these risks by waiting to proceed with the clinical trial until HGM for reproduction has developed to a point where a favorable outcome is likely, as the hypothetical assumes. Moreover, although Mary must still incur the physical risks associated with fertility drugs, egg retrieval, embryo transfer, gestation, and birth, the anticipated benefit to the Smiths is significant, for HGM is the only method by which they can conceive and bear a healthy genetic child. Under these circumstances, the risks are reasonable in relation to the anticipated benefit.[66] Moreover, if Zach has already submitted an IND application to the FDA, he should be able to provide the Smiths with enough information about risks and benefits to obtain informed consent from them.[67]

If Mary did not carry a genetic mutation and the purpose of the clinical trial was to confer an enhanced trait, such as improved memory and learning, the analysis would be similar but the risk-benefit calculus would change. Any such enhancement would have to offer significant benefits to outweigh the risks of physical and psychological harm. IRBs would likely disapprove projects aimed at achieving cosmetic changes in children or other frivolous applications.

Pregnant Women and Fetuses: In addition to the basic protections of the Common Rule, pregnant women and fetuses involved in research funded by the Department of Health and Human Services benefit from additional regulations that provide further safeguards.[68] To summarize, preclinical studies on pregnant animals and clinical studies on nonpregnant women must be conducted to create data for risk assessment.[69] If the research poses a risk to the fetus, it must either have the potential to benefit the woman or fetus directly or impose minimal risk while aiming to produce important, otherwise unobtainable biomedical knowledge.[70] If the research directly benefits the pregnant woman, alone or in conjunction with her fetus, she must give informed consent.[71] Any parent who gives consent must be fully informed about reasonably foreseeable impacts on the fetus.[72]

Assume Zach's institution has incorporated these additional regulations into its internal policies. The regulations apply only after Mary becomes pregnant and her fetus exists. "Fetus" is defined as "the product of conception from implantation until delivery,"[73] so the regulations do not apply to her in vitro embryos. Medical examinations and treatments performed during the pregnancy and the birth process may subject Mary and her fetus to some physical risk; however, they also benefit her and the fetus by increasing the odds that a healthy child will be born safely. The fetus cannot give informed consent, but the regulations are satisfied if Mary does.

The requirement of preclinical studies on pregnant animals and clinical studies on nonpregnant women should be easy to satisfy. Zach can run preclinical studies of pregnant animals using the same medical examinations and treatments planned for the clinical trial. He can also perform preclinical studies of exams and treatments on nonpregnant women to ensure that they are safe for humans to undergo.

<u>Children</u>: A child who participates in research funded by the Department of Health and Human Services also benefits from special protections.[74] Research is allowed if the child faces no greater than minimal risk.[75] Alternatively, if an intervention or procedure may provide the child with a direct benefit, the research may proceed if the anticipated benefit to the child justifies the risk, and the risk-benefit calculus is at least as favorable to the child as that offered by available alternatives.[76] Either way, the researcher must solicit the consent of the child and permission from at least one parent.[77] However, the child's consent is not required if she is not capable of assenting or the research may provide a direct benefit that is important to her health or well-being.[78]

Again, assume Zach's institution has incorporated these additional regulations into its internal policies. If the hypothetical clinical trial is successful, and Mary bears a daughter named Ariel, these additional protections apply to that child. Researchers may conduct physical or psychological examinations of Ariel to gather data. These exams will probably present no more than minimal risk.[79] Alternatively, the exams will provide a direct benefit to Ariel by ensuring she is healthy and free of the genetic mutation, thereby justifying the risk involved. The risk-benefit calculus is as or more favorable than available alternatives (*e.g.*, no exams).

At first, Ariel will be too young to consent to the physical or psychological exams. However, per the regulations, she need not consent if she is too young and/or if the exams directly benefit her health and well-being. At least one parent must grant permission, but John and Mary Smith agreed to the clinical trial at the outset and will probably agree to the ongoing exams also.

c) Fertility Clinics: Evading the Common Rule

Two assumptions underlie the foregoing analysis of the Common Rule: first, Zach, the scientist who conducts the hypothetical clinical trial, is engaged in research; second, he works at an institution that incorporates the Common Rule and related regulations into its internal policies. However, one or both assumptions are likely to be false when it comes to private fertility clinics.

To illustrate, suppose research scientists develop effective methods of editing gametes or human embryos. A fertility clinic learns of these techniques and offers HGM in conjunction with IVF. John and Mary Smith enroll as patients because all of Mary's eggs carry the mutation that causes Huntington disease. The clinic edits the mutation out of her eggs and performs IVF. Nine months later, Ariel is born.

In this scenario, the fertility clinic provides medical services to the Smiths and other patients. Because it does not conduct investigations that aim to develop or contribute to generalizable knowledge, it is not engaged in "research" within the meaning of the Common Rule[80] and regulations governing research involving pregnant women, fetuses, and children.[81] Moreover, if the clinic does not accept federal funds and is not part of an institution that incorporates the Common Rule and related regulations into its internal policies, its activities are not subject to the Rule and regulations.[82]

To be sure, as discussed in Section A.1 of this chapter, a fertility clinic cannot provide HGM services without first submitting an IND application to the FDA. The FDA cannot even receive such applications at this point in time. However, in the future, things may change. If Congress relents, and specific clinical uses become safe and effective, FDA review may not present a significant barrier to HGM for reproduction.

B STATE LAW

The focus of this chapter now shifts to state law. No state statutes address HGM specifically.[83] There are several possible reasons for this gap. State legislators are busy people, with many issues on their agendas. Some may not realize that the CRISPR/Cas9 tool exists and can be used to modify human gametes and embryos. Others may count on the FDA to regulate HGM for reproduction and/or assume that state legislation can wait until the technology is perfected.

Nevertheless, scientists, doctors, and parents must beware. Laws originally enacted to control other types of research or reproductive technologies may inadvertently restrict or even prohibit the editing of human gametes or embryos. This section examines three categories: laws against research on human embryos and fetuses, laws against human cloning, and laws against human-animal hybrids.

1 Laws against Research on Embryos and Fetuses

Some states place restrictions on research performed on human embryos and fetuses.[84] The specific nature of these restrictions varies from state to state. To illustrate how such laws may impede HGM for research and reproduction, this section adapts the John and Mary Smith hypothetical.

a) HGM for Research

Suppose a scientist named Zach wants to edit human embryos for research purposes. He solicits an embryo donation from John and Mary Smith, who are undergoing IVF because they are infertile. This scenario is risky for all three participants.

Zach cannot conduct his experiment in Louisiana because that state prohibits the culturing of IVF embryos for research.[85] He cannot proceed in Michigan, Minnesota, and South Dakota because his work could kill or injure the embryos.[86] He is at risk in Florida, New Mexico, North Dakota, Maine, Pennsylvania, and Rhode Island, where laws restricting fetal experimentation[87] may extend to in vitro embryos.[88] The Smiths must also be careful. In Maine,

Michigan, Rhode Island, and South Dakota, donation of embryos to research is illegal.[89]

Alternatively, suppose Zach decides to create his own embryos for research. Perhaps he has edited gametes and wishes to establish their viability by combining them to make embryos through the process of fertilization. Or, perhaps he plans to combine standard gametes to make embryos that can be edited afterward. In Massachusetts, he faces a stumbling block: it is illegal to create an embryo through fertilization with the sole intention of donating it for research.[90] If prosecutors decide that Zach has made embryos to donate to his own research, he may be imprisoned or fined.[91]

Finally, once embryos are edited, suppose Zach wishes to derive stem cell lines from them. He must take care not to perform his work in Arizona. It is illegal there to disaggregate a human embryo to create a stem cell line.[92] Nor should he proceed in South Dakota. Not only is destruction of an embryo prohibited there, a person cannot conduct research on cells or tissues that he knows were derived from research that killed or injured a human embryo.[93]

Zach may decide to move to a state without any of these restrictions. However, this solution is not perfect, since it requires a degree of personal and professional flexibility that he may not have. Besides, even if he does move, his new state could tighten its laws if its residents come to oppose HGM.

b) HGM for Reproduction

Now, let us suppose John and Mary Smith are fertile, but Mary's eggs contain a genetic mutation that causes Huntington disease. They undergo IVF at a fertility clinic and ask their doctor to delete the mutation from their embryos prior to transfer. Nine months later, Ariel is born.

Suppose further that HGM is still relatively new and could be considered experimental. If the fertility clinic is located in a state that bars experimentation on embryos or fetuses, as discussed earlier in Section B.1 of this chapter, a prosecutor who hears about the IVF cycle may indict the doctor. If the clinic is located in a state that prohibits the donation of embryos for research, she may indict John and Mary also.

To be sure, defenses are possible. First, consider the context. Louisiana permits the fertilization of an egg in vitro when the purpose is to bring about the birth of a child.[94] Similarly, in Pennsylvania and South Dakota, statutes against fetal or embryo experimentation do not extend to IVF.[95] The Smiths and their doctor may be protected in these states because HGM occurs within the IVF process.[96]

Second, in states that bar experimentation on embryos or fetuses, the Smiths and their doctor can argue that HGM is procreation rather than "experimentation" or "research," terms that are more often associated with lab work. If such terms are not defined in the statute, they may persuade a court that the statute is unconstitutionally vague.[97]

Third, consider purpose. Many anti-experimentation laws exempt procedures that protect the life or health of an embryo or fetus.[98] In this scenario, the Smiths and their doctor may argue that their actions are necessary to protect the life or health of their IVF embryos. However, Huntington disease does not threaten life or health until after a child is born, so the argument is a stretch.

It is difficult to predict how prosecutors and judges will respond to these defenses. The answer may depend on their underlying attitudes about HGM as a reproductive technology. Parents like the Smiths will find it simpler and safer to travel to states that do not restrict research on embryos and fetuses.

2 Laws against Human Cloning

Currently, 17 states prohibit the cloning of babies: Arizona, Arkansas, California, Connecticut, Illinois, Indiana, Iowa, Maryland, Massachusetts, Michigan, Missouri, Montana, New Jersey, North Dakota, Oklahoma, South Dakota, and Virginia. Seven of these states ban all human cloning, including research: Arizona, Arkansas, Indiana, Michigan, North Dakota, Oklahoma, and South Dakota.[99] These anti-cloning laws are relevant here because some are worded broadly and may extend to HGM.

For example, in Arizona, "a person shall not intentionally or knowingly create or attempt to create an in vitro human embryo by any means other than fertilization through the combining of a human egg with a human sperm."[100] If the word "create" applies only to the moment of conception, a scientist should be able to edit an existing human embryo without violating this law. However, if the process of creation extends beyond the moment of conception, a scientist who edits an existing human embryo, whether for research or for the purpose of creating a baby, could be found guilty of a misdemeanor.[101] Either way, the Arizona law contains a loophole: it does not bar the creation of human embryos via eggs or sperm that a scientist has altered beforehand.

In Illinois, it is against the law to clone a human being.[102] The law defines the verb "clone" as the transfer to a uterus of "anything other than the product of fertilization of an egg of a human female by a sperm of a human male for the purpose of initiating a pregnancy that could result in the creation of a human fetus or the birth of a human being."[103] Missouri also prohibits the cloning of a human being[104] and defines the verb "clone" in a similar fashion.[105] These laws define the term "clone" so broadly that the term may include the transfer of a modified embryo that is the product of *both* fertilization and genomic editing. However, because these laws ban human cloning specifically, courts should limit them to that specific context. Moreover, the laws do not bar a scientist from conceiving human embryos with edited eggs or sperm.

3 Laws against Human-Animal Hybrids

Finally, two states, Arizona and Louisiana, have enacted laws against the knowing creation of a human-animal hybrid.[106] The statutory definition of "human-animal hybrid" has multiple subsections.[107] Here, the relevant subsection defines the term to include "[a] human embryo into which a nonhuman cell or cells, or any component part of a nonhuman cell or cells, have been introduced."[108]

HGM for research or reproduction could introduce a component part of a nonhuman cell into a human embryo in at least two ways. First, the CRISPR/Cas9 tool includes the Cas9 enzyme, which is part of the immune system of the streptococcus pyogenes bacterium.[109] Other molecular editing tools employ enzymes that are native to other bacteria.[110] If a scientist inserts DNA that codes for one of these enzymes into a human embryo, he introduces a component part of a nonhuman cell in violation of the Arizona and Louisiana laws. However, he may be able to avoid this problem by building a tool that employs DNA-free sources of Cas9[111] or other enzymes.

Second, molecular tools can be used not only to delete DNA sequences but also to add new ones. Scientists will choose to add human DNA in most cases. However, if a researcher plucks DNA from a nonhuman cell and adds it to a human embryo, he introduces a component part of a nonhuman cell into a human embryo in violation of the Arizona and Louisiana laws. Whether he can circumvent the laws by synthesizing the nonhuman DNA in his lab remains an open question.

C SUMMARY

Federal law does not specifically prohibit HGM for research. However, federal funds cannot be used to support research on human embryos. Whether the NIH will grant funds to support research on human gametes is unclear at this time. In addition, scientists who work at an institution that receives federal funds and incorporates the Common Rule into its internal policies must comply as to gamete and embryo donors.

Federal law also does not directly bar HGM for reproduction. In practice, however, a moratorium exists because Congress will not allow the FDA to receive applications to conduct clinical trials in which modified gametes or embryos are transferred to a woman. To be sure, Congress may eventually relent. But even then, the FDA will not allow clinical trials to proceed as long as HGM for reproduction is unsafe. However, once HGM becomes safe, the FDA cannot block clinical trials based on moral and ethical concerns.

HGM for reproduction faces other federal regulatory obstacles. For example, if an institution accepts federal funds for any recombinant or synthetic nucleic acid molecule research, a researcher there cannot edit human gametes for reproductive use, even if her project is privately funded. Moreover, if an institution accepts federal funds for human subjects research, and incorporates the Common Rule and related regulations into its internal policies, a researcher there must comply with the

Common Rule and regulations even if her specific project is privately funded. However, scientists, doctors, and others who work at fertility clinics and other institutions that are funded entirely with private money need not comply with these federal regulations.

State laws do not address HGM specifically. However, several states have laws that ban research or experimentation on human embryos and fetuses. These laws pose a hidden threat to scientists who conduct HGM for research as well as doctors and parents who employ HGM in reproduction. Moreover, some states prohibit human cloning and human-animal hybrids. Such laws may apply to HGM due to vague or overbroad statutory language.

Readers may be surprised to learn that so little law directly addresses HGM. However, CRISPR/Cas9 and other molecular editing tools are new, and the science of HGM is in its infancy. As the technology advances, and public awareness increases, legislators may display greater interest in controlling HGM. The birth of a modified baby abroad would be a likely call to action. Chapter 9 explores laws that Congress and state legislatures may adopt in the future.

Notes

1. The United States has not signed any international treaty or convention to prohibit HGM for research or reproduction. Center for Genetics & Soc'y, Human Germline Modification: Summary of National and International Policies (June 2015), www.geneticsandsociety.org/downloads/CGS_Global_Policies_Summary_2015.pdf [hereinafter HGM POLICIES]. Thus, this book will focus on domestic law. To learn more about attempts to control HGM in other countries, see M. ARAKI & T. ISHII, International Regulatory Landscape and Integration of Corrective Genome Editing into In Vitro Fertilization, 12 REPRODUCTIVE BIOLOGY & ENDOCRINOLOGY 1 (2014).
2. For a review of laws and regulations governing IVF and PGD, see PRESIDENT'S COUNCIL ON BIOETHICS, REPRODUCTION AND RESPONSIBILITY: THE REGULATION OF NEW BIOTECHNOLOGIES 45–71, 99–100 (2004) [hereinafter REPRODUCTION AND RESPONSIBILITY].
3. See HGM POLICIES, supra note 1 (stating that the United States has no law prohibiting HGM); see also M. ARAKI & T. ISHII, supra note 1, at 10 (noting that while the 2013 NIH Guidelines for Research Involving Recombinant or Synthetic Nucleic Acid Molecules restrict the use of HGM in research, the United States has no law explicitly banning it).
4. The FDA's authority to regulate drugs and medical devices comes from the Federal Food, Drug, and Cosmetic Act; its power to regulate biological products comes from the Public Health Service Act. RICHARD A. MERRILL & BRYAN J. ROSE, FDA Regulation of Human Cloning: Usurpation or Statesmanship? 15 HARV. J.L. & TECH. 85, 107–8 (2001).

Existing Laws and Regulations 137

5. Familiar biological products include vaccines, blood and blood products, and allergy shots. U.S. FOOD & DRUG ADMINISTRATION, What Is a Biological Product? www.fda.gov/aboutfda/transparency/basics/ucm194516.htm (last updated May 31, 2016). However, the FDA also regulates more exotic biological products, such as human somatic cell therapy products and gene therapy products. Application of Current Statutory Authorities to Human Somatic Cell Therapy Products and Gene Therapy Products, 58 Fed. Reg. 53,248, 53,249 (October. 14, 1993).
6. MERRILL & ROSE, *supra* note 4, at 108–9. There are some exceptions for older drugs and certain medical devices, but these are beyond the scope of this book. *Id.* at 108 n.118.
7. *Id.* at 109.
8. *Id.*
9. *Id.* at 108, n. 118.
10. PUPING LIANG ET AL., CRISPR/Cas9-mediated Gene Editing in Human Tripronuclear Zygotes, 6 PROTEIN & CELL 363 (2015).
11. FRANCIS S. COLLINS, Statement on NIH Funding of Research Using Gene-editing Technologies in Human Embryos, NATIONAL INSTITUTES OF HEALTH (April 29, 2015), www.nih.gov/about/director/04292015_statement_gene_editing_technologies.htm [hereinafter NIH STATEMENT] (emphasis added).
12. U.S. FOOD & DRUG ADMINISTRATION, About the Center for Biologics Evaluation and Research, www.fda.gov/AboutFDA/CentersOffices/OfficeofMedicalProductsandTobacco/CBER/default.htm (last updated March 2, 2017).
13. Letter from KATHRYN C. ZOON, Dir. of the Ctr. for Biologics Evaluation and Research, FDA, to Sponsors/Researchers, Human Cells Used in Therapy Involving the Transfer of Genetic Material by Means Other Than the Union of Gamete Nuclei (July 6, 2001), https://wayback.archive-it.org/7993/20170404210748/https://www.fda.gov/BiologicsBloodVaccines/SafetyAvailability/ucm105852.htm [hereinafter ZOON LETTER].
14. *Id.* A genetic vector is designed to deliver a gene into a cell. Often, the vector is a modified virus. For more on this topic, see U.S. NATIONAL LIBRARY OF MEDICINE How Does Gene Therapy Work? GENETICS HOME REFERENCE, (March 27, 2018), https://ghr.nlm.nih.gov/primer/therapy/procedures.
15. ZOON letter, *supra* note 13. This letter ended a promising fertility technique in which doctors injected ooplasm from healthy donor eggs into the eggs of infertile women to boost fertilization and embryonic development. Before it was sent, nearly 30 children were conceived through this technique. Their cells contain mitochondria from both mother and egg donor, and they will transmit this genetic modification to future generations. KERRY LYNN MACINTOSH, Brave New Eugenics: Regulating Assisted Reproductive Technologies in the Name of Better Babies, 2010 U. ILL. J.L. TECH & POLICY 257, 271–72 [hereinafter MACINTOSH, BRAVE NEW EUGENICS].

16. *See* NIH STATEMENT, *supra* note 11 (asserting FDA authority over experiments in humans); *see also* REPRODUCTION AND RESPONSIBILITY *supra* note 2, at 113 (stating that an embryo is not a human subject).
17. Under the US Constitution, Congress has the spending power. U.S. CONST. art. I, § 8, cl.1.
18. Consolidated Appropriations Act, 2016, 114 Pub. L. No. 113, § 749, 129 Stat. 2242, 2283.
19. The section that prevents the FDA from receiving applications may not apply to every experiment in which gametes are modified. For example, suppose a man carries a defective gene that prevents him from generating sperm. A scientist may retrieve spermatogonial stem cells from the man, correct the problematic gene, and return the modified cells to the testes to see whether the man can produce normal sperm. Technically, the experiment does not involve the creation of an embryo with a heritable genetic modification, so one could argue that the provision does not apply to it. *See* STEPHEN S. HALL, The Red Line: Will We Control Our Genetic Destinies? SCI. AM., September 2016, at 54, 60–61. On the other hand, the man walks away from the experiment with the ability to create embryos with heritable genetic modifications simply by having sex. How the FDA would interpret the section in such a case is unclear.
20. The Committee on Appropriations report stated the following:

> "*Genomic Editing.* The Committee understands the potential benefits to society in the genetic modification of living organisms. However, researchers do not yet fully understand all the possible side effects of editing the genes of a human embryo. Editing of the human germ line may involve serious and unquantifiable safety and ethical issues. Federal and non-Federal organizations, such as the National Academy of Sciences and National Academy of Medicine will soon engage in more extensive scientific analysis of the potential risks of genome editing and a broader public discussion of the societal and ethical implications of this technique. In accordance with the current policy at the National Institutes of Health, the Committee includes bill language that places a prohibition on the FDA's use of funds involving the genetic modification of a human embryo. The Committee continues to support a wide range of innovations in biomedical research, but will do so in a fashion that reflects well-established scientific and ethical principles."

H.R. Rep. No. 114–205, at 69 (2015).
21. NATIONAL ACADEMY OF SCIENCES & NATIONAL ACADEMY OF MEDICINE, HUMAN GENOME EDITING: SCIENCE, ETHICS, AND GOVERNANCE (2017) [hereinafter NAS REPORT].
22. 115 Pub. L. No. 31, § 736, 131 Stat. 135, 173.
23. NAS REPORT, *supra* note 21, at 146–47.

24. *Cf. Issues Raised by Human Cloning Research: Hearing Before the Subcomm. on Oversight and Investigations of the House Comm. on Energy and Commerce*, 107th Cong., Serial No. 107-5, 78, 90 (2001) (statement of Dr. Kathryn C. Zoon, Director, Center for Biologics Evaluation and Research, FDA) (explaining that FDA could not halt a human cloning experiment that had been proven safe for the child and mother).
25. MERRILL & ROSE, *supra* note 4, at 138.
26. LISA HEINZERLING, The FDA's Plan B Fiasco: Lessons for Administrative Law, 102 GEO. L.J. 927, 942–43 (2014).
27. *See id.* at 944–50 (describing the tedious course of the litigation).
28. Legal experts have questioned whether the FDA has statutory jurisdiction over other advanced reproductive technologies. *See, e.g.*, MACINTOSH, BRAVE NEW EUGENICS, *supra* note 15, at 273–74 (arguing that FDA has no authority to control ooplasm transfer); ELIZABETH C. PRICE, Does the FDA Have Authority to Regulate Human Cloning? 11 HARV. J.L. & TECH. 619, 629–41 (1998) (questioning the agency's authority to regulate human cloning).
29. NIH STATEMENT, *supra* note 11.
30. *Id.*
31. KERRY LYNN MACINTOSH, Psychological Essentialism and Opposition to Human Embryonic Stem Cell Research, 18 J. TECH. L. & POLICY 229 (2013), 252. For a recent iteration of the amendment, see H.R. 2029, § 508, 114th Cong. (2015), which provides in full:

> "(a) None of the funds made available in this Act may be used for –
> (1) the creation of a human embryo or embryos for research purposes; or
> (2) research in which a human embryo or embryos are destroyed, discarded, or knowingly subjected to risk of injury or death greater than that allowed for research on fetuses in utero under 45 CFR 46.204(b) and § 498(b) of the Public Health Service Act." (42 U.S.C. 289g(b))
> (b) For purposes of this section, the term "human embryo or embryos" includes any organism, not protected as a human subject under 45 CFR 46 as of the date of the enactment of this Act, that is derived by fertilization, parthenogenesis, cloning, or any other means from one or more human gametes or human diploid cells."

32. Email from Dr. Kathryn Harris, Senior Outreach and Education Specialist, National Institutes of Health, to Kerry Lynn Macintosh, Professor of Law, Santa Clara University School of Law (February 4, 2016) (on file with author). To facilitate cost segregation, research institutions sometimes establish separate facilities for work that is not supported by NIH. *Id.*
33. NATIONAL INSTITUTES OF HEALTH, NIH GUIDELINES FOR RESEARCH INVOLVING RECOMBINANT OR SYNTHETIC NUCLEIC ACID MOLECULES (NIH GUIDELINES) (April 2016), *available at* http://osp.od.nih.gov/sites/default/files/resources/NIH_Guidelines.pdf (last visited June 10, 2017) [hereinafter NIH GUIDELINES].

34. The NIH GUIDELINES define recombinant and synthetic nucleic acids this way:

> "(i) molecules that a) are constructed by joining nucleic acid molecules and b) that can replicate in a living cell, i.e., recombinant nucleic acids;
> (ii) nucleic acid molecules that are chemically or by other means synthesized or amplified, including those that are chemically or otherwise modified but can base pair with naturally occurring nucleic acid molecules, i.e., synthetic nucleic acids, or
> (iii) molecules that result from the replication of those described in (i) or (ii) above."

Id. § I-B at 9.
35. Id. § I-A-1-a at 9.
36. Id. Appendix M at 100.
37. REPRODUCTION AND RESPONSIBILITY, *supra* note 2, at 115.
38. To explain, the NIH GUIDELINES apply to "[r]esearch that is conducted at or sponsored by an institution that receives any support for recombinant or synthetic nucleic acid molecule research from NIH." NIH GUIDELINES, *supra* note 33, § I-C-1-a-(1) at 10. In other words, if a research institution accepts NIH funding for some recombinant or synthetic nucleic acid molecule research, all projects of that type conducted at the institution must comply with the GUIDELINES. Id. § I-D-2 at 11. Because the RAC will not consider proposals in which edited gametes are put to reproductive use, compliance is impossible.
39. Email from Dr. Kathryn Harris, Senior Outreach and Education Specialist, National Institutes of Health, to Thomas DeGuzman, Librarian, Santa Clara University School of Law (Dec. 16, 2015 (on file with author).
40. NAS REPORT, *supra* note 21, at 31.
41. BOARD OF EDITORS, Why Embryos Should Not Be Off-Limits, 313 SCI. AM. 10 (July 2015).
42. Originally, the Common Rule revisions were to take effect on January 19, 2018. However, the Department of Health and Human Services and other departments and agencies that apply the Common Rule extended the effective date and general compliance date to July 19, 2018. Federal Policy for the Protection of Human Subjects: Delay of the Revisions to the Federal Policy for the Protection of Human Subjects, 83 FED. REG. 2885 (January 22, 2018). These entities have indicated that they plan to propose a further extension to January 21, 2019. *Id.* at 2886. Accordingly, this chapter cites sections as presented in the final rule that published the Common Rule revisions: Federal Policy for the Protection of Human Subjects, 82 FED. REG. 7149 (January 19, 2017) [hereinafter FEDERAL POLICY].
43. FEDERAL POLICY *supra* note 42 at 7149 (naming the agencies).
44. The scope provision states in relevant section: "[T]his policy applies to all research involving human subjects conducted, supported or otherwise subject to regulation by any Federal department or agency which takes appropriate

administrative action to make the policy applicable to such research." 45 C.F.R. § 46.101(a) (2019).
45. Id. § 46.103(a).
46. FEDERAL POLICY, supra note 42, at 7181.
47. 45 C.F.R. § 46.109(a).
48. Id. § 46.111(a).
49. Id. § 46.111(a)(1).
50. Id. § 46.111(a)(2).
51. Id. §§ 46.111(a)(4), 46.116(a)(1).
52. Id. § 46.116(b)(2).
53. Id. § 46.116(b)(3).
54. 45 C.F.R. § 46.102(e)(1).
55. REPRODUCTION AND RESPONSIBILITY, supra note 2, at 134.
56. The Common Rule includes definitions of intervention and interaction:

> "Intervention includes both physical procedures by which information or biospecimens are gathered (e.g., venipuncture) and manipulations of the subject or the subject's environment that are performed for research purposes.
> Interaction includes communication or interpersonal contact between investigator and subject."

45 C.F.R. § 46.102(e)(2), (3).

57. The Common Rule includes definitions of private information and identifiable private information:

> "Private information includes information about behavior that occurs in a context in which an individual can reasonably expect that no observation or recording is taking place, and information which has been provided for specific purposes by an individual and which the individual can reasonably expect will not be made public (for example, a medical record).
> Identifiable private information is information for which the identity of the subject is or may readily be ascertained by the investigator or associated with the information."

Id. § 46.102(e)(4), (5).

58. The Common Rule also defines identifiable biospecimen: "An identifiable biospecimen is a biospecimen for which the identity of the subject is or may be readily ascertained by the investigator or associated with the biospecimen." Id. § 46.102(e)(6).
59. Id. § 46.116(b)(2). Under the right circumstances, researchers may benefit from broad consent. To illustrate, suppose a married couple create a panel of IVF embryos. After their family is complete, they wish to donate the embryos to research. Such research would be considered secondary because the embryos were created for another, primary activity: procreation. FEDERAL POLICY, supra note 42, at 7191. The donors are human subjects if the embryos are linked

to their personal information and qualify as identifiable biospecimens. 45 C.F.R. § 46.102(e)(1). However, if the donors choose, they can provide broad consent to storage, maintenance, and potential secondary research use of their embryos, enabling these functions to be undertaken with only limited IRB review. Id. at §§ 46.104(d)(7)–(8), 46.116(d). Thereafter, if a researcher asks to use the embryos, the IRB will check to ensure that the proposed project is within the scope of the broad consent and that the privacy of subjects and confidentiality of the data is protected. Id. at §§ 46.104(d)(8), 46.111(a)(7).

60. 45 C.F.R. § 46.111(a)(7).
61. Id. § 46.111(a)(2).
62. See SHERMAN J. SILBER, HOW TO GET PREGNANT 174–75, 201–2, 422 (Little, Brown & Co. rev. ed. September 2005, paperback ed. August 2007; originally published 1991).
63. For an account of OHSS and treatment options, see PRACTICE COMMITTEE OF THE AMERICAN SOCIETY OF REPRODUCTIVE MEDICINE, Prevention and Treatment of Moderate and Severe Ovarian Hyperstimulation Syndrome: A Guideline, 106 FERT. & STER. 1634 (2016).
64. HONG MA ET AL., Correction of a Pathogenic Gene Mutation in Human Embryos, 548 NATURE 413 (2017).
65. In embryo transfer, a doctor introduces a catheter through the cervix and into the uterus. The embryo is transferred via this catheter. SILBER, supra note 63, at 234. Embryo transfer can be construed as a manipulation of the recipient for research purposes. See 45 C.F.R. § 46.102(e)(2) (defining intervention).
66. But cf. REBECCA DRESSER, Genetic Modification of Preimplantation Embryos: Toward Adequate Human Research Policies, 82 MILBANK Q. 195, 206 (2004) (arguing that HGM risks are not reasonable because couple who wish to raise a healthy child can adopt or use donor gametes).
67. 45 C.F.R. § 46.116(b)(2), (3).
68. Additional Protections for Pregnant Women, Human Fetuses and Neonates Involved in Research, 45 C.F.R. §§ 46.201–207 (West, Westlaw through June 8, 2017). These regulations also apply to research involving "neonates of uncertain viability, or nonviable neonates." Id. § 46.201(a).
69. Id. § 46.204(a).
70. Id. § 46.204(b).
71. Id. § 46.204(d). If the research directly benefits only the fetus, both its father and mother must give informed consent. Id. § 46.204(e).
72. Id. § 46.204(f).
73. Id. § 46.202(c).
74. Additional Protections for Children Involved as Subjects in Research, 45 C.F.R. §§ 46.401–409 (West, Westlaw through June 8, 2017).
75. Id. § 46.404.
76. Id. § 46.405.
77. Id. §§ 46.404, 46.405(c), 46.408(b).
78. Id. § 46.408(a).

79. "Minimal risk" includes the sort of harm or discomfort that one endures during routine physical or psychological exams and tests. *See id.* § 46.402 (adopting Common Rule definition of minimal risk in 45 C.F.R. § 46.102).
80. The definition of research provides in relevant section: "*Research* means a systematic investigation, including research development, testing and evaluation, designed to develop or contribute to generalizable knowledge." 45 C.F.R. § 46.102(l).
81. *See* 45 C.F.R. § 46.202 and 46.402 (adopting definitions found in § 46.102 except as otherwise noted).
82. REPRODUCTION AND RESPONSIBILITY, *supra* note 2, at 133, footnote.
83. *Id.* at 110. Although it is not one of the fifty states, Puerto Rico has a law that addresses alterations of the human genome, presumably including HGM: "Any person who uses technology to alter the human genome for purposes other than diagnosis, treatment or scientific research in the field of human biology, particularly genetics or medicine shall incur a second degree felony." P.R. LAWS ANN. tit. 33, § 4743 (West, Westlaw through the 2010 Legis. Sess. and acts from 2011 to September 2016).
84. KERRY LYNN MACINTOSH, *Human Cloning: Four Fallacies and Their Legal Consequences* 209 (2013).
85. LA. REV. STAT. ANN. § 9:122 (West, Westlaw through 2017 First Extra. Sess.).
86. *See* MICH. COMP. LAWS ANN. § 333.2685 (West, Westlaw through P.A. 2017, No. 42 of the 2017 Reg. Sess., 99th Legislature) (prohibiting nontherapeutic research that substantially jeopardizes life or health of embryo); MINN. STAT ANN. §§ 145.421-.422 (West, Westlaw through 2017 Reg. Sess. through May 21, 2017) (barring research on human conceptus except where research is harmless); S.D. CODIFIED LAWS §§ 34-14-16 to -20 (West, Westlaw through 2017 Reg. Sess., laws through April 13, 2017) (banning nontherapeutic research that destroys or poses substantial risk of injury or death to embryo).
87. FLA. STAT. ANN. § 390.0111(6) (West, Westlaw through First Reg. Sess. of the 25th Legislature, chapters through May 25, 2017) (prohibiting fetal experimentation); ME. REV. STAT. tit. 22, § 1593 (West, Westlaw through Chap. 78 of 2017 First Reg. Sess. of the 128th Legislature) (barring fetal experimentation); N.M. STAT. ANN. § 24-9A-3 (West, Westlaw through First Reg. Sess. and Special Sess. of 53rd Legislature, 2017) (prohibiting fetal research except to help fetus or where risk is insignificant); N.D. CENT. CODE ANN. § 14–02.2–01.1 (West, Westlaw through 2017 Reg. Sess. of the 65th Legislative Assembly through May 3, 2017) (prohibiting fetal experimentation unless it does not substantially jeopardize fetal life or health); 18 PA. CONS. STAT. ANN. § 3216(a) (West, Westlaw through 2017 Regular Session Act 2) (banning nontherapeutic experimentation upon unborn child); R.I. GEN. LAWS ANN. § 11–54-1(a) (West, Westlaw through Chapter 2 of the January 2017 Sess.) (prohibiting fetal research except studies that do not pose substantial risk to fetal health or life). Another state, Massachusetts, prohibits fetal research except where the work does not pose a substantial risk to fetal life or health;

however, preimplantation embryos obtained in compliance with state law are not protected. MASS. GEN. LAWS ANN. Ch. 112, § 12J(a)I (West, Westlaw through Chap. 9 of the 2017 First Annual Sess.).

88. See LORI B. ANDREWS, State Regulation of Embryo Stem Cell Research, in NATIONAL BIOETHICS ADVISORY COMMISSION, ETHICAL ISSUES IN HUMAN STEM CELL RESEARCH, Vol. II, COMMISSIONED PAPERS, A-4, A-5 (2000) (asserting state laws that protect "fetus" are taken to include any product of conception). The New Mexico and Rhode Island statutes define "fetus" to include product of conception or embryo, respectively. N.M. STAT. ANN. § 24-9A-1-G (West, Westlaw through First Reg. Sess. and Special Sess. of 53rd Legislature, 2017); R.I. GEN. LAWS ANN. § 11–54-1(f) (West, Westlaw through Chap. 2 of the January 2017 Sess.).

89. See ANDREWS, supra note 88, at A-5 (claiming that Maine, Michigan, Rhode Island make it illegal to give an embryo away for research); S.D. CODIFIED LAWS §§ 34–14-17 (West, Westlaw through 2017 Reg. Sess., laws through April 13, 2017) (providing that no one can knowingly transfer a human embryo to nontherapeutic research). Andrews also names North Dakota as a place where an embryo cannot be given away for research; but the statute she cites in support of this proposition applies only to dead or aborted embryos and fetuses. N.D. CENT. CODE ANN. § 14-02.2-02(4) (West, Westlaw through 2017 Reg. Sess. of the 65th Legislative Assembly through May 3, 2017).

90. MASS. GEN. LAWS ANN. Ch. 111L, § 89(b) (West, Westlaw through Ch. 31 of the 2017 1st Annual Sess.).

91. Id. § 89(e).

92. ARIZ. REV. STAT. ANN. §§ 36–2311.1, 36–2313 (West, Westlaw through First Reg. Sess. of the 53rd Legislature, legislation through May 3, 2017).

93. S.D. CODIFIED LAWS §§ 34–14-18 (West, Westlaw through 2017 Reg. Sess., laws through April 13, 2017).

94. LA. REV. STAT. ANN. § 9:122 (West, Westlaw through 2017 First Extra. Sess.).

95. 18 PA. CONS. STAT. ANN. § 3216(c) (West, Westlaw through 2017 Reg. Sess. Act 2); S.D. CODIFIED LAWS §§ 34–14-19 (West, Westlaw through 2017 Reg. Sess., laws through April 13, 2017).

96. New Mexico also exempts IVF but specifies that it must be done to treat infertility. N.M. STAT. ANN. § 24-9A-1-D (West, Westlaw through First Reg. Sess. and Special Sess. of 53rd Legislature, 2017).

97. See LIFCHEZ V. HARTIGAN, 735 F. Supp. 1361, 1376–77 (N.D. Ill. 1990) (Illinois statute against experimentation on fetuses held unconstitutionally vague because it did not define experimentation), aff'd, 914 F.2d 260 (7th Cir. 1990) (unpublished opinion).

98. See FLA. STAT. ANN. § 390.0111(6) (West, Westlaw through First Reg. Sess. of the 25th Legislature, chaps. through May 25, 2017) (allowing work needed to protect or preserve fetal life and health); MICH. COMP. LAWS ANN. § 333.2686 (West, Westlaw through P.A. 2017, No. 42 of the 2017 Reg. Sess., 99th Legislature) (permitting procedures intended to improve health of embryo);

MINN. STAT ANN. §§ 145.422 (West, Westlaw through 2017 Reg. Sess. through May 21, 2017) (permitting use of human conceptus to protect its life or health); N.D. CENT. CODE ANN. § 14–02.2–01.3 (West, Westlaw through 2017 Reg. Sess. of the 65th Legislative Assembly through May 3, 2017) (allowing procedures to preserve fetal life or health); 18 PA. CONS. STAT. ANN. § 3216(a) (West, Westlaw through 2017 Reg. Sess. Act 2) (permitting experimentation intended to preserve life or health of child); R.I. GEN. LAWS ANN. § 11–54-1(b) (West, Westlaw through Chap. 2 of the January 2017 Sess.) (allowing procedures to preserve fetal life or health); S.D. CODIFIED LAWS §§ 34-14-19 (West, Westlaw through 2017 Reg. Sess., laws through April 13, 2017) (allowing work to preserve life and health of embryo).

99. MACINTOSH, FOUR FALLACIES, *supra* note 84, at 185–86. Rhode Island once had a law against reproductive cloning, but the law had a sunset clause and lapsed on July 7, 2017. R.I. GEN. LAWS ANN. §§ 23–16.4–2, 23–16-4–4 (West, Westlaw statutes and Constitution current through Chapter 37 as of July 15, 2017).
100. ARIZ. REV. STAT. ANN. § 36–2312.A (West, Westlaw through First Reg. Sess. of the 53rd Legislature, legislation through May 3, 2017).
101. *Id.* § 36–2312.D.
102. 410 ILL. COMP. STAT. ANN. 110/40 (West, Westlaw through P.A. 99–938 of the 2016 Reg. Sess.).
103. *Id.*
104. MO. ANN. STAT., CONST. OF 1945, art. III, § 38(d).2(1) (West, Westlaw through November 8, 2016 election).
105. *Id.* § 38(d).6(2).
106. ARIZ. REV. STAT. ANN. § 36–2312.B.1 (West, Westlaw through First Reg. Sess. of the 53rd Legislature, legislation through May 3, 2017); LA. REV. STAT. ANN. § 14:89.6.A(1) (West, Westlaw through 2017 First Extra. Sess.).
107. For a detailed analysis of the Arizona and Louisiana laws, including a list of the various types of human-animal hybrids, see KERRY LYNN MACINTOSH, Chimeras, Hybrids, and Cybrids: How Essentialism Distorts the Law and Stymies Scientific Research, 47 ARIZ. ST. L.J. 183 (2015).
108. ARIZ. REV. STAT. ANN. § 36–2311.2(a) (West, Westlaw through First Reg. Sess. of the 53rd Legislature, legislation through May 3, 2017); *accord* LA. REV. STAT. ANN. § 14:89.6.D(1)(a) (West, Westlaw through 2017 First Extra. Sess.).
109. LIANG ET AL., *supra* note 10, at 363.
110. *See, e.g.,* BERND ZETSCHE ET AL., Cpf1 Is a Single RNA-Guided Endonuclease of a Class 2 CRISPR-Cas System, 163 CELL 1, 2 (2015) (discussing a new molecular editing tool that uses the Cpf1 enzyme found in two other types of bacteria).
111. *See* Melissa L. Kelley ET AL., Versatility of Chemically Synthesized Guide RNAs for CRISPR-Cas9 Genome Editing, 233 J. BIOTECH. 74 (2016) (explaining that chemically synthesized guide RNAs used with DNA-free Cas9 have fewer off-target effects).

9

Future Laws and Regulations

As Chapter 8 explained, human germline modification (HGM) is generally legal in the United States so long as it is limited to research in the laboratory. However, some state laws that prohibit embryo research, human cloning, or human-animal hybrids may extend to HGM for research.

By contrast, HGM cannot be used to make babies in the United States. The Food and Drug Administration (FDA) claims authority to regulate uses of the technology in humans, but Congress has temporarily suspended the ability of that agency to acknowledge receipt of applications to conduct clinical trials in which modified gametes or embryos are transferred to a woman. In effect, Congress has placed a moratorium on HGM for reproduction.

Thus, a legal regime for HGM in the United States has begun to emerge. Scientists may edit human gametes and human embryos for research in most states but may not transfer those gametes or embryos to women for gestation. This regime has certain advantages. Basic research on human gametes and embryos can add to our store of scientific knowledge about human reproduction. Meanwhile, scientists, bioethicists, and others can debate the scientific and ethical implications of modifying babies with the aid of HGM.[1]

However, this legal regime is inherently unstable. CRISPR/Cas9 and other molecular editing tools are very new, and the public knows little about them. As science advances, and public awareness grows, willingness to tolerate HGM may weaken. Moreover, if modified babies are born in foreign nations, the media, public, and politicians are sure to notice.

No one can predict the precise contours of future laws enacted in response to such events. However, it is possible to describe some possibilities. This chapter considers alternative legal strategies that the US Congress or state legislatures may pursue in the future.

A FEDERAL LAW

Analysis begins with federal law. This section argues that Congress has four available alternatives. First, it can enact a total ban on HGM that reaches research as well as reproduction. Second, it can pass a ban that permits research but prohibits HGM for reproduction. Third, it can restrict HGM for reproduction but create exceptions for therapeutic uses, such as correction of genetic mutations. Fourth, it can lift the current moratorium and allow the FDA to regulate HGM for reproduction. For each option, this section also considers the likelihood of adoption.

1 Total Ban

A total ban on HGM is the most drastic option. It bars scientists from editing human gametes or embryos, even if their only purpose is to conduct research. It also makes it illegal for doctors and lab technicians to edit human gametes or embryos for use in human reproduction.

Under this approach, scientists can still apply the CRISPR/Cas9 tool to any human cell other than a gamete or fertilized egg, inside or outside the body. Two theoretical examples illustrate the possibilities. First, suppose a man has a genetic mutation that causes liver disease. A scientist can apply the tool directly to that man's body to eliminate the mutation and substitute a functional DNA sequence.[2] Second, suppose a woman has a weak heart. A scientist can derive induced pluripotent stem cells (iPSCs) from her skin cells, use the tool to add a heart-strengthening DNA sequence, and differentiate the modified iPSCs into cardiac muscle cells for transplant back into the woman.[3] These and other therapeutic interventions can be pursued without involving the human germline.

a) Politics

In assessing the politics of a total ban on HGM, congressional reaction to human cloning provides a useful analogy. To perform human cloning, a scientist selects a somatic cell from a donor and joins it or its nucleus to an enucleated egg. He then applies chemicals or electricity to prod the egg to develop into an embryo.[4] Researchers can derive stem cells from cloned human embryos for use in research or medicine.[5] In theory, human cloning can also be used for procreation. Some predict it will emerge as an alternative fertility treatment for men and women who cannot produce viable gametes.[6] However, at this time there is no credible evidence that babies have been cloned anywhere in the world.[7]

Congress has repeatedly tried to ban human cloning to no avail. Liberal lawmakers believe that research on cloned human embryos has scientific value but want to ban the cloning of babies. Conservatives prefer a total ban on both research and reproductive cloning. A neutral observer might think a compromise is possible; after all, liberals and conservatives agree that babies should not be cloned. But pro-life conservatives have made it clear that they will never vote for a law that allows scientists to create and destroy cloned human embryos. As a result of this political impasse, there is no federal ban on human cloning.[8] The FDA has stepped into the breach, blocking clinical trials that could produce a cloned baby on safety grounds.[9]

As Chapter 8, Section A, recounted, HGM presently faces a similar federal legal regime. Scientists are free to edit and destroy human gametes and embryos in the lab but cannot use those gametes or embryos for reproductive purposes due to FDA regulation. Logically, congressional conservatives should prefer a total ban, which would protect human embryos against experimentation and death. Yet no proposal for a total ban has emerged to date.

In 2017, US scientists began to edit human embryos, and the media covered that development. Perhaps pro-life conservatives will soon introduce a bill to halt that research. They may even be able to persuade some on the left to join them. For example, while Congress was struggling to come to terms with human cloning, socialist Bernie Sanders was a member of the US House of Representatives. He repeatedly voted in favor of a draconian bill that would have banned all human cloning and sent scientists to prison for experimenting on cloned human embryos.[10] Interestingly, in a statement denouncing human cloning, Sanders also railed against eugenics and genetic engineering.[11]

One key question is whether liberals or moderates will fight to protect the right to conduct HGM for research, as they have fought to protect the right to clone human embryos for research. The answer is unclear because science has advanced since the human cloning debate began 20 years ago. Today a scientist can take a skin or other somatic cell from an existing person and derive iPSCs that match her DNA without using human eggs or creating human embryos.[12] When used in conjunction with this technology, the CRISPR/Cas9 tool opens up the possibility of creating designer stem cell lines without the need to alter human gametes or embryos.[13]

Nevertheless, liberals and moderates may oppose a total ban for three reasons. First, HGM may have other uses in research. For example, scientists are using the CRISPR/Cas9 tool to see if they can learn more about the genes that drive the development of human embryos.[14] Second, patient advocates who want babies to be born free of deadly genetic diseases will protest any attempt to curb research that could make HGM safe and effective for reproduction. Third, scientists benefit from an unstated assumption that there is freedom to conduct research in our culture. A total ban would challenge that assumption and perhaps encourage Congress to prohibit other unpopular areas of research.[15] The US Supreme Court has never held that there is a constitutional right to engage in scientific research,[16] so anyone who cherishes scientific freedom must be prepared to fight for it in the legislative arena.

2 Ban on HGM for Reproduction

Congress could also enact a law that permits scientists to modify human gametes and embryos for research purposes but prohibits the use of such altered gametes or embryos in human reproduction. This section describes this option as a ban on HGM for reproduction.

Congress has already blocked the FDA from receiving applications for clinical trials. It enacts appropriations bills annually, so it can impose this restriction year after year while drawing little notice from the public. But as the Introduction to this book discussed, scientists in other countries have begun to experiment on human embryos with disease prevention in mind. Once the technology is perfected, clinical trials in those countries may produce healthy children. Ultimately, foreign clinics may offer HGM services to paying customers. And if the FDA cannot even consider applications for clinical trials, some of the customers at those foreign clinics will be Americans.[17]

However, Congress has the power to "regulate commerce with foreign nations" under the Foreign Commerce Clause of the US Constitution.[18] If congressional intent is clear from the statutory language, a law can reach commercial acts that US citizens commit abroad.[19] Thus, if Congress wishes, it can enact a law that prohibits Americans from purchasing HGM services in foreign countries. Once such a law is in place, those who patronize offshore clinics can be arrested and charged with a crime when they return home.

To be sure, detecting violations will be a challenge. Under the Fourth Amendment to the US Constitution, people are protected against unreasonable searches and seizures. Where there is no individualized suspicion of wrongdoing, a search or seizure is usually considered unreasonable.[20] Thus, a program that tests all newborns for genetic modifications will probably be unconstitutional as well as impractical and unpopular.[21] However, a federal prosecutor may seek permission to test the DNA of a specific baby. To obtain such permission, he must have probable cause to believe that the parents utilized HGM services and show that the DNA sample is likely to yield evidence relevant to their guilt.[22]

Probable cause may arise in various ways. A woman may travel to a known haven for HGM services and return home pregnant or make admissions to friends who later turn her in. Parents can best avoid suspicion by hiding what they have done, but that strategy may have negative consequences for their children, as discussed in Chapter 10, Section C.5.

a) Politics

Suppose Congress decides that its moratorium is not sufficient and attempts to enact a ban on HGM for reproduction. The four objections are broad enough to appeal to both conservatives and liberals. To illustrate, consider the hubris objection. As Chapter 2 explained, this objection can be interpreted as a religious admonition or as a warning against violating nature. Conservatives may embrace the former meaning while liberals may prefer the latter. Either way, the result is a vote in favor of a ban on HGM for reproduction.

Before Congress votes, its members will want to know what their constituents think. According to a 2016 Harvard poll, 26 percent of respondents believe that HGM to reduce the chances that babies will be born with certain serious diseases should be legal.[23] Interestingly, those who are informed on the issue are twice as likely to approve as those who are uninformed.[24] Only 11 percent of those polled approve of editing genes to create babies with improved physical traits or intelligence. Eighty-three percent say such enhancements should be banned.[25]

At first glance, these poll results seem to support a ban on HGM for reproduction. However, the same poll reports that 44 percent of respondents believe that the federal government should fund research into techniques that could change the genes of the unborn and spare them from maladies such as cystic fibrosis, muscular dystrophy, and Huntington disease.[26] Those who are familiar with the issue are more likely to approve funding than those who are not.[27] Forty-four percent is not quite a majority, but these data suggest that the public is interested in, and may eventually embrace, therapeutic uses of HGM. Interestingly, a poll published one year later, and discussed in Section A.3 of this chapter, already indicates greater public support for therapeutic uses of HGM.

3 Ban on HGM for Reproduction with Exceptions

A third option is to restrict HGM for reproduction but create exceptions for therapeutic uses, such as correction of genetic mutations. Congress has two ways to institute this option. First, it can amend the annual appropriations bill to allow the FDA to receive applications for clinical trials, but only for specific modifications that yield verified therapeutic or medical benefits. Each year, it can survey the medical literature to identify new therapies that deserve to be added to the list of applications the agency can receive. When clinical trials succeed, the FDA will approve those modifications. Over time, some therapeutic modifications will become available to the public, but enhancing ones never will.

Alternatively, Congress can enact a new law that prohibits HGM for reproduction but exempts modifications that provide therapeutic or medical benefits. From a democratic point of view, this approach is preferable; it brings the distinction between therapies and enhancements out into the open and facilitates public debate. However, because scientists will develop new modifications over time, flexibility is important. Congress may choose to draft a broad exemption and designate the FDA (which already regulates HGM in humans) or another federal agency to issue regulations establishing and updating a list of modifications that fit within the exemption.

a) Politics

Lawmakers who favor a ban on HGM for reproduction with exceptions for therapeutic modifications face two obstacles. First, human beings tend to cling to the familiar and resist change.[28] The status quo is that HGM for reproduction is not allowed, so a proposal to create exceptions invites instinctive opposition. Second, opponents will raise a slippery slope argument, claiming that therapeutic modifications cannot be permitted without opening the door to enhancing ones.

However, recent developments indicate there may be support for this third option. In 2017, the National Academy of Sciences and National Academy of Medicine issued a report on human genome editing that included a discussion of HGM (NAS Report).[29] The report recommended that basic research on human gametes and embryos continue subject to existing regulations.[30] It suggested that clinical trials aimed at preventing a serious disease or condition might be acceptable if oversight was rigorous and reasonable alternatives were not available.[31] However, it advised regulators not to authorize clinical trials for other purposes, such as enhancement, at the present time.[32]

Also, according to a national poll published in 2017, 65 percent of respondents considered germline therapy to be acceptable. By contrast, only 26 percent thought germline enhancement was acceptable.[33] The 2017 poll demonstrates the enduring power of the therapy/enhancement distinction[34] and suggests the public may support a ban on HGM that exempts therapeutic modifications. Moreover, if other nations permit therapeutic modifications and healthy babies are born, the public may see those infants as living proof that HGM for reproduction can be compassionate and appropriate.

4 Leaving HGM to FDA Regulation (No Ban)

Finally, Congress can leave HGM to the FDA to regulate. All it need do is eliminate the provision in the annual appropriations bill that prevents the FDA from receiving IND applications. The agency will then receive applications and decide which clinical trials are safe enough to go forward. As discussed in Chapter 8, Section A.1, simple proposals aimed at correcting deadly genetic mutations will stand the greatest chance of success. Proposals to engineer complex traits such as memory or lifespan raise greater safety concerns and will be rejected, at least in the short term.

a) Politics

The FDA can probably be trusted to block clinical trials of unsafe or ineffective modifications. It has blocked trials of other advanced reproductive technologies in the past.[35] To be sure, some have questioned whether the FDA has the statutory authority to regulate reproductive technologies.[36] Nevertheless, the agency has forged ahead and will continue to regulate until a scientist or parent brings a court challenge and wins.

FDA regulation offers flexibility as an advantage. As molecular tools are perfected, and knowledge of genetics expands, the FDA can adjust its responses to proposed clinical trials and permit safe ones to proceed. By contrast, if Congress enacts a ban, and later decides to amend or repeal it, the process will be slow and may fail for lack of political consensus.

However, the FDA's power is limited in two ways. First, as Chapter 8, Section A.1, explained, the agency bases its decisions on safety and effectiveness. Once a modification is proven safe and effective in humans, the agency must approve it, even if it is an enhancing modification. Second, the FDA cannot control scientists and doctors in other nations. HGM clinics may sprout up abroad. Without a federal law to stop them, Americans may go offshore and come home pregnant or with a modified newborn. Thus, some legislators, particularly those who are adamantly opposed to enhancements, may conclude that FDA regulation alone is not an adequate solution.

B STATE LAW

Congress is not the only arbiter of what is legal in the United States. Each of the 50 states has its own legislature. States with a dominant political party may find it relatively easy to achieve consensus and adopt a ban on HGM.

Again, human cloning offers a useful analogy. Seven states ban all human cloning, while ten others ban only reproductive cloning.[37] In general, total bans are found in conservative states such as Arizona. Reproductive cloning bans are found in liberal states such as California, where biotechnology companies require a clear legal environment to support their research.[38] Still, after more than 20 years of anti-cloning hysteria, 33 states have no bans on human cloning.

A similar pattern may emerge in this new field. Legislators in conservative states may enact total bans to protect embryos from being harmed or killed in the course of HGM research. From a pro-life perspective, such legislation is necessary. The FDA can stop scientists from conducting clinical trials that result in the birth of modified babies, but it has no authority to halt destructive embryo research.

Meanwhile, legislators in liberal states may enact a ban that permits HGM for research but not reproduction. In doing so, they can please biotech companies that need a stable legal regime to support their research. They can also assuage constituent concerns about the prospect of superbabies. However, public support for therapeutic modifications of HGM may grow as the technology improves. Thus, it is also possible that legislators will enact a more compassionate law that prohibits HGM for reproduction but carves out exceptions for established therapeutic modifications.

Finally, if experience with human cloning is at all predictive, many states will not enact laws to regulate HGM. Legislators in conservative states may choose to rely on existing laws barring research that destroys or harms human embryos.[39] Their counterparts in liberal states may depend on FDA regulation to halt HGM for reproduction.

C SUMMARY

In the United States, scientists can freely edit human gametes and human embryos, except in states with laws that impinge indirectly upon such work. However, they cannot use modified gametes and embryos to make babies. As Chapter 8 stated, Congress has forbidden the FDA to acknowledge receipt of applications to conduct clinical trials in which modified gametes or embryos are transferred to a woman, thereby rendering it impossible to conduct such trials.

This legal regime may not last for long. Multiple factors threaten to destabilize it: pro-life opposition to experimentation on human embryos; the four objections, with their focus on the bad consequences of HGM; limits on FDA authority; and the eventual birth of healthy babies in foreign countries, which may encourage the American public to approve therapeutic uses of HGM.

This chapter has presented four possible options for federal law. First, Congress can enact a total ban on HGM. Second, Congress can enact a ban that permits HGM for research but prohibits HGM for reproduction. Third, Congress can block most HGM for reproduction but carve out exceptions for specified therapeutic modifications. Fourth, Congress can lift its current restrictions on the FDA and permit the agency to review applications for clinical trials. This last option opens the door to enhancements that are safe and effective. Which option Congress chooses will depend on the factors enumerated earlier and the fortunes of the major political parties.

If state legislatures jump into the fray, a diverse array of state laws will emerge. This chapter predicts total bans in some conservative states, bans on reproduction with or without exceptions in some liberal states, and no bans in the majority of states.

Notes

1. DAVID BALTIMORE ET AL., A Prudent Path Forward for Genomic Engineering and Germline Gene Modification, 348 SCIENCE 36 (2015).
2. Id. at 37 (citing an experiment in which scientists applied the CRISPR/Cas9 tool to mice to correct a genetic mutation that causes liver disease).
3. Cf. id. (suggesting that scientists could use the CRISPR/Cas9 tool to alter DNA sequences in embryonic stem cells before turning them into cardiomyocytes).
4. See KERRY LYNN MACINTOSH, Human Cloning: Four Fallacies and Their Legal Consequences 1–3, 11–15 (2013) (describing Dolly experiment and later variations on that experiment) [hereinafter MACINTOSH, HUMAN CLONING].
5. MASAHITO TACHIBANA ET AL., Human Embryonic Stem Cells Derived by Somatic Cell Nuclear Transfer, 153 CELL 1 (2013). For example, if the somatic cell donor has a disease, drugs aimed at that disease can be tested on the stem cells derived from the cloned embryo. Perhaps, scientists will one day be able to differentiate the stem cells into transplantable tissues that match the donor's DNA. See THE PRESIDENT'S COUNCIL ON BIOETHICS, Human Cloning

6. *E.g.*, MARK D. EIBERT, Human Cloning: Myths, Medical Benefits and Constitutional Rights, 53 HASTINGS L.J. 1097 (2002).
7. MACINTOSH, HUMAN CLONING, *supra* note 4, at 44.
8. *Id.* at 181–85.
9. *Id.* at 179–80.
10. In the Senate, Clinton and Sanders Didn't Always Agree, U.S. NEWS & WORLD REPORT (April 2, 2016), www.usnews.com/news/politics/articles/2016-04-02/clinton-sanders-had-opposing-views-on-biomedical-research.
11. As Representative Sanders stated: "While I support stem cell research, the cloning of a human being for any purpose raises the deepest and most profound ethical and moral questions: questions about the sanctity or the uniqueness of each human person; questions about the evil of eugenics and genetic engineering in humans; and, equally important, questions about the ownership and use of cloned humans by an unregulated corporate biotechnology industry motivated almost exclusively by their quest for venture capital, short-term profits, and higher stock prices." 149 CONG. REC. H. 1397, 1414 (2003).
12. MACINTOSH, HUMAN CLONING, *supra* note 4, at 201–2.
13. In a recent proof-of-principle experiment, scientists harvested skin cells from a patient with retinitis pigmentosa, converted them to iPSCs, and applied CRISPR/Cas9 to the stem cells in an effort to repair the point mutation that causes the disease. The mutation was corrected in 13 percent of the gene copies. ALEXANDER G. BASSUK ET AL., Precision Medicine: Genetic Repair of Retinitis Pigmentosa in Patient-Derived Stem Cells, 6 SCIENTIFIC REPORTS (2016), doi: 10.1038/srep19969.
14. *See* ANNEESA AMJAD, Swedish Scientist Edits Genomes of Healthy Human Embryos, 870 BIONEWS (September 26, 2016), www.bionews.org.uk/page_704671.asp (discussing Swedish scientist Fredrik Lanner, who edits out genes in healthy human embryos in order to observe the effect on development).
15. *Cf.* JOHN CHARLES KUNICH, THE NAKED CLONE 107 (2003) (arguing that a ban on research cloning could set a precedent affecting other worthy avenues of scientific inquiry).
16. *Id.* at 94–95.
17. NATIONAL ACADEMY OF SCIENCES & NATIONAL ACADEMY OF MEDICINE, HUMAN GENOME EDITING: SCIENCE, ETHICS, AND GOVERNANCE 104 (2017) [hereinafter NAS REPORT].
18. U.S. CONST. art. 1, § 8, cl. 3.
19. For example, the Ninth Circuit upheld the conviction of Michael Clark, an American citizen who traveled to Cambodia and purchased sex from minors there in violation of the Prosecutorial Remedies and Other Tools to End the Exploitation of Children Today (PROTECT) Act. UNITED STATES V. CLARK, 435 F.3d 1100 (9th Cir. 2006), cert. denied, 127 S. Ct.

2029 (2007). Because Clark was a citizen, the court reasoned, there was a nexus between his conduct and the United States, and he could be prosecuted for extraterritorial acts without violating the Due Process Clause of the Fifth Amendment. *Id.* at 1108. Furthermore, the court stated, the statute under which Clark was convicted bore a rational relationship to Congress's power under the Foreign Commerce Clause: it required both travel in foreign commerce and participation in a commercial sex act while abroad. *Id.* at 1114.

20. CITY OF INDIANAPOLIS V. EDMOND, 531 US 32, 37 (2000). The Supreme Court has recognized limited exceptions to this principle and has permitted random drug testing of student-athletes and certain public servants. *Id.*
21. This author has not found any opinions evaluating the constitutionality of programs that collect DNA from a segment of the population in the absence of any individualized suspicion of wrongdoing. *Cf.* MARYLAND V. KING, 133 S. Ct. 1958 (2013) (upholding state law authorizing collection of DNA from individuals arrested for serious crimes).
22. No case directly on point exists, in part because babies born through HGM do not yet exist. However, the case of COMMONWEALTH V. DRAHEIM is instructive. There, a woman was charged with the statutory rape of two teenage boys, each of whom was alleged to have sired a child by her. The trial court denied the Commonwealth's motions to compel saliva samples from defendant, her two children, and the teenage boys for the purpose of DNA testing. On appeal, the Supreme Judicial Court of Massachusetts addressed the constitutional rights of third parties who are not suspects. It reasoned that "the Commonwealth must show probable cause to believe a crime was committed, and that the sample will probably provide evidence relevant to the question of the defendant's guilt." 849 N.E.2d 823, 829 (Mass. 2006). The seriousness of the crime, significance of the evidence, and unavailability of less intrusive means of procuring the evidence were also factors to be considered. *Id.* The court vacated the trial court's orders and remanded for proceedings consistent with its opinion. *Id.*
23. HARVARD T.H. CHAN SCHOOL OF PUBLIC HEALTH, The Public and Genetic Editing, Testing, and Therapy 2 (January 2016), https://cdn1.sph.harvard.edu/wp-content/uploads/sites/94/2016/01/STAT-Harvard-Poll-Jan-2016-Genetic-Technology.pdf [hereinafter HARVARD POLL].
24. *See id.* (41 percent of those familiar with the issue approve of HGM performed to avoid disease; only 20 percent of those unfamiliar with the issue approve).
25. *Id.*
26. *Id.* at 3.
27. *See id.* (54 percent of those familiar with the issue support funds for research; only 39 percent of those unfamiliar with the issue support funds for research).
28. RONALD M. GREEN, BABIES BY DESIGN: THE ETHICS OF GENETIC CHOICE 8–9 (2007).
29. NAS REPORT, supra note 17.
30. *Id.* at 142.

31. *Id.* at 145–46. The NAS REPORT provides that clinical trials aimed at disease prevention should not occur unless regulatory mechanisms are in place to keep the technology from being used for other purposes. *Id.* at 146.
32. *Id.* at 147–48.
33. DIETRAM A. SCHEUFELE ET AL., U.S. Attitudes on Human Genome Editing, 357 SCIENCE 553 (2017). The polling data came from 1600 adults in the United States who responded to a YouGov survey conducted in December 2016 and January 2017.
34. *See id.* (explaining that survey respondents found the distinction between therapy and enhancement more salient than the distinction between somatic and germline interventions).
35. KERRY LYNN MACINTOSH, Brave New Eugenics: Regulating Assisted Reproductive Technologies in the Name of Better Babies, 257 U. ILL. J.L. TECH & POLICY 271–72 (2010).
36. *Id.* at 272–74.
37. MACINTOSH, HUMAN CLONING, *supra* note 4, at 185–86.
38. *Id.* at 186.
39. *Id.* at 209.

10

Prohibiting Human Germline Modification Harms Scientists and Science, Parents, Children, Foreigners, and Society

Federal law currently allows scientists to perform human germline modification (HGM) for research. However, the US Congress has placed a *de facto* moratorium on HGM for reproduction. Due to funding restrictions, the Food and Drug Administration (FDA) cannot acknowledge receipt of applications to conduct clinical trials in which modified gametes or embryos are used in reproduction. Moreover, as Chapter 8, Section A.1, discussed, even if Congress lifts this moratorium, the FDA will not allow clinical trials to proceed until it finds them to be safe for mothers and babies. Thus, it may seem as if the federal government has HGM for reproduction under control.

This appearance is deceptive, however. The FDA has no power to regulate HGM in foreign countries. Chinese scientists have corrected genetic mutations in viable human embryos[1] and have inserted a gene variant associated with resistance to HIV-1 infection into nonviable human embryos.[2] Eventually, they may learn how to help parents have children who are free of genetic disease and/or immune to viruses. Once HGM services are offered in China or elsewhere, Americans can travel to receive them.

Thus, although Congress could maintain its moratorium indefinitely, it may decide to pursue other legislative options. As Chapter 9 noted, Congress can enact a total ban that prohibits any modification of a human gamete or embryo. The ban will halt HGM for reproduction and also protect human embryos against experimentation. Alternatively, it can adopt a law that bans HGM for reproduction but leaves research alone. Finally, it can enact a law that bans HGM for reproduction but exempts specific therapeutic applications. No matter which option it selects, Congress will probably cite one or more of the four objections as rationales. It will make violations a crime and impose prison sentences or fines.[3]

This chapter examines the consequences of the existing moratorium and new bans Congress may enact in the future. It focuses on potential harms to scientists and science, parents, children, foreigners, and society. This chapter ends with a discussion of state bans on HGM and their effects.

A HARM TO SCIENTISTS AND SCIENCE

The Federal Food, Drug, and Cosmetic Act (FFDCA) makes it illegal to put a new drug into interstate commerce without FDA approval or exemption.[4] Similarly, the Public Health Services Act (PHSA) prohibits the introduction of a biological product into interstate commerce without a biologics license or exemption.[5] Thus, scientists who conduct clinical trials in defiance of the prevailing moratorium risk being charged with a crime. A first-time offense under the FFDCA draws a prison sentence of no more than one year and/or a fine of no more than $1000.[6] The PHSA punishes violations with a fine of no more than $500 and/or a prison sentence of no more than a year.[7]

Most scientists probably do not care about these penalties, which apply only to those who perform HGM for reproduction. However, they should worry that Congress may criminalize the modification of a human gamete or embryo. This part focuses on the harms a total ban could inflict on scientists and science.

CRISPR/Cas9 and other molecular editing tools can facilitate at least two areas of pure research that are unrelated to HGM for reproduction. First, scientists can switch key genes on and off in human embryos and observe the impact on embryonic development.[8] Second, in principle, stem cells derived from modified human embryos can be used to study genetic diseases or test drugs.[9] Under a total ban, such research will be illegal. Valuable knowledge may be lost.

Further, a total ban can harm science more generally. Today, scientists in the United States enjoy a remarkable freedom. For the most part, they can conduct whatever research they wish as long as they can obtain funding. To be sure, there are limits: the FDA will not permit anyone to clone human babies,[10] and some states outlaw embryo research, human cloning, and human-animal hybrid research, as discussed in Chapter 8, Section B. Still, laws that criminalize research are the exception and not the rule.

Most scientists are not lawyers. They do not realize that their freedom of inquiry rests on the shifting sands of American culture and not legal bedrock. The US Supreme Court has never held that there is a constitutional right to engage in scientific research.[11] Although some academics believe the First Amendment of the US Constitution supports such a right,[12] their theories have never been tested in the Supreme Court and may not hold up. Moreover, although scientific research may be a liberty protected under the Due Process Clause,[13] the Supreme Court is unlikely to designate this liberty as a fundamental one.[14] Thus, the rational basis standard of review will apply, meaning that a total ban may be held constitutional as long as it bears a rational relationship to a legitimate government interest.[15] For example, Congress can argue that a ban on research is a rational means of ensuring the technology is never perfected and put to reproductive use, which it condemns on the basis of the four objections.

To understand the threat to science, consider a hypothetical. After Congress enacts a total ban on HGM, a handful of researchers who wish to modify human gametes or embryos challenge the ban under the First and Fifth Amendments. They lose at trial and on appeal to an intermediate appellate court, so they petition for certiorari to the Supreme Court. The Court grants their petition. It reasons that the First Amendment does not safeguard scientific research. Moreover, although it concedes that scientific research is a liberty protected under the Fifth Amendment, it finds that the liberty is not fundamental. Therefore, it applies the lenient rational basis standard of review and upholds the ban.

The Court's decision is a precedent; thus, going forward, bans on other controversial fields of research are more likely to be upheld. Realizing this, scientists begin to avoid experiments that may offend the public out of fear that legislators will prohibit their work and ruin their careers. Scientific knowledge is lost, much of it unconnected to HGM.

Meanwhile, foreign scientists continue to perfect molecular editing tools and their HGM research opens up entire new fields. Inventions follow, and the patents go to foreign companies. Thanks to the total ban, the United States loses its place as a leader in biotechnological research and invention.

B HARM TO PARENTS

Federal law may also harm men and women who wish to become parents with the aid of HGM. This section covers three topics: infringement of procreative rights, relegation to foreign providers, and exposure to criminal penalties.

1 Procreative Liberty

The first injury that parents may suffer is to their constitutional rights. A detailed examination of this topic is beyond the scope of this book. However, this section will briefly discuss the threat that a ban on HGM for reproduction poses to procreative liberty.

Skinner v. Oklahoma[16] is the foundational case. There, a state law mandated the sterilization of persons convicted three times of certain felonies involving moral turpitude. The Supreme Court reasoned that sterilization deprived a person of a basic liberty: procreation. For that reason, it subjected the classification in the law to strict scrutiny.[17] Oklahoma did not prove that those singled out for sterilization had heritable traits that others who committed intrinsically similar crimes did not have. Therefore, the Court invalidated the law on equal protection grounds.[18]

Constitutional law experts view *Skinner* as the wellspring of the modern right of privacy that protects such personal decisions as the use of birth control.[19] Since it decided *Skinner*, the Supreme Court has not directly addressed the constitutionality of laws that impede procreation. However, its opinions on the right of privacy have asserted that there is a right to make personal decisions regarding procreation without unjustified governmental interference.[20] Relying on these *dicta*, a federal district court has held squarely that the right of privacy protects access to assisted reproductive technologies that are designed to achieve, rather than prevent, pregnancy.[21]

Generally, a law that places a significant burden on the right of privacy is subject to strict scrutiny.[22] Under that standard of review, the government must prove that a law is narrowly drawn to achieve a compelling governmental interest.[23] Speculative harms do not qualify as compelling.[24]

a) Illustration #1: Therapeutic Modification

Assuming the right of privacy includes the right to procreate, the next question is whether HGM qualifies as procreative. Law professor John Robertson argues that an activity is procreative if it promotes the traditional goal of having healthy children to rear.[25] Elimination of genetic mutations from gametes or embryos enables carriers to have healthy children.[26] Put to that use, HGM is indeed procreative, and a ban on it threatens constitutional rights.

Chapter 1, Section B.1, provides a hypothetical that can be used to illustrate this point. Suppose that all of Mary Smith's eggs contain a mutation that causes Huntington disease; thus, all of her embryos are affected. HGM is the only technology that can eliminate the genetic mutation and allow her to bear a child free of the disease. However, suppose further that Congress has banned HGM, either through its moratorium or a new law enacted in response to safety concerns and the four objections. Mary has three options: forgo a genetic child, bear a child who will inherit the disease, or (if not expressly prohibited) travel abroad to access HGM services. By restricting Mary to these undesirable options, the ban significantly burdens her privacy right and thus is subject to strict scrutiny.[27]

As long as HGM remains unperfected, the government can prove that its ban is necessary to achieve a compelling interest: that is, protecting mothers and children against an unsafe technology. However, scientists may soon learn to correct genetic mutations in gametes or embryos safely. Once healthy children are born abroad, the government will find it difficult to persuade a court that safety concerns are compelling and must justify its ban on other grounds.

As Part I of this book noted, the four objections and related concerns are weak when applied to therapeutic modifications. Correction of a genetic mutation is consistent with religious traditions of healing. It does not impair genetic diversity to any meaningful extent, nor does it constitute human manufacture. A child free of a genetic disorder meets parental expectations at birth and has more rather than less autonomy. Moreover, allegations that HGM leads to class divides, competitive pressure, democratic collapse, eugenics, ossification, genocide, and harm to future generations generally relate to enhancing modifications, not therapeutic ones.

Two remaining concerns are pertinent to therapeutic modifications. First, the government may argue that many people cannot afford HGM. Second, it may contend that HGM stigmatizes people who have genetic disorders. However, a court applying strict scrutiny may suspect that these arguments are pretexts. The government has not attempted to ban IVF, even though some cannot afford it. Nor has it outlawed the practice of discarding or aborting embryos and fetuses with genetic or chromosomal abnormalities, which is more stigmatizing than HGM as discussed in Chapter 5, Section B.3.

If the government has no strong reason to prevent therapeutic modifications, it may claim that it has a compelling interest in halting enhancing modifications. But even if it can identify such an interest (a point addressed later), its law must be narrowly tailored to achieve the interest. Prohibiting all reproductive uses of HGM goes much further than necessary. As detailed in Chapter 9, Section A.3, Congress can prohibit enhancing modifications while exempting therapeutic modifications.

The government may counter that it must ban all HGM for reproduction. Otherwise, doctors and technicians licensed to provide therapeutic modifications may secretly provide their patients with enhancing ones. However, this slippery slope argument is unpersuasive. Laws routinely distinguish between legal and illegal activities and punish those who indulge in the latter. Experts who provide therapeutic modifications have little incentive to risk their livelihoods and freedom by going too far. Thus, once therapeutic modifications become safe, Mary has a good argument that the ban is unconstitutional as applied to her and other carriers of genetic mutations.[28]

b) Illustration #2: Enhancing Modification

This section addresses enhancing modifications. Robertson argues that procreative liberty is not implicated unless parents refuse to reproduce without enhancing modifications. Even then, he reasons, because the goal of procreation is to have a healthy child, the right to procreate may not protect access to enhancing modifications.[29] Thus, whether a ban on HGM for enhancement infringes procreative liberty is uncertain, and alternative analyses are necessary.

The Chapter 1, Section C.2, hypothetical provides a framework for analysis. Suppose John and Mary Smith can conceive a healthy child through sex. However, they wish to add certain single nucleotide polymorphisms (SNPs) to their gametes to give their child improved memory and learning. Suppose further that Congress has banned HGM on the strength of safety issues, the four objections, and related concerns. John and Mary have no legal means of achieving their goal and will not reproduce.

On the one hand, if the right to procreate protects enhancement, the ban significantly burdens the Smiths' exercise of their right, and strict scrutiny applies. Presently, the government has a compelling interest in protecting mothers and children from an unsafe technology; however, if enhancing modifications can be perfected, safety concerns may dwindle. Moreover, under strict scrutiny, the government cannot simply allege that enhancing modifications are bad. It must *prove* that they impair genetic diversity, transform human reproduction into manufacture, deprive children of an open future, subject children to unreasonable parental expectations, stratify society, create access issues and competitive pressure, and/or lead to apocalyptic outcomes that harm future generations. Doing so will be difficult: as Part I of this book demonstrated, the four objections and related concerns are often inaccurate, exaggerated, or speculative, even when raised against enhancing modifications. Thus, if enhancing modifications become safe, the ban may be unconstitutional as applied to the Smiths.

On the other hand, if the right to procreate does *not* protect enhancement, and no other fundamental right is implicated, a court must uphold the ban if it is rationally related to a legitimate governmental interest.[30] A court will rule for the government if there is any possible basis for concluding that this test has been met.[31] Even if HGM is perfectly safe, the government may be able to derive legitimate interests from the four objections and related concerns. For example, Robertson suggests that worries about class divides or unreasonable parental expectations may provide a rational basis for a ban.[32] Thus, the ban will be upheld as constitutional.

Before moving on, this section offers a caveat. Parents who wish to enhance their children may be able to mount a successful constitutional challenge to a ban on alternative grounds. Although a full discussion of alternatives is beyond the scope of this book, one is worth noting: some commentators believe the fundamental right to rear a child as one sees fit includes genetic enhancement.[33]

2 Cross-border Reproductive Care

Laws that restrict access to assisted reproductive technologies and interfere with the right to procreate are nothing new. Some nations ban gamete donation or surrogacy outright. Others demand that gamete donors or surrogates provide their services for free, which decreases supply. Even when a country allows heterosexual married couples to access a technology, it may deny access to gay couples or singles, forcing them to travel to a country with fewer restrictions to get the care they need.[34] Such care is so common that a term has been coined to describe it: "cross-border reproductive care."[35] Most nations do not penalize citizens who obtain cross-border reproductive care.[36]

As Chapter 1 noted, HGM will often be conducted in the context of a cycle of in vitro fertilization (IVF). Chinese scientists have already begun to research therapeutic modifications that could help parents bear healthier babies. Enhancing modifications may take longer to perfect; but once a market for them exists, clinics willing to meet that demand will pop up around the world. If Congress refuses to lift its moratorium, or enacts a ban on HGM, it may drive parents to nations with more accommodating legal regimes. Although parents may be glad to have such options, international travel will add time, effort, and expense to their reproductive project. In addition, cross-border reproductive care may pose physical risks to them and their children if foreign medical facilities are substandard – a topic taken up again in Section C.1 of this chapter.

3 Prison Sentences, Fines, and Other Consequences

Finally, laws against HGM may subject parents to prison and fines. For example, if scientists conduct clinical trials in defiance of the existing moratorium, parents who participate can be charged with aiding and abetting and will face the same punishment if convicted.[37] They can also be charged with conspiracy, which is punished as a misdemeanor if the underlying offense is a misdemeanor.[38]

To be sure, few if any parents will be charged and convicted of these offenses because scientists will not conduct illicit trials. The risk to their careers and liberty is simply too great. However, as Chapter 9, Section A.2, noted, Congress can craft a ban that punishes US citizens who purchase HGM services abroad. Such a law poses a greater threat, because if HGM services are not available in the United States, parents will be tempted to pursue cross-border reproductive care in countries where HGM is legal. It seems likely that many will commit crimes without realizing it, and those who do will face severe penalties.[39] Those who pay fines will suffer financial hardship. Those who go to prison will be separated from their babies and lose their jobs. Once they are released, their criminal convictions will make it difficult to find new employment.

The type of modification may influence outcomes. Parents who commission therapeutic modifications may get off lightly. For example, if Mary Smith uses HGM to correct a genetic mutation in her eggs, prosecutors, jurors, and judges who have sought medical attention for their own sick children may relate to her plight. She may receive a favorable plea bargain, be acquitted,[40] or draw a lesser prison sentence or fine.

By contrast, parents who purchase enhancing modifications may be treated with hostility. If John and Mary Smith use HGM to give their child improved memory and learning, prosecutors, jurors, and judges may believe that the child has a competitive advantage in life and experience envy. As Chapter 7, Section A, explained, envy is associated with resentment and hostility. Yet, there are few opportunities in life to punish those whom we envy. Parents like the Smiths make perfect targets, for the violation of an accepted standard (the law) facilitates the transmutation of envy into righteous outrage. Tough charges, convictions, and sentences will bring emotional satisfaction and thus are virtually guaranteed.

C HARM TO CHILDREN

Lawmakers may believe that the moratorium and/or a permanent ban on HGM are necessary to prevent the birth of children with genetic modifications. However, in a world where cross-border reproductive care is a reality, such children will be born in any event. This section delineates the damage that laws against HGM will inflict on them. It addresses physical, familial, social, legal, and personal harms.

1 Physical Harm

Laws against HGM can lead to the birth of children with diseases or disabilities in two ways.

a) Standard Reproduction Poses a Risk

Recall Mary Smith, who carries a mutated gene that causes Huntington disease. All of her eggs, and thus all of her embryos, are affected. Once HGM becomes reasonably safe and effective, she could correct the mutation in her eggs. But if the technology is unavailable because Congress refuses to lift the moratorium or enacts a ban, she may reproduce through sex instead and bear a child who will grow up to suffer from Huntington disease.

b) Cross-border Reproductive Care Poses a Risk

Alternatively, suppose the Smiths become frustrated with their inability to access HGM in the United States. They travel to a foreign clinic, where technicians try to correct the mutation in Mary's eggs. Nine months later, Mary gives birth to a baby girl named Ariel. Tragically, Ariel has a serious birth defect because the clinic provided incompetent services. If Congress had allowed the FDA to receive applications for clinical trials, and the agency had rejected them due to safety concerns, the Smiths might have realized that cross-border reproductive care was risky and stayed home.

2 Loss of Parents and Financial Support

Laws against HGM can also harm children by depriving them of parents and financial support. As Section B.3 of this chapter noted, parents are unlikely to be lured into illicit clinical trials but may run afoul of a ban that extends to offshore activities.

To illustrate, suppose Congress enacts a new law that prohibits HGM for reproduction. The Smiths know of the law but never hear of a little-known provision that punishes those who purchase HGM services abroad. They travel to a nation where HGM is legal, and technicians correct the genetic mutation in Mary's eggs. Mary later gives birth to Ariel, who is healthy and free of Huntington disease. Mary foolishly confides in Ariel's pediatrician, who reports the Smiths to the Federal Bureau of Investigation. A federal prosecutor charges them with a crime. Following a trial, both are convicted of felonies and sent to prison.

Ariel is left without parents. If no relatives step forward to care for her, she may be sent to a foster home. When John and Mary complete their sentences and are released, they may regain custody of her. By then, however, her ability to bond with them may be impaired. Moreover, as convicted felons, John and Mary may find it difficult to obtain new jobs and support their daughter. In the end, Ariel suffers as much as or more than her parents do.

As speculative as this hypothetical may seem, it is grounded in hard realities. Some 3 million children in the United States have a parent who is either in prison or newly released from prison. When parents are lost to incarceration, children experience economic insecurity and familial dysfunction. A compromised upbringing may encourage them to commit crimes of their own.[41] Congress should ponder these facts before enacting any law that could send more parents to prison.

3 Stigma and Its Consequences

Laws against HGM can cause psychological harm to children born in defiance of them. To explain this point, this section addresses two types of stigma: social and legal.

Social psychologists use the term "stigma" to describe a mark that identifies a person as abnormal or less worthy than others. *Social stigma* is often linked to conditions such as race, religion, nationality, mental disorder, and physical abnormality.[42] Stereotypes play a key role in promoting stigma by degrading their targets.[43] Those who bear a social stigma may be unpopular and face discrimination in employment, housing, insurance, and other services.[44]

Legal stigma arises when a law marks a person or class as immoral or unworthy.[45] For example, in *Brown v. Board of Education*,[46] state laws separated blacks and whites in public education. The Supreme Court recognized that the laws harmed black children by branding them as inferior.[47] It concluded that the laws violated the Equal Protection Clause of the Fourteenth Amendment.[48] *Brown* stands as a powerful reminder that legal stigma can be actionable. In addition, once a person or class has been legally stigmatized, the public may feel emboldened to commit further acts of discrimination or violence.[49]

Will children of HGM face social and legal stigma? To assess the risks, a detailed analysis is required. The type of modification makes a difference, so this section will employ Chapter 1 hypotheticals to render the analysis concrete. The first hypothetical evaluates a therapeutic modification, and the second discusses an enhancing modification.

a) Illustration #1: Therapeutic Modification

Suppose John and Mary Smith use HGM to correct a genetic mutation in Mary's eggs. When their daughter Ariel is born, she is free of Huntington disease. Two marks distinguish Ariel from other people: her mode of conception and the indelible edits on her genome. These marks will not be obvious to casual observers but may be revealed through genetic testing or disclosures.

Some may wonder if the Smiths have crossed divine and natural boundaries or engaged in human manufacture. However, upon examination, such claims founder. To summarize the analysis from Chapter 2, Sections A and B, correction of a genetic mutation is consistent with religious traditions of healing and does not threaten genetic diversity. Moreover, as Chapter 3, Section C.1, explained, correction of a genetic mutation does not transform human reproduction into manufacture, deprive a child of an open future, or subject her to undue parental pressure. Because the hubris and manufacture objections and related concerns are weak in this context, the stereotypes listed in Chapters 2 and 3 will be as well. Few people will view Ariel as evil, unnatural, artifact-like, pitiful, controlled, anxious, or stressed. That is good news, for the weaker the stereotypes, the lower the risk that Ariel will face social stigma.

In this scenario, most people probably will not care how Ariel was conceived. However, a possible exception should be noted. If HGM is generally perceived as unsafe, employers and health insurers who learn of Ariel's origins may develop concerns about her health. In theory, she benefits from the Genetic Information Nondiscrimination Act of 2008 (GINA),[50] a federal law that prevents health insurers and employers from discriminating on the basis of genetic information.[51] In practice, however, she may find it difficult to persuade her state insurance commissioner or the Equal Employment Opportunity Commission (EEOC) that a refusal to insure or hire her was based on genetic information.[52]

EFFECT OF BAN. Now, assume the same facts, but add that John and Mary travel abroad to conceive Ariel, either because the moratorium remains in place or because Congress enacts a new law that bans HGM for reproduction. The Smiths' conduct may or may not be criminal, depending on the legality of cross-border reproductive care. Ariel has committed no crime. However, the question here is whether the law intimates she has negative traits or marks her as someone who should not exist because of those traits.

At present, Congress has not clarified the reasons for its refusal to allow the FDA to receive applications for clinical trials of HGM. As mentioned in Chapter 8, the only available committee report states that HGM involves unspecified safety and ethical issues.[53] At a minimum, this statement insinuates that Ariel and other children of HGM should not exist because they are likely to be sick or disabled.

In the future, Congress may issue more detailed statements in justification of the moratorium or enact a new ban with its own extensive legislative history. For the sake of analysis, suppose it asserts the hubris and manufacture objections along with concerns about lack of open future and parental pressure. By asserting these objections and concerns, Congress validates them as true. In so doing, it promotes stereotypes about children of HGM that flow naturally from the objections and concerns. In other words, Congress *encourages* the public to view Ariel as evil, unnatural, artifact-like, pitiful, controlled, anxious, and stressed. In this manner, it imposes a legal stigma on her and others who share her modification.

This legal stigma attaches even if the law in question applies only to HGM performed in the United States. In that event, John and Mary Smith will have committed no crime. However, a law that forces them offshore still sends the message that HGM is wrong and that Ariel has negative traits. If Ariel lives in the United States, she may experience discrimination if others become aware of her genetic status.

b) Illustration #2: Enhancing Modification

Next, suppose John and Mary Smith use HGM to add several SNPs associated with memory and learning to their sperm and eggs. Their goal is to have a child who excels in school and grows up to become a wealthy doctor or lawyer. Nine months later, their daughter Cora is born.

As noted in Chapter 2, Sections A and B, religious authorities generally do not tolerate enhancement, and nature worshippers reject all modifications of the human genome, so the Smiths appear to be transgressors. Further, the Smiths have added SNPs in an attempt to give Cora an advantageous trait. As Chapter 3, Section C.3 emphasized, most of Cora's genome is unaltered; nevertheless, when faced with this deliberate attempt to shape a child, critics may complain that the Smiths have manufacture Cora, deprived her of an open future, and pressured her to achieve.

More importantly, because this hypothetical involves an enhancement, the stratification and apocalypse objections come into play, *shifting the focus from the Smiths to Cora herself*. To demonstrate this point, let us apply the claims and concerns presented in Chapter 4, Section B.3, and Chapter 5, Sections A, B, and D, to these facts. Allegedly, Cora and her descendants will bring about class divides, social inequalities, democratic collapse, market-driven eugenics, and genocide.[54] Parents will feel pressure to modify their own children to keep up with Cora, yet be unable to afford to do so, and future generations will suffer on account of Cora.

The hubris and manufacture objections are aimed at the scientists and parents who employ HGM. Thus, they only *imply* that Cora is evil, unnatural, artifact-like, and so on. By contrast, the stratification and apocalypse objections are aimed directly at Cora. As Chapter 4, Section C, and Chapter 5, Section F, make clear, predictions of bad outcomes *depend on* stereotypes about her: she is superior (due to the enhancement) and divisive (due to her ability to transmit the enhancement to descendants). If not for her, and others like her, social inequalities would not exist, democracy would not collapse, the market would not generate faddish cohorts, and genocide would not occur. In other words, Cora's superiority and divisiveness make her unjust, violent, anti-democratic, coercive, fungible, artifact-like, superficial, and genocidal.[55] Similarly, concerns about pressure and consent of future generations frame Cora as the problem. If not for her, and others like her, parents would not feel pressured to enhance their own children, and future generations would not suffer the consequences of her existence. She is a competitive threat and the dangerous product of anti-democratic decisions.

Concededly, certain claims within or related to the stratification and apocalypse objections are not aimed directly at Cora. Yet, even these claims associate her with negative events. For example, some predict that HGM will cause the government to revive mandatory eugenics programs. As Chapter 5, Section F.2, mentioned, this claim links Cora with coercion and evil. Others worry that most parents will not be able to afford HGM. Cora is not to blame for unequal access; yet, the concern implies that she is a privileged rich kid, a stereotype that many find disagreeable.

These negative stereotypes present a threat to Cora. Collectively, they create a hub around which social stigma can form. If Cora's genetic status is exposed, her social status may begin to fray. She may succeed in making friends with others who share her academic or career interests. However, classmates and coworkers may envy her alleged superiority and find covert ways to undermine her.

Teachers and employers who know about Cora's genetic status may value her abilities but hesitate to confer deserved awards or promotions that could provoke resentment among her peers. An employer may even decide that it is easier to fire Cora than to deal with unrest in the workplace. As stated in Section C.3 of this chapter, GINA prohibits employers from discriminating on the basis of genetic information. However, the EEOC is responsible for investigating and evaluating claims of employment discrimination in violation of GINA. For Cora to bring a private claim against her employer, she must first file a claim with the EEOC and obtain a Right to Sue notice.[56] If an employer asserts a legitimate reason for discharging Cora, she may find it hard to persuade the EEOC that discrimination occurred.

EFFECT OF BAN. Now, assume the same facts, but add that John and Mary travel to conceive Cora, either because the moratorium is in effect or because Congress enacts a new law that criminalizes HGM for reproduction. Their act may or may not be criminal, depending on the legality of cross-border reproductive care. Cora has committed no crime. The question is whether the law sends the message that she has negative traits or stigmatizes her as someone who should not exist because of those traits.

Once again, suppose Congress issues statements in support of the moratorium or enacts a new ban with its own legislative history. This time, however, the evidence indicates that its members rely on the stratification and apocalypse objections. Some also voice concerns about competitive pressure, unequal access, and future generations who cannot consent.

By citing these objections and concerns in support of its law, Congress validates them as correct. It sends a message that Cora should never have been born because she is superior and divisive.[57] Congress also promotes additional stereotypes that flow naturally from the objections and concerns. In other words, it marks Cora, and others with enhancing modifications, as violent, anti-democratic, fungible, superficial, genocidal, competitive, and the product of anti-democratic decisions. It also links them to coercion, evil, and privilege.

In this manner, Congress subjects Cora to the legal stigma on the basis of her genetic status. The stigma attaches even if cross-border reproductive care is legal: by forcing the Smiths offshore, Congress implies that Cora has dangerous traits and should not exist. If she resides in the United States, she will suffer the effects of this stigma. Depending on how angry the public is about enhancement, she may even face violence.

Revisiting *Brown v. Board of Education*, an interesting comparison can be made between laws that mandate racial segregation in schools and laws that prohibit HGM. The former implicitly assume that black children have inferior qualities, while the latter openly presume that genetically altered children have superior and divisive qualities. At their core, however, the two types of law are similar: both rest on stereotypes and both stigmatize the members of a minority group.

c) IVF and Test-tube Babies Distinguished

Readers who are familiar with assisted reproduction may question the foregoing analysis. As many remember, when Louise Brown was born in 1978, IVF was controversial.[58] Test-tube babies were seen as unnatural and a stigma attached to the term.[59] Robert Edwards and Patrick Steptoe, the doctors who pioneered IVF, warned their patients to keep quiet about their treatments and not answer questions from the media.[60] Yet, eventually, the public realized that IVF produced healthy babies and the furor subsided.[61] Today, more than 5 million babies have been born through the technology worldwide.[62]

Unfortunately, this happy ending does not predict that children of HGM will be accepted, for three reasons. First, although some critics assert that IVF is unnatural and/or akin to a manufacturing process,[63] while others charge that gamete donation has eugenic overtones,[64] no one claims that IVF babies are superior beings who, along with their descendants, will bring about the collapse of democracy and other apocalyptic outcomes. Unfortunately, one does hear such dire predictions about children of HGM, whom critics have portrayed as an incipient threat to society and the species.

Second, IVF has never been banned, even though 85 percent of the American public initially thought it should be.[65] In other words, there is no legal stigma associated with IVF. By contrast, Congress has already imposed a moratorium on HGM for reproduction by decreeing that the FDA cannot receive applications for clinical trials. If it renews the moratorium year after year or enacts a permanent ban, its actions will impose a legal stigma on children of HGM, especially if it justifies its decision in terms of the stratification and apocalypse objections.

Third, while some IVF patients prefer to keep quiet about their use of the technology, many others feel comfortable sharing their medical histories and personal stories with family and friends, or even strangers.[66] As a result, the public has had enough vicarious experience with IVF to develop familiarity with the technology and the babies born through it. But if Congress prohibits HGM for reproduction, parents who travel to gain access to it will be scofflaws at best and felons at worst. Most will be too intimidated to share personal stories that could humanize them and their children. Instead, as discussed in Sections C.5 and C.6 of this chapter, they and their children will hide the truth. Secrecy will keep the public from realizing that the children born with genetic modifications are human beings and not that different from anyone else.

4 Envy and Violence

Chapter 7 discussed envy in Section A.2. As it explained, people who experience that toxic mix of inferiority, resentment, and hostility can act on it in various ways. They can denigrate the character and accomplishments of their rivals or search for other ways to undermine or defeat them. Moreover, as noted in Section D, the envious can perpetrate violence against their rivals, or scapegoat them in tough social or economic times. Chapter 7 also argued in Sections B, C, and D that the stratification and apocalypse objections, which warn against the advent of superior beings, foment envy and encourage physical aggression against children of HGM.

Suppose Congress bans HGM on the strength of the stratification and apocalypse objections, reasoning that superior beings should not exist. Nevertheless, John and Mary Smith use HGM to conceive a daughter with improved memory and learning in violation of the ban. The ban is a type of social norm, and Cora's existence runs counter to it. Faced with this norm violation, those who envy Cora are empowered to transmute their feelings to indignation or resentment proper. These emotions can fuel physical aggression, as acknowledged in Chapter 7, Section A.3. In this manner, the ban heightens the risk of violence against Cora.

5 Loss of Medical and Personal History

The foregoing analysis indicates that laws against HGM place parents at risk of prosecution and children at risk of stigma and violence. These risks create a strong incentive for parents to conceal their use of HGM to protect themselves and their children. Unfortunately, such concealment can harm children in two ways.

First, secrets can lead to medical harm. Suppose, for example, that John and Mary Smith do not inform Cora or her doctors that she was conceived through HGM. As a result, Cora's medical history is incomplete. Later, if Cora suffers from health problems related to HGM, uninformed doctors may make incorrect diagnoses and administer the wrong treatments. Grandchildren and other descendants may face the same problems.

Second, secrets can also impose psychological harm, by undermining trust and damaging family relationships.[67] Cora may sense that her parents are hiding important facts from her but not know why. She may blame herself or imagine all kinds of dire scenarios, without ever realizing that the secret concerns the technology used to conceive her.

As with any secret, there is a risk of inadvertent disclosure. A family member may let the secret slip, or genetic testing may reveal the modification. A gene cleansed of a mutation or a naturally occurring genetic variant that confers immunity to HIV-1 may not raise any red flags. However, multiple genetic variants added in the hopes of conferring an enhanced trait may be easier to spot.

For example, imagine that Cora undergoes genetic testing as an adult. The test detects 12 SNPs associated with improved memory and learning. The lab may not understand the significance of these data; but if it does, Cora will learn of her enhancement. She may resent her parents for hiding the truth from her and feel stigmatized by the law that opposes her existence. Hopefully, the lab will respect the confidentiality of her private information; but if the test results fall into the hands of authorities, her parents may be prosecuted if the statute of limitations has not expired.

6 Passing

Children who know how their parents conceived them face different challenges. They must protect their parents against prosecution and themselves against stigma, discrimination, and violence. Passing offers a possible solution. Just as blacks have passed as whites, and gays and lesbians have passed as straight,[68] the children may pass as the product of standard reproduction and hide their genetic status from friends, coworkers, and others. Passing will be easy for them because people will not be able to discern their genetic status simply by looking at them.

However, as social psychologists note, passing imposes costs of its own. The more the mind tries to suppress a secret, the more the secret rises to the surface, forcing the mind to redouble its efforts at suppression. In this manner, passing, which requires one to hide a stigma, induces psychic distress.[69] Passers also may experience inability to trust, isolation from peers who share their stigma, and the sense of powerlessness that comes from being unable to challenge an unjust social and legal order.[70]

To illustrate, suppose that the Smiths circumvent or violate a federal moratorium or ban to conceive Cora. She excels at her studies, in part due to her improved memory and learning, but primarily because she has a strong work ethic. She conceals her genetic status to protect herself and her parents and lives in fear that the truth may be discovered. She dares not confide in her friends and suffers in silence as jokes, pop culture references, and school lessons depict people like her as too problematic to exist. Over time, her self-esteem and well-being erode. Sadly, Cora never realizes that her classmates Sarah and Tom were born with the same modification and are also passing.

D HARM TO FOREIGNERS

Thus far, this chapter has focused on harms that the moratorium and future bans may inflict on Americans. However, other nations may tolerate HGM for reproduction. In that event, foreigners will be born with therapeutic or enhancing modifications. If these individuals travel to the United States, they will confront some unpleasant realities.

To illustrate, suppose John and Mary Smith are citizens of a nation that permits HGM. They employ HGM to conceive Cora, who has improved memory and learning. When Cora is older, she comes to the United States for education or work. If her genetic status is known, her American classmates or colleagues may envy her and undermine her goals and projects. Moreover, if HGM for reproduction is illegal in the United States, her existence will contradict an accepted norm, facilitating the transmutation of envy to resentment proper, and encouraging her peers to commit physical aggression against her. She may choose to pass to protect herself, but even passing imposes psychological costs, as discussed in Section C.6 of this chapter.

Now, assume Cora meets and marries an American man and transmits her altered genes to her own children. As explained in Chapter 4, Section B.3, such genes will be diluted with every passing generation and have little impact. Nonetheless, if a ban is enacted to prevent the development of hereditary castes and other imaginary disasters, the public may develop a hysterical fear of foreigners and genetic contamination.

The federal government will have few viable means of avoiding such conflicts. Excluding citizens of nations that permit HGM will offend those nations. Screening foreigners for genetic modifications at the border will be burdensome and yield results that are inconclusive because many SNPs occur naturally. Realistically, foreigners with genetic modifications will enter the country; once they do, monitoring and controlling their sexual activities will be impossible.

Eventually, however, foreigners with genetic modifications will realize the risks that they face. Some may choose to forgo education, employment, and vacations in the United States. An interesting analogy can be found in reactions to President Donald Trump's initial decision to bar nationals of Iran, Iraq, Libya, Somalia, Sudan, Syria, and Yemen from entering the United States for 90 days to deter terrorism.[71] Online searches for air flights to the United States declined, as did tour bookings.[72] Many American universities and colleges also reported a decrease in applications from international students, especially those from the Middle East.[73]

E HARM TO SOCIETY

Last but not least, when Congress prohibits HGM for reproduction, it threatens the egalitarian ideals undergirding our society. This threat is particularly keen if it bases its decision on the stratification and apocalypse objections, thereby sending the message that human beings born with enhancing modifications are superior, divisive, and unjust and thus unfit to exist. This message contradicts political principles that affirm the equality of all persons.[74] Moreover, if cross-border reproductive care is available, such human beings *will* exist and suffer the harms described in Section C of this chapter. By eroding core principles, and habituating the public to the abuse of genetic minorities, Congress opens the door to discrimination against other unpopular minority groups.[75]

What if Congress acts solely on the strength of the hubris and manufacture objections, which protest HGM and adults who wield it? These two objections do not oppose the existence of children of HGM as such and thus do not contradict egalitarian ideals directly. However, they do imply that children of HGM are evil, unnatural, and artifact-like. Thus, children born in defiance of a legal regime that rests on these objections will still be stigmatized and suffer all the other harms described in Section C of this chapter. Once again, the public will become accustomed to the degradation of genetic minorities.

Of course, experience can serve as a check on prejudice. For example, those who study and work alongside members of racial, ethnic, national, religious, or sexual minorities have an opportunity to learn that derogatory stereotypes are false. Likewise, personal experience with children of HGM could dispel negative stereotypes about them. However, a ban incentivizes children of HGM to conceal their genetic status and thus eliminates opportunities to learn from interaction with them.[76]

One final point is in order. In the short term, HGM will be used to correct deadly genetic mutations. In the long term, genetic knowledge and technology may improve to the point where other modifications become feasible. If Congress bans HGM, it may unwittingly slam the door on interventions that can benefit individuals and society as a whole. One example makes the point. If, as suggested in Chapter 1, Section C.3, maximum lifespan can be safely extended, but HGM is illegal, people may be more likely to suffer from age-related diseases and certainly will die sooner. It would be ironic if a ban brings about the dreaded nursing home world discussed in Chapter 5, Section C.2.

F STATE BANS ON HGM

As Chapter 8, Section B, indicated, state laws do not address HGM directly. However, 50 state legislatures have it within their power to enact bans. The birth of a child through HGM may spark controversy and prod them into action.

In Chapter 9, Section B, this book predicted that a legal patchwork will eventually emerge. Conservative states may enact total bans that protect human embryos against research. Liberal states may favor bans that prohibit HGM for reproduction only. Some may make exceptions for specific therapeutic modifications intended to secure the health of children. Finally, many states may do nothing at all and rely instead on the federal government to regulate the technology.

State bans will inflict harms similar to those associated with a federal ban. Total bans will impede scientific discoveries and erode scientific freedom, as discussed in Section A of this chapter. Bans on HGM for reproduction, particularly those that impose criminal penalties, will harm parents and children for the reasons detailed in Sections B and C of this chapter. Foreigners with genetic modifications who travel to a state that bans HGM for reproduction will endure the indignities described in Section D of this chapter. Lastly, a state with a ban will damage its own commitment to egalitarian values, as recounted in Section E of this chapter.

However, state bans differ from a federal ban in that people can evade them by traveling within the United States. Scientists can move to states where their research is legal. If Congress lifts its moratorium, and the FDA approves specific genetic modifications, parents can receive HGM services in states that either have no laws or permit those modifications. Children or foreigners who suffer from legal stigma in one state can move to another with more tolerant attitudes and no ban.

However, the reverse is also true. Residents of states that have no bans may move to states that do, with unfortunate results. Scientists may be compelled to give up research. Parents and children who have committed no crime may be forced to hide their involvement with HGM to avoid stigma and discrimination. Foreigners may wish they had stayed home.

Optimistically, states with bans may face a backlash. Consider North Carolina. In 2016, the state enacted a law requiring individuals to use the restrooms or locker rooms in public facilities that corresponded to the gender on their birth certificates, even if their current gender identities were different. Many perceived the law as discriminatory. North Carolina lost more than $395 million to litigation and canceled business expansions, conferences, concerts, and sporting events[77] before repealing the law in 2017.[78] By analogy, once children with genetic modifications are born in tolerant states, their parents, relatives, friends, and sympathizers may lobby against or boycott states that have stigmatizing laws.

G SUMMARY

Before lawmakers prohibit a controversial technology, they should consider the damage that their own actions can inflict. Laws are more than line items on a political resume. They are blunt-edged public policy tools that can have harmful consequences, not only for offenders, but for others. This chapter has examined the effects of the existing moratorium on HGM for reproduction and bans that Congress or states may enact in the future. It has argued that such prohibitions hold the potential to harm scientists and science, parents, children, foreigners, and society. By fully accounting for these costs, this chapter seeks to bring balance to the public policy debate.

Notes

1. LICHUN TANG ET AL., CRISPR/Cas9-mediated Gene Editing in Human Zygotes Using Cas9 Protein, 292 MOLECULAR GENETICS AND GENOMICS 525 (2017).
2. XIANGJIN KANG ET AL., Introducing Precise Genetic Modifications into Human 3PN Embryos by CRISPR/Cas-mediated Genome Editing, 33 J. ASSISTED REPROD. & GENETICS 581 (2016).
3. Cf. KERRY LYNN MACINTOSH, ILLEGAL BEINGS: HUMAN CLONES AND THE LAW 76–79 (2005) (discussing federal bills that proposed stiff sentences and fines for those convicted of human cloning).
4. 21 USC §§ 331(d), 355(a), (i) (West, Westlaw through P.S. 115–43).
5. 42 USC § 262(a)(1), (a)(3) (West, Westlaw through P.L. 115–43). The PHSA also provides that the FFDCA applies to biological products. Id. at § 262(j).
6. 21 USC § 333(a) (West, Westlaw through P.L. 115–43).
7. 42 USC § 262(f) (West, Westlaw through P.L. 115–43).
8. NORAH M. E. FOGARTY ET AL., Genome Editing Reveals a Role for OCT4 in Human Embryogenesis, 550 NATURE 67 (2017).
9. Cf. THE PRESIDENT'S COUNCIL ON BIOETHICS, Human Cloning and Human Dignity: An Ethical Inquiry 130–32 (2002) (mentioning cloned human embryos as a source of stem cells for such experiments).
10. For a discussion of FDA actions and authority with respect to human cloning, see MACINTOSH, ILLEGAL BEINGS, *supra* note 3, at 82–85.
11. JOHN CHARLES KUNICH, THE NAKED CLONE: HOW CLONING BANS THREATEN OUR PERSONAL RIGHTS 94 (2003).
12. See, e.g., id. at 97 (arguing that research may be protected as symbolic speech under certain circumstances); ROY G. SPECE JR. & JENNIFER WEINZIERL, First Amendment Protection of Experimentation: A Critical Review and Tentative Synthesis/Reconstruction of the Literature, 8 S. CAL. INTERDISC. L.J. 185 (1998) (claiming that research is protected as a step within the scientific method); JOHN A. ROBERTSON, The Scientist's Right to Research: A Constitutional Analysis, 51 S. CAL. L. REV. 1203 (1977) (arguing that research must be protected as predicate to dissemination of scientific information).
13. US CONST. Amends. V, XIV, § 1; RICHARD DELGADO & DAVID R. MILLEN, God, Galileo and Government: Toward Constitutional Protection for Scientific Inquiry, 53 WASH. L. REV. 349, 392–95 (1978).
14. ROBERTSON, *supra* note 12, at 1213–14.
15. WASHINGTON V. GLUCKSBERG, 521 US 702, 728 (1997).
16. 316 US 535 (1942).
17. Id. at 541.

18. *Id.* at 541–42.
19. JOHN E. NOWAK & RONALD D. ROTUNDA, CONSTITUTIONAL LAW § 14.27, at 797–801 (5th ed. 1995).
20. CAREY V. POPULATION SERVICES INT'L, 431 US 678, 684–85 (1977); see also EISENSTADT V. BAIRD, 405 US 438, 453 (1972) (making a similar statement in an equal protection case).
21. LIFCHEZ V. HARTIGAN, 735 F. Supp. 1361, 1377 (N.D. Ill. 1990), aff'd, 914 F.2d 260 (1990) (unpublished opinion).
22. E.g., CAREY, 431 US at 688–89 (finding that a law permitting only licensed pharmacists to dispense condoms imposed a significant burden on right of privacy and applying strict scrutiny to invalidate it). In recent years, the Supreme Court has applied a modified standard to uphold laws that regulate but do not outlaw abortion. It asks whether a law imposes an undue burden on a woman's right to abort a nonviable fetus by placing a substantial obstacle in her path. If not, the law can be upheld as an expression of respect for the lives of the unborn. *See* GONZALES V. CARHART, 550 US 124, 146 (2007). This author believes strict scrutiny is the correct standard for assessing the constitutionality of laws that place a significant burden on procreative decisions but will address the undue burden standard as an alternative as appropriate.
23. CAREY, 431 US at 686.
24. *Cf.* MACINTOSH, ILLEGAL BEINGS, *supra* note 3, at 193 (explaining that the government cannot establish a compelling interest by asserting that a cloning ban is needed to eliminate speculative harms).
25. JOHN A. ROBERTSON, Procreative Liberty in the Era of Genomics, 29 AM. J.L. & MED. 439, 449 (2003).
26. *Id.* at 476.
27. If the undue burden standard used in abortion cases applies, the result should be the same. A federal ban that forces Mary Smith to forgo a genetic child, bear a sick child, or travel abroad places a substantial obstacle in her path and thus should not be upheld absent a compelling governmental interest.
28. *See* MICHAEL C. DORF, Facial Challenges to State and Federal Statutes, 46 STAN. L. REV. 235, 236 (1994) (explaining that a court can hold that a law is unconstitutional as applied to certain circumstances).
29. ROBERTSON, *supra* note 25, at 478.
30. WASHINGTON, 521 US at 728.
31. NOWAK & ROTUNDA, *supra* note 19, § 11.4, at 390.
32. ROBERTSON, *supra* note 25, at 479.
33. *See* JASON GLAHN, I Teach You the Superman: Why Congress Cannot Constitutionally Prohibit Genetic Modification, 25 WHITTIER L. REV. 409 (2003) (arguing that a parent's constitutional right to rear a child as she sees fit and without government interference includes a right to use HGM as long as the child suffers no physical or psychological harm).
34. *See* I. GLENN COHEN, PATIENTS WITH PASSPORTS: MEDICAL TOURISM, LAW, AND ETHICS 381–89 (2015) (discussing laws around the world that

prohibit or restrict certain reproductive technologies and describing patient efforts to circumvent the laws).
35. RICHARD F. STORROW, Assisted Reproduction on Treacherous Terrain: The Legal Hazards of Cross-border Reproductive Travel, 23 REPRODUCTIVE BIOMEDICINE ONLINE 538, 539 (2011).
36. COHEN, *supra* note 34, at 389.
37. *See* 18 USC § 2 (West, Westlaw through P.L. 115–43) (providing that one who aids and abets the commission of a federal offense is punishable as a principal; 42 USC § 262(f) (West, Westlaw through P.L. 115–43) (providing that person who aids and abets a violation of PHSA is guilty of an offense).
38. *See* 18 USC § 371 (West, Westlaw through P.L. 115–43) (defining separate crime of conspiracy but providing that conspiracy to commit misdemeanor is punishable as misdemeanor).
39. By analogy, when Congress tried to outlaw human cloning, the proposed bills imposed 10-year prison sentences and/or fines of $1 million. MACINTOSH, ILLEGAL BEINGS, *supra* note 3, at 76–79.
40. Juries are supposed to apply legal rules to facts to determine whether a criminal defendant is guilty beyond a reasonable doubt. However, juries sometimes acquit a person despite his guilt, a controversial practice known as jury nullification. DARRYL K. BROWN, Jury Nullification within the Rule of Law, 81 MINN. L. REV. 1149, 1150 (1997).
41. AMERICAN BAR ASSOCIATION, Children Are Unintended Victims of Mass Incarcerations, Say Researchers (March 2017), www.americanbar.org/publications/youraba/2017/march-2017/children-of-those-behind-bars-are-unintended-victims-of-mass-inc.html.
42. MACINTOSH, ILLEGAL BEINGS, *supra* note 3, at 119.
43. MONICA BIERNAT & JOHN F. DOVIDIO, Stigma and Stereotypes, in THE SOCIAL PSYCHOLOGY OF STIGMA 88, 111 (TODD F. HEATHERTON ET AL. EDS. 2003).
44. *Id.* at 119.
45. MACINTOSH, ILLEGAL BEINGS, *supra* note 3, at 120.
46. 347 US 483 (1954).
47. *Id.* at 494.
48. *Id.* at 495.
49. MACINTOSH, ILLEGAL BEINGS, *supra* note 3, at 120–21.
50. Pub. L. No. 110–233, 122 Stat. 991 (2008) (codified in scattered sections of 29 and 42 USC).
51. THE GENETIC ALLIANCE, GENETICS AND PUBLIC POLICY CENTER, & NATIONAL COALITION FOR HEALTH PROFESSIONAL EDUCATION IN GENETICS, GINA and Your Health Insurance and GINA and Your Job, GENETIC INFORMATION NONDISCRIMINATION ACT, www.ginahelp.org (last visited on November 20, 2017) [hereinafter THE GENETIC ALLIANCE ET AL.].
52. Under GINA, state insurance commissioners handle complaints regarding discrimination in health insurance. *Id.* at GINA and Your Health Insurance,

How GINA Works, Who Should I Contact if I Feel I Have Been Discriminated Against? The EEOC investigates complaints regarding discrimination in employment. *Id.*

53. H.R. Rep. No. 114–205, at 69 (2015). Congress renewed the moratorium in 2017, shortly after the National Academy of Sciences and National Academy of Medicine issued their report on human genome editing in early 2017. NATIONAL ACADEMY OF SCIENCES & NATIONAL ACADEMY OF MEDICINE, HUMAN GENOME EDITING: SCIENCE, ETHICS, AND GOVERNANCE (2017) [hereinafter NAS REPORT]. However, this author has not found any legislative history referencing that report or the concerns raised therein.
54. Societal ossification, which is discussed in Chapter 5, Section C, applies only to lifespan extension and is not relevant to this hypothetical.
55. The stereotypes of self-absorbed, selfish, controlling, and parasitic elders discussed in Chapter 5, Section F.3, do not apply to Cora because she did not receive genes intended to extend maximum lifespan.
56. THE GENETIC ALLIANCE ET AL., *supra* note 51, at GINA and Your Job, How GINA Works, Who Should I Contact if I Feel I Have Been Discriminated Against?
57. *Cf.* MACINTOSH, ILLEGAL BEINGS, *supra* note 3, at 121–22 (discussing legal stigma that anti-cloning laws impose on human clones).
58. *Id.* at 13.
59. KATE BRIAN, The Amazing Story of IVF: 35 years and 5 Million Babies Later, THE GUARDIAN (July 12, 2013), www.theguardian.com/society/2013/jul/12/story-ivf-five-million-babies.
60. *Id.*
61. MACINTOSH, ILLEGAL BEINGS, *supra* note 3, at 13.
62. BRIAN, *supra* note 59.
63. MACINTOSH, ILLEGAL BEINGS, *supra* note 3, at 13, 19.
64. *E.g.*, CYNTHIA R. DANIELS & ERIN HEIDT-FORSYTHE, Gendered Eugenics and the Problematic of Free Market Reproductive Technologies: Sperm and Egg Donation in the United States, 37 SIGNS: J. WOMEN IN CULTURE & SOCIETY 719 (2012).
65. MACINTOSH, ILLEGAL BEINGS, *supra* note 3, at 13.
66. *E.g.*, MELANIE COLE, This IVF Story Might Never Have Happened, URBAN MOMMIES (July 14, 2016), www.urbanmommies.com/my-ivf-story/.
67. MACINTOSH, ILLEGAL BEINGS, *supra* note 3, at 126.
68. *Id.* at 128.
69. *See* LAURA SMART & DANIEL M. WEGNER, The Hidden Costs of Hidden Stigma, in THE SOCIAL PSYCHOLOGY OF STIGMA 220, 222–24 (TODD F. HEATHERTON ET AL. EDS. 2003).
70. MACINTOSH, ILLEGAL BEINGS, *supra* note 3, at 128–29.
71. Exec. Order No. 13,769, § 3(c), 82 Fed. Reg. 8977, 8978 (January 27, 2017). President Trump chose these seven nations because the Obama Administration had already restricted visa-free travel for individuals who had

traveled there, citing concerns about foreign terrorism. KYLE BLAINE & JULIA HOROWITZ, How the Trump Administration Chose the 7 Countries in the Immigration Executive Order, CNN (January 30, 2017), www.cnn.com/2017/01/29/politics/how-the-trump-administration-chose-the-7-countries/. President Trump's original executive order was later superseded by a second executive order that barred entry of nationals from Iran, Libya, Somalia, Sudan, Syria, and Yemen for 90 days. Exec. Order No. 13,780, §§ 2(c), 13, 82 Fed. Reg. 13,209, 13,213, 13,218 (March 6, 2017). This second order removed Iraq from the list. The President deemed Iraq a special case for several reasons, including the nation's assistance in battling ISIS, a terrorist organization. *Id.* § 1(g), at 13,211.

72. BRAD TUTTLE, 'Trump Slump' Could Mean Well Over $10 Billion Per Year in Lost Tourism Revenues, TIME.COM (March 2, 2017), http://time.com/money/4687114/trump-slump-foreign-tourism-us-immigration-travel/.

73. STEPHANIE SAUL, Amid 'Trump Effect' Fear, 40% of Colleges See Dip in Foreign Applicants, N.Y. TIMES (March 16, 2017), www.nytimes.com/2017/03/16/us/international-students-us-colleges-trump.html.

74. *See* US CONST. Amend. XIV, § 1 (securing right of all persons within the United States to equal protection of law); *see also* THE DECLARATION OF INDEPENDENCE, para. 2 (US 1776) (declaring all men created equal).

75. *Cf.* MACINTOSH, ILLEGAL BEINGS, *supra* note 3, at 131 (explaining that anti-cloning laws undermine egalitarianism).

76. *Cf. id.* at 131–32 (making a similar point about anti-cloning laws).

77. EMMA GREY ELLIS, Guess How Much That Anti-LGBTQ Law Is Costing North Carolina, WIRED (September 18, 2016), www.wired.com/2016/09/guess-much-anti-lgbtq-law-costing-north-carolina/.

78. JASON HANNA ET AL., North Carolina Repeals "Bathroom Bill," CNN (March 30, 2017), www.cnn.com/2017/03/30/politics/north-carolina-hb2-agreement/.

Conclusion

CRISPR/Cas9 and other molecular editing tools are not yet safe or effective enough to be used in conceiving babies. For many observers, that judgment is sufficient to justify imposing legal restrictions on human germline modification (HGM). However, in the future, such tools may improve. Thus, it is important to consider objections that go beyond safety.

Critics complain that scientists and parents who dabble in HGM transgress divine and natural boundaries and transform human reproduction into manufacture. They also claim that enhanced beings and their descendants will stratify society and produce apocalyptic outcomes. Part I of this book analyzed these four objections and concerns related to them. It concluded that most are inaccurate, exaggerated, or speculative. Moreover, the objections and concerns are linked to negative stereotypes about children of HGM. If such children are born in the future, they will encounter a society conditioned to believe in these stereotypes.

Part II investigated the psychology behind the four objections and related concerns. Psychological essentialism, a heuristic that the mind uses to make sense of natural kinds and artifacts, facilitates biological misunderstandings that, in turn, contribute to the objections and concerns. Moreover, the stratification and apocalypse objections, together with related concerns, encourage others to envy children of HGM and commit violence against them.

Finally, Part III of this book discussed laws and regulations that affect HGM. Scientists engaged in pure research can modify human gametes and embryos as long as they find private money to support their work and do not violate state bans on embryo research, human cloning, or human-animal hybrids. However, those who wish to use HGM for reproductive purposes face a major roadblock: the Food and Drug Administration (FDA) cannot acknowledge receipt of applications to conduct clinical trials in which modified gametes or embryos are transferred to women because Congress has refused to allocate funds for that purpose. In effect, there is a federal moratorium on HGM for reproduction. As long as clinical trials are stalled, babies cannot be born from modified gamete or embryos in the United States.

Yet, Congress does not control events outside the United States. Once babies with genetic modifications are born abroad, Americans will travel to obtain HGM services. Congress and state legislatures may respond by enacting laws that seek to ban HGM permanently and punish those who obtain cross-border reproductive care. Chapter 10 explained that the moratorium and other bans hold the potential to harm scientists and science, parents, children, foreigners, and society.

Therefore, before that first baby is born, it is important to implement an alternative to punitive legislation: public education. In 2017, the National Academy of Science and National Academy of Medicine took a commendable first step by releasing a report that discussed HGM in some depth.[1] However, these organizations are not the only ones responsible for informing the public. Scientists, academics, policymakers, and other thought leaders can also make a positive contribution. In doing so, they should address four points.

First, thought leaders should disseminate accurate scientific information about HGM for research and reproduction, so that the public can learn to understand and distinguish the two. The science and technology of HGM are progressing rapidly. The primary challenge will be to keep information up-to-date.

Second, thought leaders should explain that HGM for reproduction presents physical risks to mothers and children, without exaggerating those risks in a manner that invites public skepticism. They should monitor foreign developments and warn against rogue offshore clinics that offer unregulated services. Further, they should make it clear to the public that HGM for reproduction involves time, effort, and considerable expense. Therapeutic modifications, such as the elimination of dangerous genetic mutations, may justify such burdens, but enhancing modifications often will not.

Third, thought leaders should teach the public that many traits, from height to intelligence, involve hundreds of genes and thus are extremely difficult to engineer. Moreover, they should emphasize that even if HGM produces a child who manifests a particular trait, the trait alone cannot guarantee a desired life outcome. For example, a child with an excellent memory may not achieve academic or career success, a child with an extended lifespan can still die young, and so on.

Fourth, thought leaders should advise the public that intuition can distort beliefs about HGM. As Chapter 6 explained, psychological essentialism makes it all too easy to conclude that HGM impairs the human essence of a child. Essentialism also fosters the misimpression that HGM can create children with intended traits, uses (e.g., achieving academic success or a living to a specific age) and types (e.g., doctor or lawyer). Further, it promotes the notion that enhanced beings can easily hand their traits down through the generations like family heirlooms. These and other fallacies have poisoned the well of public policy. It is important that people learn to recognize and combat misleading intuitions.

In addition to advocating public education, this book proposes a wait-and-see approach to HGM. Perfecting molecular editing tools and learning how to apply them to human gametes and embryos will take time. Because therapeutic applications are easiest to perform, scientists will produce them first, long before enhancement is possible or practical. Given the present regulatory obstacles in the United States, the initial clinical trials will probably occur abroad. Legislators and regulators will have the opportunity to observe, collect data, and reflect calmly upon the situation. There is no need for a preemptive legislative strike that may be difficult to overturn later. Very few people have a medical need for HGM, but those who do deserve a fighting chance at gaining relief when the technology matures.

Enhancing modifications will come much later and will lean in the direction of modest alterations that can be executed without undue risk. Again, existing regulatory hurdles ensure that the first clinical trials will occur abroad. The American public will face the news with equanimity if it has been educated beforehand. People will then understand that attempts at enhancement face technical challenges and produce limited results. Those who understand will eschew HGM for enhancement.

Forty years ago, people thought that in vitro fertilization (IVF) would create a generation of soulless test-tube babies. Instead, IVF has helped men and women conceive millions of ordinary children. Today, some people fear that HGM will create enhanced beings who dominate others and destroy valued social institutions. However, in the short term, HGM can do no more than help parents conceive healthy children. Eventually, it may also make it possible for parents to give their children modestly enhanced traits. However, even those children will be ordinary human beings and not the genocidal supermen and superwomen that some imagine. Going forward, as policymakers and legislators contemplate regulating HGM, they should restrain their own hubris and take only baby steps.

Note

1. NATIONAL ACADEMY OF SCIENCES & NATIONAL ACADEMY OF MEDICINE, Human Genome Editing: Science, Ethics, and Governance (2017).

Index

Andrews, Lori, 73, 100
Annas, George, 73, 100
apocalypse objection, 3, 4, 9, 62–79, 89, 91, 98–100, 102–3, 107, 112–15, 116, 117, 121, 162, 167–68, 169, 170, 172, 180
   collapse of democracy, 3, 9, 62–65, 77, 78, 79, 89, 99, 102, 107, 112, 113, 116, 160, 167
   defined, 62
   eugenics. *See* this entry
   genocide. *See* this entry
   ossification, 62, 68–72, 79, 89, 99, 100, 102, 107, 112, 114, 160

Bailey, Ronald, 72
base editing, 11, 13, 14, 89, 121
   defined, 2
beta thalassemia, 1, 2
Brave New World, 39, 42, 44
Brown v. Board of Education, 165, 169
Buck v. Bell, 65
Bush, George W., 9

Calment, Jeanne, 19, 55
Center for Biologics Evaluation and Research (CBER), 124
children of HGM
   defined, 3
chromosomes
   artificial, 48, 54, 57, 64, 73, 74–75, 78, 99, 103
Clinton, Hillary Rodham, 72
Common Rule, 127–32, 135
   children, research on, 131
   human subjects, defined, 128
   informed consent, 128
   pregnant women and fetuses, research on, 130–31

competitive pressure, 48, 50, 51, 54–55, 56, 57, 58, 91, 100, 111–12, 160, 162, 167, 168
Consolidated Appropriations Act, 2016, 124–25
Consolidated Appropriations Act, 2017, 125
Conyers, John, 72
CRISPR/Cas 9, 1–2, 9, 11, 13, 14, 15, 16, 30, 33, 40, 42, 89, 121, 132, 135, 136, 146, 147, 148, 158, 180
cross-border reproductive care, 125, 162, 163, 164, 166, 168, 169, 173, 181
Cuddy, Amy, 110, 115
cystic fibrosis, 13, 32, 150

deoxyribonucleic acid (DNA)
   chemical bases, 14, 18
   nucleotide, 2, 14, 18
design stance, 96
Dickey-Wicker Amendment, 126, 127

enhancement
   bizarre, 74
   defined, 16, 21, 93
   height, 16–17, 18, 181
   intelligence, 17–18, 63, 150, 181
   lifespan, 17, 19–21, 22, 31–32, 33, 42, 43–44, 45, 55–57, 58, 62, 66, 68–72, 73, 74, 75–76, 77–78, 102, 111, 112, 114, 125, 151, 173, 181
   memory and learning, 17, 18–19, 21, 22, 31, 32, 33, 34, 42, 43, 44–45, 52–55, 57, 58, 63–64, 66, 67, 73, 75, 78, 94, 97–98, 99, 111, 112, 115, 125, 130, 151, 161–62, 163, 167–69, 170–71, 172, 181
envy, 4, 58, 75, 76, 79, 89, 107–17, 121, 163, 168, 170, 172, 180
   aggression and, 89, 107, 109, 115–17, 170, 172
   benign, 111–12
   BIAS map, 115–16
   elements of, defined, 107
   jealousy, distinguished from, 108

envy (cont.)
  resentment proper, distinguished from, 108
  scapegoating, ideological model of, 116–17, 170
  secrecy, 108–9
  stereotype content model, 89, 111, 113, 114
  transmutation of, 89, 109–10, 117, 163, 170, 172
Equal Employment Opportunity Commission (EEOC), 166, 168
equality
  human, 31, 64, 73, 172–73, 174
  opportunity, 65
  outcome, 64–65
eugenics, 9, 49, 62, 76, 77, 78, 89, 99, 100, 102, 107, 112, 113–14, 148, 160, 167, 168
  market forces, 68, 78, 113–14, 167
  negative, 65
  positive, 65
  sterilization laws, 65–66, 159
  stigmatizing the disabled, 67, 77, 78, 160–61

Federal Food, Drug, and Cosmetic Act (FFDCA), 158
Feinstein, Dianne, 72
fertility rate, 69
Fiske, Susan, 110, 114, 115
Food and Drug Administration (FDA), 123–26, 129, 130, 132, 135, 146, 147–48, 149, 150, 151–53, 157, 158, 164, 166, 169, 174, 180
foreigners, 4, 67, 121, 157, 172, 174, 175, 181
Frankenstein, 33, 34
Fukuyama, Francis, 70, 71, 173
future generations, consent of, 62, 91, 100, 102–3, 114–15, 126, 160, 162, 167, 168

Galton, Francis, 65
gamete
  artificial, 12
  defined, 1
gamete intrafallopian transfer (GIFT), 31
Gattaca, 39, 48
genes
  beta globin (HBB), 1, 14–15
  CCR5 receptor, 16, 31
  defined, 1
  huntingtin, 13–14
genetic diversity, 32, 34, 35, 101, 160, 161, 166
Genetic Information Nondiscrimination Act of 2008 (GINA), 166, 168
genetic mutation
  off-target, 2
  point, 14–15, 125
genocide, 3, 9, 32, 62, 73–76, 77, 78, 79, 89, 99, 100, 102, 107, 112–13, 116, 160, 167

Glick, Peter, 110, 115, 116
Green, Ronald, 31, 32, 68

HIV-1 virus, 15–16, 20, 31, 42, 51, 93, 157, 171
hubris objection, 3, 9, 30–35, 89, 95–96, 100–1, 149, 165–66, 167, 173, 180
  defined, 30
  Frankenstein myth, 30, 33, 34–35, 96, 101
  offense against God, 30–32, 33–34, 35, 95, 101, 149, 167
  offense against nature, 30, 32, 34, 35, 95, 101, 149, 167
human cloning, 35, 48, 73, 132, 134, 136, 146, 147–48, 152, 158, 180
human germline modification (HGM), 11–12
  compared to standard reproduction, 40–41
  defined, 1
  experiments, 1–2
  methods, 31, 40
  public polls, 149–50, 151
Huntington disease, 13–14, 31, 32, 33, 41, 49, 67, 94, 129, 131, 133, 134, 150, 160, 164, 165
  autosomal dominant, 13
Huxley, Aldous, 39, 42
hypertrophic cardiomyopathy, 2

in vitro fertilization (IVF), 11–12, 13–15, 16, 19–20, 31, 40–42, 44, 49, 50, 52, 55, 63, 66, 67, 68, 78, 94, 97, 123, 129, 131, 132–34, 161, 162, 169–70, 182
induced pluripotent stem cell (iPSC), 12, 147, 148
informed consent, 129, 130
inheritance, principles of, 53
intracytoplasmic sperm injection (ICSI), 12
intrauterine insemination (IUI), 11
Isasi, Rosario, 73, 100

Kim, Sung Hee, 107, 108, 109

legal stigma, 173, 174
life expectancy, 19, 21, 56, 69, 71
  defined, 19
lifespan, maximum
  defined, 19
  human, 19, 20, 55–56
Lombardo, Paul, 66

manufacture objection, 3, 9, 39–45, 89, 91, 97, 101, 160, 161, 165–66, 167, 173, 180
  defined, 39
Medin, Douglas, 91
Mehlman, Maxwell, 55, 62, 64, 65

Index

meiosis, 13, 53
   defined, 13, 53
mitosis, 54
Mlodinow, Leonard, 52
mosaic, 2, 14
   defined, 2

National Academy of Sciences and National Academy of Medicine
   NAS Report, 3, 9, 110, 111, 125, 151, 181
National Institutes of Health (NIH), 124, 126–27, 135
   NIH Guidelines for Research Involving Recombinant DNA Molecules, 126–27
Nazi Germany, 65, 116
North, Michael, 114
nursing home world, 69, 70–71, 78, 114, 173

open future, 39, 41, 42, 43, 44, 45, 91, 98, 101, 161, 166, 167
Ortony, Andrew, 91
ossification, 9

parental expectations, 39, 41, 42, 43–44, 45, 91, 98, 101, 160, 162, 166, 167
passing, 171, 172, 173, 174
pleiotropy
   defined, 18
polygenic trait
   defined, 18
preimplantation genetic diagnosis (PGD), 12, 13–14, 39, 40, 49, 50, 67, 77, 123
President's Council on Bioethics, 9, 20, 49, 68, 70, 71
psychological essentialism, 4, 89, 91–104, 121, 180, 181
   artifacts, 44, 91, 96–99, 100, 101, 102–3, 107, 180
   defined, 91
   DNA as essence, 92–93, 94–95, 103
   human genome as essence, 95
   living kinds, 92–94, 95, 96
   natural kinds, 91–96, 101, 102, 103, 107, 180
   philosophical essentialism, distinguished from, 104 n.6
   stereotypes, 89, 100–3, 121
Public Health Services Act (PHSA), 158

Recombinant DNA Advisory Council (RAC), 126–27
Rifkin, Jeremy, 32
Robertson, John, 160, 161, 162
Roman Catholic Church, 30–31, 66

Sanders, Bernie, 148
Shelley, Mary, 33
sickle cell disease, 14–15, 32, 33, 49, 50
   autosomal recessive, 14
Silver, Lee, 9, 31, 32, 48, 54, 64, 73, 74
single nucleotide polymorphism (SNP), 18–19, 31, 34, 43, 52, 54, 63, 73, 94, 97, 115, 167, 171, 172
   defined, 18
Skinner v. Oklahoma, 65, 159
Smith, Richard H., 107, 108, 109
spermatogonial stem cell (SSC), 11, 31, 40, 41
standard reproduction, 39–41, 57, 164, 171
   defined, 1
state laws, 4, 121, 132–35, 136, 146, 152, 153, 157, 174, 180, 181
   embryos and fetuses, 132–34, 136, 146, 180
   human cloning, 134, 136, 146, 180
   human-animal hybrids, 135, 136, 146, 180
status quo bias, 93
stereotypes about children of HGM, 3, 4, 10, 33–35, 44, 48, 57, 58, 62, 76–78, 79, 89, 91, 100–3, 121, 166, 167–69, 172–73, 180
stigma, 165–70, 171
   defined, 165
   legal, 165, 166–67, 168–69
   stereotypes, relation to, 165, 166, 168–69
stratification objection, 3, 4, 9, 48–58, 77, 89, 91, 98–100, 101–2, 107, 110–11, 115, 116, 117, 121, 162, 167, 168, 169, 170, 172, 180
   defined, 48

therapy
   correction of genetic mutations, 13–15, 22, 31, 41–42, 44, 49–50, 58, 66, 73, 94, 97, 129–32, 133–34, 147, 150–51, 152, 160–61, 164–67, 171, 173–74
   defined, 12, 21, 93
   immunity, 15–16, 20, 22, 31, 42, 44, 51, 58, 66, 93, 171
therapy-enhancement distinction, 11, 20–21, 22, 89, 91, 93–95, 103, 151
Trump, Donald John, 72, 172

unequal access, 48, 50, 51, 55, 56–57, 58, 67, 91, 100, 102, 160–61, 162, 167, 168
United States Congress, 3, 4, 72, 123, 124–25, 132, 135, 136, 146–52, 153, 157, 158–59, 160, 161, 162, 163, 164, 165, 166, 168–70, 172–73, 174–81
United States Constitution, 158–59
   Due Process Clause, 158
   Equal Protection Clause, 65, 159, 165
   First Amendment, 158–59

United States Constitution (cont.)
   Foreign Commerce Clause, 149
   Fourth Amendment, 149

right of privacy, 66, 159–62
United States Supreme Court, 65–66, 72, 148, 158–60, 165

For EU product safety concerns, contact us at Calle de José Abascal, 56–1°,
28003 Madrid, Spain or eugpsr@cambridge.org.